**OXSTALLS
LEARNING CENTRE**

Oxstalls Lane  Gloucester
Gloucestershire  GL2 9HW
Telephone: 01242 715100

UNIVERSITY OF
GLOUCESTERSHIRE
at Cheltenham and Gloucester

# WEEK LOAN

# TRAVEL WORLDS

Journeys in Contemporary Cultural Politics

EDITED BY

RAMINDER KAUR AND JOHN HUTNYK

ZED BOOKS
London & New York

*Travel Worlds* was first published by
Zed Books Ltd, 7 Cynthia Street, London N1 9JF, UK,
and Room 400, 175 Fifth Avenue, New York, NY 10010, USA
in 1999

Cover photograph by Karoki Lewis
Cover designed by Andrew Corbett
Laserset by Long House, Cumbria, UK
Printed and bound in the United Kingdom
by Biddles Ltd, Guildford and King's Lynn

A catalogue record for this book
is available from the British Library.

Library of Congress Cataloging-in-Publication Data
Travel worlds : journeys in contemporary cultural politics / edited by
Raminder Kaur and John Hutnyk.
p. cm.
Includes bibliographical references (p.    ) and index.
ISBN 1–85649–561–2 (Hb). — ISBN 1–85649–562–0 (Pb).
1. Tourist trade—Social aspects.   I. Kaur, Raminder, 1967–   .
II. Hutnyk, John, 1961–   .
G155.A1T674    1998
338.4′791—dc21                              98–46656
CIP

ISBN 1 85649 561 2 Cased
ISBN 1 85649 562 0 Limp

# CONTENTS

*Acknowledgements*
The editors would like to thank all the contributors for their work on this collaborative venture, with special thanks for extra tours of duty to Koushik, Peter, Virinder and Saurabh. Thanks also to Raj Patel, Caroline Hellyer, Rajeev Vinaik and Kevin Hetherington. John would like to acknowledge the travelling cheques of the European Science Foundation and ESRC/ICCCR with whom he held Research Fellowships during the years this project was under construction.

# 1

## INTRODUCTION

### RAMINDER KAUR AND JOHN HUTNYK

The industrialization of travel explodes into the major mercantile force of our times. Occidental culture on the march extends now to new crusades for pleasure and power. The Holy Grails and Promised Lands are repackaged in luminous ways for ravenous consumption. Travel scenes signal pleasure and perfect harmony, the possibility of romance, the satisfaction of desire, the consummation of every whim. Fantasy landscapes and brochures of identity configure us now by distance, by a well-defined geographical lack. Travel media portray searching selves, constituted in movement by separation and respite from the everyday world and through purchased access to the holiday dreamtime.

Travel practices bring worlds into being which are always contested terrains, travel arenas with whose dynamic reactions and contradictions this book is most concerned. We do not separate travel into the distinct realms one often finds in the extant literature, whether it be exploratory travel, trade, crusades, colonial expansion, ethnography and spiritual quests, or entailing migrancy, exile, displacement, tourism and transnational commoditization. Whilst noting the differences between variant travel modes, the contributing writers combat the fallacy of allocating attention to demarcated travel worlds as if remote from other motivated travels, or from 'home'. Nor do we only focus on North–South or West–East traffic, which tends to be the predominant emphasis of critical texts.[1] Rather, we consider various corrosive overlaps and antagonisms in travel so as to provoke the hegemony of the North, or West, and its hold on travel privileges. Our view is that travel in contemporary times is so powerfully associated with the articulation of privilege that, for instance, the experience of travel as one of survival through movement is occluded in the celebratory obsession with adventure tours and the like. In taking a broad swipe at travel, we want

1

to bring other ways of travelling and diverse limits to travel alongside
and on board.

In this project, our understanding of cultural politics invokes a variety
of critical strategies: approaches which provide transnational perspectives; accounts which apply a more complex consideration of identity
politics in travelling cultures; and investigations which undermine the
often 'hidden' hierarchies of phenotype values in travel worlds.
Alongside these concerns we advance critiques which are conscious of
the class, commodity and capital underpinnings of travel worlds. We also
provide reworked narratives attentive to the coordinates which authorize
travel conventions, and pointing to the conjunction of tourism and
commodity culture with social science or cultural studies disciplinarity.
Rather than present a unified mono-picture, we celebrate the numerous
roads to a critical appreciation of travel politics. It is with a broader
notion of travel as contested tension between the physical and the
imaginative, or the material and the ideological, that the idea of journey
as a means of recuperating travel stories from hegemonic folds comes
into force. Our objective in writing this book is to think and act out
ways of travel that avoid both violent incursions and the converse
frame of romanticized exoticism. Perhaps here the search is for pointers
to confront and challenge on the paths that lead from the transit lounge.

Cartographers, explorers, navigators, adventurers, discoverers, re-
discoverers – call them what you will, but all under the travelling rubric
– started the familiar process that extends not only across the planet but
also surges into the sky with the discovery, naming and surveying of
stars that epitomizes the traveller's imagination. Still more or less
confined to the dominant classes, this notion of travel propels the
modern-day travellers who desire to find and appropriate 'new' places
in their personal worlds. Travel, in this perspective, becomes a claiming
and stamping of space with national, religious or more personal signa-
tures. Status, as a consequence, is enhanced: but 'been there, seen that,
done that' mantras affirm ignorance rather than sagacity. Descartes'
epitaph very much becomes, 'I travel therefore I am': the enlightenment
project repackaged as a regimented mission (see Saurabh Dube in
Chapter 3). Here we see how the growth of capitalism and the rapacious
drive to discover new markets and resources have pre-empted the rush
to 'know' paradise settings, or rugged ravines away from signs of civilization, desired objects comparable to the symbiotic tropes of exotic and
sensuous women, and the wild and unruly men of the Orient in Said's
analysis (1978). These 'discoveries', of course, mean only new names
branded on previously 'untouched' bodies (see Koushik Banerjea in
Chapter 2) as, all too evidently, violence and romance walk hand in hand.

The figure of the lone adventurer exploring jungles, charting seas or collecting ethnographic data is a familiar emblem. But the traveller is not an innocent, nor just curious. The linkage here between the investigative directives of knowledge and power is explicit, and does not need reiterating (Foucault 1966). Where we remain content to make apologies for the business-as-usual of travel knowledge we may need to rethink our politics, the ways in which our proclamations and prefaces are mere devices for the same old arrogance of those with the privilege to write travellers tales (Robertson *et al.* 1994). How different are we to the troops on the march? Armed with glossy brochures and exemplary credentials, destroying all possibilities of transformation simply by being able to go, come back and tell the tale. In an uneven global culture, the travel stories of the enabled classes amount to the new currency that transmutes all values. There is good reason to be concerned that we may deceive ourselves too, for the convoluted incorporations of critique and the tricks of the ever-expanding market are all-pervasive. But not all experience of travel fits so snugly into the protocols of circulation. Some are forced to stay at home, others are forced to run – a pivotal theme to which we frequently return in the course of this book.

Our book is not a corrective to travesties of travel, but rather an agenda for further research addressing the contemporary legacy of travel fiction and fabulation from Homer to Neil Armstrong. Faced with Euro-centric travel accounts – academic or picaresque – we signal the need to rewrite the travel records from other perspectives. The project of rewriting eclipsed worlds is fraught with difficulties, however, and we do not imagine this book as the only antidote. Our focus is on inter-acting scapes of capitalist circulation (Appadurai 1990), which allows us to include tourism as the colonization of pleasure and desire; exploita-tion of labour in the production and travel of goods and people; and the political strain of identity checks at immigration desks, visa regulations and back-room searches, hurried departures and forced destinations.[2]

Rather than triumphal passages of freedom, discovery and 'multi-cultural' encounters, we ask what are the factors that hinder travel? Borders and boundaries are overwhelmingly defined by nation-police-states. In the last few years alone, in Europe, the far right have forced social democratic parties and even less liberal types to further secure the fortress walls. Asylum seekers find no sympathy, but rather detention and deportation. The right to travel is only for those with the right credentials to travel.[3] Long-resident 'guest-workers' and their children born 'inside' the boundaries of Europe – Turkish families resident in Germany, for example – are not accorded any of the rights of citizens. Black urban youth are subject to 'stop and search' rather than free passage on the streets. Travel here is a grim itinerary designed to benefit business and not (these) travellers. It has long suited capital to move workers here and there when needed – be it for post-war industrial reconstruction and night shifts in the northern mills or, earlier, for the plantations and mines of the colonies (see Shirin Housee in Chapter 10). The violence of the slave trade did not come to a halt just because home support for that trade became untenable – and the narrative of British naval might and righteous intervention against rogue traders has served too long as a fairytale alibi. In the wake of ongoing violence, a political response to travel needs to do more than write subaltern anti-colonial narratives – however necessary – and is obliged to participate actively in campaigns of redress. The small contribution we want to make here is to illustrate some of the ways in which practices such as indentured trade projects, racialized exclusion, and orientalist ideological work continue today as the underbelly of the travel industry.

## Transit Lounge

It is no longer news that, in the form of tourism, travel has become a multi-billion dollar industry that has a major impact throughout the world (Greenwood 1989; Lett 1989; Lafant and Graburn 1992). Yet tourism studies seem to be entrenched in a leisurely school of anaesthetized and unchallenging thought. This book is less about the character of tourism or of the tourist, for there has been ample literature that has concentrated on these debates (Cohen 1972, 1979; MacCannell 1976; Crick 1985, 1988; Smith 1989 and Lafant 1995). Instead, we work at the edges of tourism studies, with detailed case studies of travel worlds and through attention to a politics of travel. This book's remit is to erode tourism's case for privileged focus in relation to other travel motivations and directives.

Theorizing travel in its broader sense has itself become an industry of sorts and James Clifford (1997) has become something of an avatar for diverse members of the cultural studies writing corps. In travel theory, however, there is a tendency to isolate commoditized travel as if it operated in a different world from other travel. We are wary of falling into mere enumeration of etymologies or types (Cohen 1979, Urry 1995), or of resting only with better ethnographies (see Raminder Kaur in Chapter 11), or merely celebrating 'refusals' and 'alternatives' which seem to us to be just more in the same old train. Good news appraisals of 'alternative' tourism are the big deceit here, for how alternative are they? (see Hutnyk 1996).

Our view is that the emerging moment of social scientific approaches to travel as a legitimate subject – anthropology reinvented as travel stories (Clifford 1997: 8), multiplying sociologies of place and space (Urry 1995) – requires us to interrogate this scene for the same adventurisms that characterize travel narratives themselves. The viability of this approach is marked if we consider how the anthropological institutionalization of fieldwork by Malinowski as a prerequisite for the project of comprehending otherness now transmutes into so many ethnographies of travel.[4] We suspect that this does little to disrupt the frame. That old 'I was there in the remote wild jungle' approach still filters in and out of traveller accounts, guidebooks and scholarly searches for the 'untouched' and 'authentic'. The inherited lattice of orientalism in newer guises, ironic reflexive explorations of the traveller's self, and detailed awe at the wondrous incongruity of the 'post-colonial' world, remains caught within the commodity economy, and prefigured by the shades the scholarly selves wear.[5]

Many of the alternative perspectives of cultural studies continue to be particularly Eurocentric,[6] and, even in 'anthropology' with its world-wide (-conquering) remit, Eurocentrism ensures that many studies still imagine a pristine other world and proceed by excluding altogether any mention of commoditized travel.[7] Evidently, travel stories cut out much – they are a censor, excluding as they include, travelling here but leaving there, ruptures, departures, abandonment. The conventionally authorized tales blank out Southern perspectives, and often an implicit bifurcation of the West and the Rest persists in the travel genres even after scholarly critiques have rendered their moves (see Seán McLoughlin and Virinder S. Kalra in Chapter 9). Obviously we think there are sides to travel stories which are rarely told, and which demand more attention. In this book the focus is on the tales that deliver with a twist – occlusions.

Another take on exotic subjects as the damning construct of travel guides our political critique of so-called post-coloniality (Spivak 1990). In some ways, of course, we are governed by the protocols and established themes, even though the angles seem tangential. We wish to bring to these topics a perspective not grounded in an unexamined Eurocentrism, an untroubled nation-category accepting geographism (see Peter Phipps in Chapter 7) or on the discursive missionary zeal of naïve pop-culture. Our travel stories are anti-colonial more than post-, they are concerned with political marginalization and resistance rather than with the philosophic status of the border metaphor (see Virinder S. Kalra and Navtej K. Purewal in Chapter 5, and the poems of Joyoti Grech); and with extending the cultural politics of appropriation rather than with a discursive critique of meaning which appreciates much, but does less than is required (see John Hutnyk in Chapter 8). Here, some of our perspectives grow out of campaign politics for redressing the limits and inequities of particular travel worlds. With the inclusion of essays, poetry and fiction on travel worlds, this book is meant to be something of a travel guide, something of a hold-all backpack, and something of another compass. We are seeking other passages here – not just the middle passage (Gilroy 1993), nor the fast ride to the third space (Bhabha 1994). We multiply directions rather than specify favourite routes, choose diverse angles, many ways to and from the South and the hegemonic Northern lights.

## Pathways

Koushik Banerjea opens our foray with a consideration of hegemonic practices of travel and their ruptures (Chapter 2). Contemporary travel is rooted in a colonial past: it is acquisitive, exoticizing, and, to a large extent, dependent on the racial associations of the traveller. Moreover, the territorial acquisitions of global travel are rehearsed in a compressed and transmuted form in the context of the multi-racial Western metropole. Beginning with the 'crusading element' implicit in the 'adventure', the chapter elaborates a notion of travel being more about confirming prior assumptions than about discovering new realms. The self-images invested in travels oscillate between assertion of a Self and search for an Other – the latter invariably constitutes the seeking Self. Banerjea then introduces the notion of 'propertied whiteness' to demonstrate how skin tone becomes a privileged passport to the acquisition of property and a prerequisite to appropriation of territories and people. Mapping of bodies, characteristic of sex tourism, acts as an extension of mapping of territories. This mode of racialized travel parallels other narratives such as those of Gilroy's model of Africa's diaspora in *The Black Atlantic,* although to differing ends: Banerjea goes further by problematizing the bounded arenas of territoriality and travel. By noting paradigmatic ruptures suggested by the dissonant footfalls of stellar African-American performers such as Jeru Davis, John Coltrane, Sonny Rollins and Don Cherry, the chapter shows that another register is possible for assessing the traffic of cultural gods and goods between North–South termini.

Saurabh Dube puts the spotlight on crusading missionaries (Chapter 3). On one hand, he notes the dissonant strands of missionary and colonial administrators' discourse, which in the end coalesce; on the other hand, he highlights the subversion of hegemonic powers and meaning in relation to indigenous reception of missionaries' 'bible-brandishing' (-bashing) antics. Noting that it was not a uniform Western mentality which constructed those all-powerful images of the non-Western other, it is possible to see that traveller-missionaries did participate in the promulgation of the empire mission in specific ways. In the uneven and diffuse spread and contradictions of such a project, 'hierarchies of otherness' can be compared with the 'severalty of Western selves'. The missionaries in colonial India attempted to create travel worlds commensurate with their sense of Christian mission, yet these were also worlds which, although influential, could not readily dominate the local. What was taken as acknowledgement of greatness and accordance of respect or deference, on the part of the native, might be better read as ways in which the performative rituals of empire could suit home-grown agendas. Here 'arenas defined by Western travels ... became rather different journeys at the hands (and in the minds) of other peoples'. In his chapter the institutional setting of inquiry allows Dube to show how these assumptions about the East are still rife in the academy where a persistent desire still finds non-Western informants unchanged beneath the changes, simple amongst complexity, and pre-modern amidst the post-modern.

Joyoti Grech provides another vessel for communicating views about travel. The poem 'Anthem' continues the focus on Christian imperialism but turns it on its head, as it does the notion of migration (Chapter 4). Identifying the patron of English nationalism, Saint George, as an Arab nobleman demands a complex re-examination of normalized assumptions, as it does the process of hegemonization by state and religion through-out history. In this poem we see an Arab migrant, or perhaps a colonizer, landing on the shores of a dark unknown landmass, the edge of the heart of darkness, to face naked painted natives engaged in unashamedly sexual rituals. The poem poses the questions of who's who – migrant or colonizer – and who is the barbaric 'dragon', without determining our interpretations. In effect, the images of this poetry leave resonances which can percolate over time to form new, richer and more complex understandings, memories, and experiences.

Exploration of the convoluted entanglements of colonialism and migrancy is continued in Virinder Kalra and Navtej Purewal's per-spectives on the construction, closure and negotiation of borders – specifically the one drawn between India and Pakistan in 1947 after the period of colonial rule (Chapter 5). Even though separated by only a few miles of no man's land, the gulf between the two nations seems immeasurable. The movements of population and violent encounters in the border-crossing zone have left deep social and historical scars. Land, train tracks and roads, including the famous Grand Trunk Road, are bifurcated. Similarities in cultural practices are noted across the artificial, yet potent, divide known as the Zero Line. While stringent measures are taken against Indian and Pakistani residents in their travels across the border, Western tourists are allowed access with comparatively little fuss. This parallels the easy flow of multinational capital into the two territories which, along with multinational corporations themselves, can be noted as the more 'powerful' mode of travel. The authors find defiant and creative negotiations of the border by indigenous South Asian travellers across what is otherwise seen as an 'insurmountable mountain'. This is not, however, to celebrate meekly the small resistances of those who struggle to find ways under the wire, as we often find in Border studies – for, in the end, such practices do not defeat the border patrols.

Another poem by Joyoti Grech considers the composite aspects of the lives of Jumma people engaged in the struggle for human rights and self-determination in the Chittagong Hill Tracts of south-eastern Bangladesh (Chapter 6). 'Bordercrossing' explores ways in which the nation state seeks to control free movement of the people living within its domain, whilst collaborating across national boundaries to effect the surveillance and control of people perceived to be dangerous to state power. One of the poem's basic premises is that travel is not a luxury, or a pastime of the privileged, but a life-assuring necessity, albeit one conditioned by the criterion of state citizenship. People are endowed with relevant paperwork to prove the state's recognition of their existence, where forged IDs as legitimization of births 'irrelevant to the soul' are the order of the travelling package. In its multi-layered illustration of the lives of individuals and their community, the poem documents the rich validity not only of the lives of members of a 'tribal' collective and their imaginative resistance to nation-state power, but also of the effectiveness of their political organizations.

Peter Phipps considers the psyched-out selves of border crossers in the (dis)guise of tourists and 'terrorists', traversing the interrelations between tourism and violence (Chapter 7). The two categories are distinct in that the tourist is more of a consumer, perhaps in denial or on a personal quest, while the terrorist/freedom fighter travels with deadly serious intent, or may be on the run trying to pass as 'merely' a tourist. Yet both demonstrate certain similarities as 'living symbols of another nationalism'; and they each exemplify parallel negotiations of state and border control involving stringent surveillance and passage. Despite the tourist's celebrations and appreciations of 'other' and 'different' culture as the signifier of authenticity in travel, the incommensurability of such travel worlds with the aspirations of some locals are brought to a head as tourists become markers of exchange value in the international hostage trade. While it has been acknowledged (Crick 1988) that tourists suffer a form of self-loathing and strive to get 'off the beaten track', in this chapter the dynamic is recognized as operating at an abstract level even where tourists stray into dangerous geographical zones. Here the violence directed against them for a myriad of reasons confirms the structure of tourist shame which seemingly borders on a kind of homicidal-suicidal self-sacrifice.

Offering a comprehensive critique of exoticism and romanticism on the part of those Western youth travellers to the subcontinent who are fascinated by temples, incense and half-comprehended notions of mysticism, John Hutnyk shows how such exoticizing and trinketizing approaches alibi a wider ideological and political project (Chapter 8). Taking on the 'soft target' of Crispian Mills, lead singer of the pop group, Kula Shaker, this chapter focuses on 'spiritual' touristic practices, as seen on MTV travel documentaries, where 'alternative' becomes just another lifestyle choice in the phantasmagoric market of the West. Such an approach highlights the imbrication of touristic practices with other manifestations of transnational flows, including those of capital, media and ideologies. With the half-baked 'souveniring' of aspects of Indian culture in Kula Shaker's music, it becomes possible to note that exotic commodities are presented as emblems of alterity – signifying nostalgia for a spiritual and harmoniously magical 'India' which can be recovered from any complicity in ongoing colonial plunder. The dynamics of appropriation and unequal exchange of cultural commodities are highlighted when this appropriation ensures compound contradictions in the travel of such products via televisual transmission and Sony Corporation sponsorship.

In Chapter 9, Seán McLoughlin and Virinder Kalra provide another means by which South Asia is utilized as a resource. Beginning on a bus talking with young women travellers in Pakistan, they offer a slamming critique of academic, media and social work conventions of under-standing and representing diasporic South Asian culture as derivative of its regional manifestations in the subcontinent. Geographical South Asia is commonly seen as the privileged place in which keys to unlock England's 'multi-cultural riddles' are found. This effectively marginalizes the position of minority groups in the UK with regard to constructions of residency, and assumes a highly problematic notion of 'dislocation'. The authors ask whether 'dislocation' is not more applicable to Western travellers in South Asia. By highlighting the multiple journeys and tropes of self-representation articulated in discussions amongst diasporized Mirpuri youth in Britain on their travels to, and in, Mirpur, the narratives of travelling diasporised Asians demonstrate the creative fusion of cultural reference points, rather than exemplifying an entrapment between the 'two cultures' of East and West. Their dynamic discourse entails both narratives of roots with regard to Mirpur, and of routes with regard to multitudinous points of reference.

Following on from such travels, Shirin Housee furthers the discussion of roots and routes by narrating the journeying self, and the intricate entwining of travel and identity (Chapter 10). Life journeys conflate with journeys across the globe – India, Mauritius and England – along with travel experience as a black woman in other parts of the world. This chapter brings much-needed perspectives to the black woman's travels, overlooked or homogenized in Eurocentric accounts and guides on travel. The notion of 'black' is produced as a political category at particular moments. It is a category which is informed by her birth in Mauritius into a family of Indian ancestry, their emigration to England, and her self-representation and political alliances in an overtly racist world. It encapsulates her positional identity in the white society of her place of residence and travel worlds in various locations. The question of gender acts as a further factor in tempering her encounters with hosts on her travels. Her fluid negotiations of identity offer a stark contrast to reified visions of Mauritius and Mauritians in travel brochures. Nonetheless, her identifications with a Western country, for better or worse, particularly in countries of the South, afford her a certain privilege of manoeuvrability denied to others in the global ecumene.

Raminder Kaur (Chapter 11) develops Housee's anecdotal and autobiographical style for a fictive-factual conclusion to the volume which revisits strands in preceding chapters. The account provides imaginative material with which to recall arguments about the awkward affinities between tourists and social scientists in touristic sites (MacCannell 1976; Pi-Sunyer 1981; Crick 1985, 1988; Clifford 1997), as well as highlighting the gulf between travel experiences and academic reportage. The fictional contents permit communication of the nuance of travel worlds and harsh views generally censored for circulation in 'polite society'. The chapter opens possibilities at the same time as closing them down, violating those that have been found to be dead ends in this book.

## Departure Gates

Travel is a ubiquitous phenomenon practised universally – but the sense of travel practice that we adopt in this project is intended as a corrective for trends that we see in tourism studies, theories of globalization and explorative or adventure literature. We need to conceive of travel as premised on alternative possibilities without falling into the trap of exoticizing, as with an uncritical adoption of pilgrimage and exodus. We do not say, of course, don't leave home, but we do want to think otherwise about departures and itineraries. We attempt to present a travelator, a moving pathway through various sites of contestation and construction. Travel research need not be only a collection of journey anecdotes or metaphors on the theme of travel, but should seek to look at the full range of cultural practices associated with travelling and their sociopolitical implications. This book starts from the premise that everything is drawn into travel; which at its furthest extension seems to subsume all cultures and all spaces, things, and times, into its consumptive logics. Within this incorporation there are, of course, differences of intensity and counter-hegemonic moments which it is the task of localized studies in a global context to explore.

Everyone has a traveller's tale to tell. In this book we tell each other tales that ask what might be some of the things required for transformatory projects in the regions that link the traveller. How does one narrate and enact travel that works for solidarity-in-difference alongside a division-free union of the world; that tries to get rid of that nauseous sickness associated with a focus that dwells mainly on the pleasures of passengers in ships, trains, buses, cars, aeroplanes and space vehicles, and their ports of call? We argue for a travel unafraid of upsetting authenticity regulators, culture vulture brokers, scavengers of spice and devotees of dilettant difference. This calls for a politics of culture which takes as its context the various transitions and trajectories of travel and transformation: citing movements and struggles, from those against forced migration and enslavement, through mercantile extraction and cyber-highway robbery, right on up to musical appropriation and liberal appreciation in a global scenario of cannibalizing capitalism.

Rewriting the guidebooks is our humble project in the context of circulations and flows, of objects, images and peoples, through diverse spaces and sites, with varied emotional and political charges, and told in a variety of storied modes, proliferating regardless. We would like to re-plot (and re-televise) some of the accepted, cherished and overly-privileged trails, not by refusing travel or travel stories, but by way of them, through them, up, under and around them. This project carries a political weight, and the burden of difficult journeys. Perhaps such a narrative is itself a violation, but this book travels with travel worlds wanting to renew the vistas of what is possible in the social sciences, to extend the access points, passport and passageways of what can be said and done, to chart other directions and dimensions, and to anticipate other neglected horizons. Necessarily utopian, this is not a journey that is impossible, but one that seeks to map out a variety of plausible paths not yet trodden flat by the dull protocols of scholarly package tourism, and, of course, books like this. There is nothing that requires us to always and only go for fun in the sun – the world is no resort haven, for most of us. Those that do blindly travel to brochure land carry their own baggage of travel sickness.

## Notes

1  The authors of this book use the terms West and North interchangeably. They are, of course, a reference to the First World, or what may be called the high-income countries. Consequently, the terms East or South refer to countries of the 'Third World' – those found on the wrong side of international divisions of labour and privilege.

2  Appadurai offers the useful model of '-scapes' as perspectival constructs with which to consider global cultural flow. Rather than premising his argument on centre–periphery models, he explores the global economy in terms of disjunctures and relationships between (1) ethnoscapes; (2) mediascapes; (3) technoscapes; (4) finanscapes; and (5) ideoscapes. We do not view tourists as simply one aspect of the movement of people under 'ethnoscapes', but look to see how this interacts with other global flows of media imagery and distribution (mediascapes), technology (technoscapes), global capitalism (finanscapes), and ideologies of states and counter-state movements (ideoscapes).

3  The European Union (EU) has recently agreed to track asylum seekers with recorded fingerprints to provide a Europe-wide rebuffing system. Assumed criminality and 'illegal' status allows the most brutal treatment to be sanctioned by official laws and conventions (*The Guardian,* 20 March 1998).

4  Malinowski's own project is now reconfigured as multi-site travelling anthropology (Marcus 1995: 106) in recognition of the mobile institutional and power arrangements which enable ethnography to take place at all.

5  On reflexivity in a travel frame, see Arshi *et al.* (1994: 234–7). This text offers a critique of Pratt (1992) and her avoidances and limits on the subject of trans-culturation, focusing upon a strict bookkeeping (as in keeping to books) in an otherwise attentive reading.

6  Examples of this could be multiplied: we refer only to recent texts such as that of Falk and Campbell (1997), Bell and Valentine (1997), but note the scope of Lowe and Lloyd (1997).

7  Euro-privilege applies even where anthropologists would finally recognize their kinship with tourists and other visitors: if their texts mention these relations they do not get promoted into the Sociology or Cultural Studies sections of the

bookshops, but languish in the bottom shelf Anthropology or Development sections. Paul Gilroy's book *The Black Atlantic* (1993) is a floating corrective to those cultural studies approaches which demarcate the metropolitan West as site for cultural studies and the 'rest' of the world for a primitivist anthropology.

# 2

## NI-TEN-ICHI-RYU
### Enter the World of the Smart Stepper[1]

### KOUSHIK BANERJEA

[T]he blacks have their own thing and the music lets whites get in on their life a bit, but the Indians, they're another story, just do it and live it and there's a single attitude … and it's easy to see how history is just the winners telling everyone how bad the losers are, Johnny Rotten said that … classic line which sums the whole thing up … maybe that was what started me thinking about all that punk stuff, how everything's gone back to square one again, and then those stories on the telly, about the BNP in the East End, and the NF have changed their name as well, just like the SPG, and I would have thought that was all in the past now, that we'd gone through a bit of a breaking point with those two Southall riots, and I grew up with Indians and Pakistanis and know the difference, they killed hundreds of thousands just to get that border, and don't forget Bangladesh, and that was the starting point (King 1996: 180).[2]

By the time that the 'Punky Reggae Party' was in full swing during the long hot summer of 1976, the image of 'Williams'[3] suspended in horrific animation in the carceral vaults of Mr Han's island palace was already a fading celluloid memory. Bruce Lee, star of the seminal 1973 martial arts 'action' feature, *Enter the Dragon*, was some years dead although his enduring iconographic presence entitled him to remain the one South-East Asian import still unequivocally welcome in the Western metropole. Meantime, immigration to England from the Indian subcontinent had all but dried up as a credible statistic not long after the Beatles, on their own hippy trail, 'discovered' for themselves the rare mystical pleasures of the East.

More than two decades have elapsed and the spirit of Williams is alive and well in the musical, monastic guise of hiphop 'playa' Jeru Davis, aka Jeru the Damaja, aka Sifu Jeru of the Perverted Monastery.[4] In a sense, too, he is going home, eastward bound back to Hong Kong to film the video for his single, *Ya Playin' Yaself*. This time, though, the ebony warrior, mindful of the pitfalls of performative excess, gets to leave in one piece and rescue his 'sister' from evil Triad kidnappers. By Jeru's own admission, the video 'was made to be like a Jet Lee movie' replete with battle-cipher MC-ing ('mike chanting' of improvised lyrics over the instrumental cut), more kicks than kung-fu flicks by Run Run Shaw, and obligatory happy ending.[5]

Similar eastern overtures by Staten Island crew the Wu-Tang Clan on their critically acclaimed *Enter the Wu-Tang* (36 Chambers) debut, and its chart-busting sequel, *Wu-Tang Forever*, have also enjoyed global favour as transnational visual documents within a sonic diaspora.[6] Those 'in the west but not of the west' could apparently look east again without embarrassment, perhaps for the first time since John Coltrane, and the video would be their tool for self-actualization. However, lest we allow ourselves to be seduced by the optimistic undercurrents of this wave of fortuity – travel as perennially hybrid release or as productive marginal realignment, etc. – we might profit from the timely reminder that

> perhaps it was inevitable that the term would vie with 'culture' as a signifier of tremendous scope, because – if we go back to the agricultural etymology of the term – cultures do not just spring up ready-planted in their native soils; very often cultures are the result of transplantation – in other words, of a form of travel.... To examine travel is to examine theory' (Arshi *et al.* 1994: 225).

This is no simple task, containing as it does the implicit demand that we divest ourselves of our own itinerant narcissism long before casting a roving eye over that intellectual trajectory which always already delimits. In any case, as a basic precaution against carelessness, we have to possess some notion of just what it is that we understand 'travel' to mean. Which, and whose, hazardous enterprise are we talking about? After all, the jaundiced alternative is that our wandering spirits, our figures of heroic adventure, remain forever locked in dispute within the confines of an idealized self-image.

Searching for some clarity we might profitably turn to Graham Dawson, who in his martial tale of 'soldier heroes' offers the helpful proposition:

> there is no structural reason why adventure should not relate to contradictory flows of desire, drawing the domestic imaginary into connection with those other imaginaries … that furnish the adventure landscape and the themes of the quest (Dawson 1994: 66).

He subtly hints at the crusading elements never far from the contrived altruism of 'adventure's' seductive surface and, importantly, draws our attention to the paradoxical tension between risk and control which remains at the heart of the whole adventure 'experience':

without risk there can be no adventure; but since both gain and loss remain possible outcomes, excessive risk may cause the experience of excitement to give way to anxiety. Adventure in the modern sense is balanced between anxiety and desire (Dawson 1994: 53).

The suggestion here is that travel, far from being some transgressive actuality of 'the postmodern condition', just as often serves as the conduit for redrawing the boundary between what is acceptable and unacceptable ever more tightly around the norm of the 'known'. Ironically, what is actually being transported is a version of conservative conformism whose purposive limits are defined by the constant search for a philistine 'outside' against which to pit a puritan 'inside'. As the wily Afrikaner might have observed of his less-detached countrymen during a careless moment in southern Africa: 'it's those Protestant motherfuckers up to their old tricks again'.

It is worth remembering that empire was the condition, and its colonies the performance of an exaggerated imperial psyche. India, Africa and the Caribbean – with their connotations of danger, excitement, and the special allure of their uncharted 'darkness' – were the farthest points in that imaginative (Christian) geography rooted in a dichotomy between Home and the World. These were the wilderness to be transformed through what Dawson has ingeniously called 'enlightened cultivation'. Moreover they were the location for that most popular of Orientalist conceits: the irresistible dualism of enlightened despotism and sexual conquest as key features in a narrative of re-invention or at least self-idealization for a whole class of colonial opportunists. Said's epochal expose of such practices in *Orientalism* (1978) helps focus our gaze on those Europeans who spent much of the nineteenth century looking to the East for its purported sensuality, its promise of erotic adventure. French Orientalist painting was chiefly concerned with slave markets, houris, and harems. And none less than Lord Tennyson was writing about swapping dreary England for 'yonder shining Orient [where] the passions cramped no longer shall have scope and breathing space.... I shall take some savage woman, she shall rear my dusky race' (Tennyson cited in *The Guardian*, 4 May 1996).

Meanwhile the French author, Pierre Loti, was off to Japan to look for 'a little yellow-skinned woman with black hair and cat's eyes ... not much bigger than a doll' (Loti, cited in *The Guardian*, 4 May 1996). It is worth noting that although he duly acquired and married such a specimen through his laundryman in Nagasaki, he promptly abandoned her once her mysteries had been 'revealed' to him.

Martin Green, narrating the practice of an 'imagined' imperialism, points out, in more measured fashion, that Empire was: 'a place where adventures took place and men became heroes' (Green, cited in Dawson 1994: 59) – in other words, empire as the site of heroic deeds to make the natives blush with envy and the colonials beam with pride. Within this schema, then, travel clearly assumes the function of a sort of rite of passage; it is only through travel that boys can become men and those men in turn become heroes ... or so the story goes. Moreover, it is only when such journeys are undertaken within the rubric of a colonial power dynamic that 'the zone of occult instability where the people dwell' (Fanon 1963: 183) can be effectively bypassed. It bears repetition that it is precisely such instability of cultural signification which allows the national culture to be articulated as a dialectic of various temporalities – which is why the very notion of travel is always peculiarly problematic.

Borrowing from both Fanon (1963: 196) and Kristeva (1986: 194), I want to suggest that travel be read more productively as the means through which a social imaginary is marked out, discursively ordained and identified with as psychic property. Bhabha adds his chorus of approval, exhorting us to profit from the interrogative currency of such a move: 'These ... postcolonial temporalities ... challenge us to think the question of community and communication without the moment of transcendence: how do we understand such forms of social contradiction?' (Bhabha 1994: 153) Indeed there is nothing contradictory *per se* in viewing travel as both the reinscription of an antique power play and, in more diffuse terms, as engaging sites of liminal possibility via the new-fangled routes of diaspora. Travel is the performative interpretation of Shaolin Buddhist philosophy and aesthetics for a Brooklyn hiphop constituency with all the attendant concerns around issues of appropriation, transplantation and regeneration. It is the perverted, nappy-haired monk in Asia whose presence amongst the bemused and the always already aware connotes a distinct form of psychic identification. Yet all too often it is also the *mission civilatrice* of that latter-day army of Freikorps paedophiles dispersed across the pubescent fleshpots of South and South-East Asia.[7] Of those men who would be kings as they cast a roving eye across their neo-colonial domain ... and process the commodified bodies of little native boys with a paedophilic Prussianism matched only by the eager exchange of Western currency for a poverty-struck native complicity.

At stake, then, is how we might unravel the mysteries of travel as a process of becoming. What is being ventured, for instance, in hiphop's eastern gaze? And what is gained?

Crucially, the answer is contained in that psychic space between the discordant journeys of inspirational pilgrimage and purposive paedo-

philia. Perhaps this is a crude dichotomy, yet its exaggerated polarities
allow for a useful lucidity. Both are return trips from the West to the
East yet with wildly differing connotations. Ultimately both speak of a
particular 'need' to travel: one which can be conflated with the ever-
ascendant premium placed within overtly political doctrine and its
nefarious organic practice upon the fractious notion of 'territoriality'.
Indeed, the polyglot narratives of West/East return travel are diverse
enough to encompass such disparate motivations as comparatively
deregulated psycho-sexual fulfilment *and* the pursuit of a spiritual ethics
suffused with a mobile aesthetic. Our interest, then, must lie in
unravelling the symbolic currency of travel branded on the very bodies
of those who travel.

This much is clear: when the self-professed need to travel enters the
confessional narrative of mercantile academia, the resonances with a
climate of imperial adventure, conquest and the white man's burden are
rarely absent. We can trust to the spectacle of frontiersmen from Albert
Camus to Michael Taussig engaging in various physical and literary
sojourns to the terrains of a fraught neo-colonial humanism or that ever-
elusive apparition of the noble savage. These are the epic journeys, the
transnational quests to circumvent the totality of a particular discursive
sensibility – the jaundiced eye and illiberal practices of 'defective'
anthropology[8] – summarily translated as perspectival supremacy. But it
is their formulaically heroic stars, usually white and European, who
exhort our attention in the unseemly spectacle of a self-professed
methodological absolution from stigmatized anthropological tribute.
(We might care to observe in the spirit of The Last Poets that 'the white
man's got a god complex'). So we may heave a collective sigh of relief,
then. No matter that these whites travelled to distant climes with their
unfamiliar instruments and unremarkable perceptive regimes, they came
bearing the greatest gift of all: the self-reflexivity in their hearts and
minds. No longer the untutored gaze of a Malinowski emerging 'wise'
from the dramaturgy of participant observation. Rather the tirelessly
self-aware purveyor of 'discursive practice' in the field, that space which
Clifford has wryly conceded: 'is a home away from home, a place of
dwelling.... The field as spatial practice is thus a specific style, quality,
and duration of dwelling' (Clifford 1992: 99). In the playful spirit of
empire, then, is forged a kind of ethnographic diaspora literally made up
of ethnographers: a hermetically sealed enclave of knowledge, integrity
and science – social, political and always handy – with which to translate
the natives' baffling rituals. India, for instance, becomes a site of secular
pluralism yet irreconcilable communalism; of *sati*, pantheism *and* funda-
mentalism; and importantly of ancient mysticism and ennobling poverty.

Ultimately, the subcontinent is returned intact to the colonial centre as a degenerate totality.

If trickery, pragmatism and coercion styled their own syncretic pact to appropriate Indian territories in the 'Old World', then this was merely coterminous with pioneering strategies of the 'pilgrim fathers' to assume Indian lands in the 'New'. This would be achieved through a legitimation discourse premised on investment in whiteness as uniquely valuable property in a society predicated on the power differentials inscribed in phenotype. And, significantly, this would appear most frequently as a metaphysical assertion informing the physical claim to the rights and privileges conferred by 'ownership' of land and, for that matter, of the law of the land:

> In many ways so embedded that it is rarely apparent, the set of assumptions, privileges and benefits that accompany the status of being white have become a valuable asset that whites sought to protect.... The origins of property rights ... are rooted in racial domination.... Race and property were thus conflated by establishing a form of property contingent on race – only Blacks were subjugated as slaves and treated as property. Similarly ... in native American land ... only white possession and occupation ... was validated and therefore privileged as a basis for property rights (Harris 1993: 1713–16).

Our interest here lies in the critical import of a propertied whiteness (in those fleshpots) as *the* ontological fact of personhood, both in terms of its reified political connotations and in terms of the access it provides to the acquisition of materials: be it land, peoples or simply brown boys and girls. Whilst the law may have constructed whiteness as an objective fact, there remains little doubt as to its actuality as ideological proposition. We should be under no illusions: whiteness as property fruitfully (for whites at least) engages the law in a protective function. Under such conditions it would not only be useful but also legitimate for whites to buy into the Benthamite promise that 'property is nothing but the basis of expectation'. For if by 'white supremacy' we mean the systemically ordained primacy of a political, economic and cultural order defined by the conscious and implicit hegemony of white interests and entitlement, the consequences are clear for our story.

When folks speak of 'border crossing' or 'transgressing boundaries' they are frequently referring to the radius of their own psychic circumference. Take the notion of social space, for instance: these buildings, those trees, this community centre, that *martial arts cinema*. Such are the cognitive markers of an eminently reducible *terra firma* – the forms through which the very idea of social space is mapped. Yet this bricks and mortar geography is itself subordinate to the territorial document of entitlement. Places become 'ours' through the grandly pragmatic gesture of asserting property rights. No matter that the propertied characteristics of whiteness and a symbiotic blackness historically allowed, as Walter Rodney so eloquently points out in *How Europe Underdeveloped Africa* (1981), the sequestering of the latter's agency as condition for the former's primacy. Of course Indian land claims as 'first possessors' were discounted as being of dubious merit when those claims conflicted with the pioneering aims of 'civilizing' the North American 'wastelands'.

What matters is the import, in the first instance, of a legal discourse underpinning the mobile narrative of land acquisition whereby the very expectation of that land as a condition of propertied whiteness is something to be sacralized and unswervingly defended. This is the great cause worth bowing down before and at its heart stirs the nascent form of an omnipotently constitutive whiteness. Thus do we witness the complicity of a requisite native 'irrationality' with the 'reason' invoked by a peculiarly colonial hegemony: enter 'the space of death where the Indian, African, and white gave birth to a new world' (Taussig 1991: 5).

How, then, does this poetics of control operate? Think of the 'coolie', that archetypal beast of burden, whose very existence is predicated upon the (frequently human) cargo with which he is laden. Imagine that quotidian Hegelian space which propels: 'the notion of hegemony into the lived space of realities ... as in the sweaty warm space between the arse of him who rides and the back of him who carries' (Taussig, 1991: 288). This construct is useful in so far as it allows us to 'explore', though not perhaps in such an overtly penetrative fashion, the dynamic which binds the ravages of paedophilic adventurism to the presumed solipsism of 'native' children.

Try to look at things in a linear sort of way. It helps. White men 'going abroad' to fuck brown children is *not* such an amazing story, mired as it is in mythology and a historical precedent longer than a gibbon's arm. We can engage Raymond Williams's (1981) notion of a 'structure of feeling' productively to underline the extraordinarily ephemeral ways in which substantive concerns, beliefs and their strategic corollaries are handed over to 'communal possession'. These ways are at once sacrosanct from yet implicitly suggested by the discrete parcels of social, economic and political life subsuming individual or collective identities.

When white 'adventurers' first laid eyes on the opulence of 'the East', their overarching desire was acquisitive. Treasure would serve as a tribute to their seafaring prowess, boldness of vision and loyalty to that idea of identity as inextricably bound to their propertied status as 'white men'. The East may well have been a career but only a particular 'version' of humanity would be entitled to pursue that rapacious vocation.

Consider for a moment that conventional narrative of expectation which underscores the promise and practice of propertied whiteness. This is a useful point of return as it is implicated in the imperial design of adventure as a sort of boys' own quest; a romantic mode of engagement which allows its heroes to project and sustain an imaginative utopia. From 'soldiers of fortune' to James Bond; Lawrence of Arabia to Richard Branson and beyond – these are the archetypes for the imagination of the ultimate paradox: the dramaturgy of excess performed within a theatre of self-containment. And what could be more excessive yet utterly self-absorbed than the image of (the white man as) God fucking *his* children on the virginal sands of Sri Lanka?

Meanwhile, back in the Shaolin Temple compound another kind of itinerant performance is taking place. In the spirit of Said we might observe that the north–south, south–north traffic in hiphop disciples seeking to learn 'the mystery of Chess Boxing'[9] implicitly enlarges and complicates the back-and-forth colonial trajectory mapped by the limits of a particular geopolitical discourse. How, then, might we begin to understand such dissident movements within the context of a global village growing urbanely high on the flavours of transnational capital? Said's narrative is a helpful compass to our own messy navigations:

> As the struggle for independence produced new states ... it also produced ... nomads ... unassimilated to the emerging structures of institutional power ... And in so far as these people exist between the old and the new ... their condition articulates the tensions, irresolutions, and contradictions in the overlapping territories shown on the cultural map of imperialism (Said 1993: 402).

Jeru Davis, then, as obdurate, unintegrated rebel? Jeru the Damaja as transnational vagrant whose 'logic of daring' puts flesh on the bones of that predicament which disfigures modernity? A touch of griotic Zen reminds us in the nick of time:

> ... with all that Ra-Ra-Ra, ya playin' yaself
> with all that gun talk, ya playin' yaself
> with all that big willy talk, ya playin' yaself ...[10]

The question, however, remains: why make such journeys at all? Even if we accept that a degree of travel has always characterized the ambivalent nature of diasporic community in 'the West', received wisdom to date has usually attempted to contain such movement by introducing nationalist paradigms as the lens through which vernacular culture is mapped. Thus an otherwise helpful formation such as 'the Black Atlantic' (Gilroy 1993) still falls some way short of acknowledging, at its points of conceptual closure, the complex, intercultural negotiations frequently taking place beyond the proscribed limits of diaspora. Why, for instance, did modal giant John Coltrane make his Indian pilgrimage and Alice keep the fires burning?[11] And what of the Asian sojourns undertaken, amongst others, by former Coltrane sideman, Pharaoh Sanders or contemporaries, Sonny Rollins and Don Cherry?

Circular breathing patterns and tantric scales aside, my point is not to provide an inventory of transnational delegations and cultural appropriations. Rather, it is to highlight the dangers of a too-neat, too-linear reading of vernacular geography. Buying into such a projection is fraught with the risk that a unique opportunity to re-envision the emergent politics of transnationality will be missed. It is not even a question of the legitimacy of the ensuing vernacular – such concerns were bankrupt long before the master revealed *A Love Supreme* and an essentialist needle first failed to fit its stylistically contoured groove. Rather, at issue is not the 'what' but the 'why' underscoring the trail blazed across the East by these children of the African diaspora.

Bhabha elides us to look at such dissident footfalls as 'a meditation on the disposition of space and time from which the narrative of the nation must begin' (Bhabha 1994: 155). And there are other voices hinting at the seductive allure (for 'Western' dissidents) of Asian popular culture when married to Buddhist principles and the performative ethics of Hong Kong cinema:

> Learning martial arts in order to strengthen the body, helping the weak, eliminating the strong, heroism and righteousness ... these ideological values are embedded in kung-fu movies (Yu-Mo-Wan, Hong Kong film archive, *Kung-Fu Fighting*, BBC2, May 1996).

The writer and self-professed martial arts fanatic, Bey Logan, offers more sociologically satisfying fare:

> Particularly for minorities (or) ... for people who feel downtrodden, they feel their lives are controlled by richer people who have their own agenda, and they see this underdog hero and generally kung-fu cinema is the cinema of the underdog.... As the age becomes more dangerous and more technologically advanced people feel that they are powerless ... but there's a sense of looking at a hero who only relies on his hands, his feet and his courage to effect the world around him to an enormous degree' (*Kung-Fu Fighting*, BBC2, May 1996)

Perhaps we should pause for a moment and consider why such a premium is being placed (indeed has long been placed) within prominent sections of the hiphop community on both sides of the Atlantic, black or otherwise, upon an imagistically reified, performatively imagined version of South-East Asian body symbolism. If we are to believe what we are told – that martial arts is an expression of speech or a physical language – then we must demand the following details: who is doing the 'talking' and what might they be 'saying'? Typically, for a discipline which prides itself on its pantheistic mutability, its major proponents are not short of explanatory fuel. Actor-director Donnie Yuen offers the poetic vision: 'A punch is a punch. A kick is a kick. It's an expression. But it takes kung-fu movies to deliver that expression from each and every one of us.' (*Kung-Fu Fighting*, BBC2, May 1996). His contemporary, Jet Lee, is somewhat more expansive:

> The Chinese physique can't really be compared to that of Westerners ... but the Chinese are swift in movement and can express that movement well. Everyone wants to see a hero. Body movement expresses heroism, so many people like these movies ('Kung-Fu Fighting', BBC2, May 1996).

It is not hard to see how those bodies 'in the west but not of the west', subjected to the most appalling history of brutalization and dehumanization, would choose to reinvent themselves 'as the precious container of mythology and folklore' (Banerjea and Barn 1996: 193). Foucault, for one, recognised how the micro-politics governing regulation of the body might have implications for the macro-politics concerned with the surveillance of whole communities. He describes such preoccupations with body and population as 'the two places around which the organisation of power over life was deployed' (Foucault 1981: 139). However, he only really focused upon those 'rational' disciplines of the body and populations which emerged in response to the urban crises (in Europe) of the eighteenth and nineteenth centuries, obliging attention here of a less anaemic and parochial variety.

Those displaced bodies historically manipulated as the dehumanized tools of a relentless labour are thus forced to seek solace from the cruellest excesses of productivism in the bittersweet folds of a vibrant vernacular. Gilroy cogently reminds us that:

> the black body is here celebrated as an instrument of pleasure rather than an instrument of labour. The night time becomes the right time and the space allocated for recovery and recuperation is assertively and provocatively occupied by the pursuit of leisure and pleasure. (Gilroy 1993: 36)

That this search for the raw materials of redemption is never complete should alert us to the possibilities contained within its condition of being always already 'in motion'. Little wonder, then, that its balletic grace coupled with its swashbuckling excess should transform kung-fu in the

East into such an attractive narrative of performance and pedagogy to those in the West whose relationship to an untutored version of 'modernity' with its grand promise of freedom of movement has always been at best ambiguous and at worst a cruel fallacy.

Jeru went to Asia as much to recover an ethic of performance as his 'kidnapped sister'.[12] Wingchung conflict at close quarters, moves to make the Williams Brothers blush, and the clash of the Brooklyn style with the predatory Crane are ample testament to that, almost in the same breath that they are served up as vicarious fodder for an insatiable MTV generation. Bodies for so long forbidden to perform in all but the most sanctioned environments would find playful release within the excessively active idiom of kung-fu fighting; and in so doing would flaunt the rigidly ordained universe managed by a supremacist gaze. As ever, though, such moments can appear transient or disturbingly unsustainable while the ubiquitous reach of transnational capital exacts its corporate toll on the head of dissident cultural strategy. Performance, ironically, has become as much a cipher of containment as defiant expression of bodily excess. We should be mindful that pugilism with its connotations of those (black) men 'who fought the good fight' has in no way unsettled supremacist wisdom governing the spatial and temporal regulation of the 'native' body.

Notwithstanding, the resonances of Jeru's eastern journey are clear. Retracing the unequivocally black steps taken by the ultimately doomed figure of Williams, he floats into Hong Kong's congested carnivalesque just as those other 'adventurers' who have also re-entered Asia, though with delusions of *Mai-Bap* grandeur to her catatonic children, are about to 'pull out'. What his presence prefigures, however, is a dissonant mode of travel. Not the paedophilic recovery of some fictive colonial pasture when all the natives just liked to say '*Ji!*' and would oblige with supple limbs and terrorized silence. Rather the paradoxical response to massive dislocations and perceived intransigence within the corporate interior and neo-imperial wastelands of the West by the practice of an itinerant transnationality and performance of cultural refabulation: 'Precision, concreteness, continuity, form – all these have the attributes of a nomadic practice whose power ... is not aggressive but transgressive' (Said 1993: 402).

*Ni-Ten-Ichi-Ryu*? Occupy the liminal space between the notes, ride the Spartan drum'n'bass rhythm of this instrumental cut by London-based producer, Robert 'Photek' Parkes, and our story appears to have come full circle. Sup the meditative chalice of this booming junglist tiger, profit from its breakbeat choreography of combat philosophy. Surf the airwaves with the rest of the sonic 'pirates' and enjoy that fulsome riposte to those grey men at the DTI. *Yes! Yes! Yes! London Town, pushing this one out to all diasporic Massive, you know who you are!* Take a trip to Soho, weave your way through the Arcade Funk and witness the journeymen children of diaspora plotting with clever metal the fantastic, stellar routes of astral travel to 'Cyberia' and beyond. Revel in its protozoan chaos, then consider how such 'mutant' travel narratives are the wholly logical product of that long and profound interface, recovered across historical time by such 'playas' as Coltrane, Rollins and Jeru, between the more contingent and happily profane organs of diaspora.

Travel, and its spatial imperative, is a serious business. People can and frequently do die over territorial disputes. The land itself is etched with the memory of the millions killed or exiled during the trauma of Indian Partition, and in more recent times, the perversion of high-profile, prime-time 'ethnic cleansing' in Rwanda and Bosnia has once more raised the spectre of nationalisms whose prerogative is always already territorial. Enforced migrations subsequently visited upon whole populations give the lie once and for all to the myth of travel as a uniquely democratic cipher. For while it may contain other peripheral possibilities, at its dominant heart lies the implicit violence of acquisitive zeal: for people, for products, but above all for land.

Yet this primitive urge for territorial monopoly is alive and well much closer to home, too. There is a point during the John King novel, *The Football Factory*, when one of the characters, several *bhang lassis* to the credit, starts to talk about 'the Thar desert right here in Southall' (King 1996: 181). London becomes the compressed site of an opportunistic post-colonial encounter: the character's itinerant gaze is filtered through the mobile body politic of a football hooligan 'firm' and the usual obsessions with concepts of territory, honour and loyalty are played out to their bloody conclusion. Just fiction? Away from the text it is worth remembering that white flight from 'those inner cities', and the resort to a politics of virulent parochialism where the expectations of 'propertied whiteness' have not been met, collude to wreak a mobile narrative of havoc on those dark 'others' unlucky enough to be caught in the path of this Oregon Trail.

Stephen Lawrence, the black teenager murdered in a racist attack at a bus stop in south London on 22 April 1993, is a case in point, whose only remaining journey would be an ethereal one to his parents' ancestral land, Jamaica:

> At issue is a subject most of us probably consider too primitive to concern us much – territoriality (which) mostly unseen, often elaborately genteel in its manifestations, remains a power in our land ... the white working class has fled in huge numbers for the outer suburbs ... and race has been a factor

in this Great Trek.... The accused ... young hooligans to the outside world, in their own imaginings they are protecting their community from alien incursion. They are taking the furtive, tacit, disguised territoriality that permeates our society and turning it into a perverted crusade (Popham, *The Independent*, 15 February 1997).

Perhaps it is apt that we land finally on the metaphor of the crusade, as this is both the means and the mission of a terrifyingly anaemic travel narrative. Indeed, the covetousness of crusading travel owes an almost equal debt to the transnationality of imperial capital and the border patrols of ethnic parochialism. This, after all, is the promise and practice of a disturbingly mobile body politic whose sharply transported terrors are only briefly interrupted by the resourceful cultural trajectories of diaspora.

## Notes

1 *Ni-Ten-Ichi-Ryu* or Two Swords Technique is the title of a sparse drum 'n bass instrumental by the London-based producer, Robert 'Photek' Parkes. The 'Smart Stepper', weaned on a stylistic diet of drum'n'bass 'hardstep', is presented here as an emblematic figure – one which is engaged in a different mode of travel to mercantile academia, class-conscious backpackers or Freikorps paedophiles (see below). The suggestion here is that both the music and its mobile constituency hint at those 'other' versions of travel defiantly produced within the context of metropolitan diaspora. Perhaps it is also worth emphasising how both are uniquely sustained and transformed by the fluid dynamics which underscore such a peculiarly British cultural form as Jungle or drum'n'bass.

2 John King's 1996 novel, *The Football Factory*, offers an appropriate induction into the world of the smart stepper. It is useful in that it provides a distinctive cartographic treatise on both physical *and* cultural journeys being made within contemporary Britain, yet its narrative remains refreshingly aware of the global dimensions of such post-imperial travel. It speaks clearly of how the daily pursuits of popular culture cannot be disentangled from the often fractious contours of diaspora which emerge within the British metropolitan context. As such it deserves consideration as a key text for travel theorists.

3 Williams is best remembered as the black fighter in *Enter the Dragon* reviewing the tyranny of Mr. Han's operation (as the invitee to a martial arts competition) with the political eye of post-COINTELPRO Black Power activism. COINTELPRO, otherwise known as the Counter Intelligence Programme of the FBI, relied heavily during the late 1960s and early 1970s on a network of police informers and specially primed infiltrators of the black body politic, particularly the metropolitan chapters of the Black Panther Party. It was remarkably successful in delivering a retrogressive of counter-insurgency politics and ushered in a new era of heightened cynicism within African-American political movements.

4 Jeru Davis  prides himself on what he sees as the didacticism within his rhymes.

Having made his critical debut back in 1991 on Gangstarr's *Daily Operation* album, he has since set about climbing what he calls 'Moral Mountain', high up on which is perched 'The Perverted Monastery', the natural home of its abbot, Sifu Jeru. Like his contemporaries, the Wu-Tang Clan, Jeru is happy to be closely associated with the aesthetics and ethics of kung-fu, which features significantly in his rhymes. He sees such Eastern philosophy and style as being absolutely compatible with his own upbringing in Brooklyn, New York, as a Rastafarian. As such he offers a useful link to the past and those earlier journeys to and from the East made by such influential African-American musicians as John Coltrane or Sonny Rollins, to name but two.

5 Sir Run Run Shaw was perhaps the most influential producer in the history of kung-fu film-making, having worked with all its major players, including Bruce Lee, Jackie Chan and Maggie Cheung.

6 Hiphop crew the Wu-Tang Clan are another chart-topping example of the Eastern flavours currently proliferating throughout the genre. The title, Wu-Tang, is borrowed from the name given to an ancient order of martial arts monks. It is also one half of the martial arts film, *Shaolin and Wu-Tang*, from which the Wu-Tang Clan took three samples for their debut LP.

7 I am thinking here of the quasi-revolutionary zeal with which so-called 'sex tourists', primarily economically privileged white Western males, continue to march across the contact zones of South and South-East Asia. For the record, 'Freikorps' were that self-styled militia of German men seeking to restore some sense of their emasculated selfhood following their nation's humiliation and territorial losses in the wake of the First World War. Their party pieces included, amongst others, gang rape and mutilation of any woman unlucky enough to be in their 'contact zone'. While the modern-day paedophile may curb his activities short of murder, he is not averse to flexing his imperial muscle nor to exercising his imperial capital in the former colonies in ways long outlawed across the over-developed world. Such recent high-profile cases as that of Arthur C. Clarke in Sri Lanka merely serve to underline this point.

8 What remains unclear is precisely what might constitute an ethical anthropology. From Taussig to Clifford and beyond there is much browbeating on the 'defective practice' of non-reflexive anthropology and its propensity to delimit the object of study by superimposing its own metanarrative, consistent with the actualities of Western political, social and economic privilege. Conversely there is a strong sense, in such texts as *Shamanism, Colonialism and the Wild Man* of 'the good white man' redeeming his fallen discipline (anthropology) amongst the natives. Self-reflexivity becomes the key to this redemptive strategy, yet in a curious paradox the power to call upon this ethical tool lies uniquely with the same individual who is seeking to divest his thinking of its neo-colonial trappings: the anthropologist. Hence the subsequent farce of 'self-professed methodological absolution'.

9 The phrase is taken from the single release of the same name by the Wu-Tang Clan. On the video which accompanies the single, the members of the Clan appear like hooded Samurai warriors on a massive, black and white chess board. The imagery opted for is self-consciously stylised and plays havoc with any notion of an originary hiphop aesthetic, owing more to the traditions of Run Run Shaw than Run DMC.

10 In his 1997 release, *Ya Playing Yaself,* Jeru has a laugh at the expense of all those folk who, so to speak, 'give it the large' but keep getting busted: the big talk, little pork merchants who litter the airwaves.

11 Modal jazz was exemplified throughout the 1950s and 1960s by such visionaries as John Coltrane and Miller Davis on albums like *Blue Trane* and *Kind of Blue.* Alice Coltrane made her pilgrimage to India following the death of her husband in 1967 and, like Trevor Howard, stayed on. However, unlike Mr Howard, she subsequently became a disciple to a Hindu religious order, and made several recordings with such influential musicians as Zakir Hussain and Carlos Santana. More recently her version of the Coltrane classic, *A Love Supreme*, appeared on the *Red, Hot and Cool* compilation, dedicated to raising awareness of the spread of HIV and AIDS within African-American and Hispanic-American communities.

12 The nominal plot around which the video for *Ya Playin' Yaself* is shot involves Jeru rescuing his Asian 'sister' from Triad kidnappers. The video incorporates all the major martial arts combat styles, such as Wingchung, the Crane and Jeru's own invention, the Brooklyn style, in a playful nod to the seminal martial arts flick, *Enter the Dragon.* The Williams Brothers were famous in the 1930s for their Jazz-Dance routines in Harlem's Cotton Club and, in the video, Jeru parades his own nimble steps, showing admirable fleetness of foot and a healthy respect for his zoot-suited predecessors.

# 3

## TRAVELLING LIGHT
Missionary Musings, Colonial Cultures
and Anthropological Anxieties[1]

### Saurabh Dube

An immaculate conception of the epiphany of travel spells the end of
memory. But memory strikes back – as empires have done, again and
again – to be reunited with travel through an excess of longing. From
the dim recesses of a dark memory emerges a fragment of forgetting –
the transcendental trick of the true traveller. Here is Clastres quoting
Montaigne on Socrates on travel: 'Someone said to Socrates that a
certain man had grown no better in his travels. "I should think not," he
said. "He took himself along with him"' (Clastres 1989: 7).[2]

A little over fifteen years ago, Bernard Cohn invoked the image of
'missionaries in the row boat' to remind us of some of the ways in which
memory, forgetting, and travel are bound to each other through a surplus of longing. In the fragment that follows, the tireless anthropologist-
historian is primarily questioning a model of anthropology as ahistorical
practice, but the metaphorical charge and the critical force – and the
contemporary resonances and the current implications – of his writing
extend rather wider.

> the missionary, the trader, the labour recruiter or the government official
> arrives with the bible, the mumu, tobacco, steel axes or other items of
> Western domination on an island whose society and culture are rocking along
> in the never never land of structural-functionalism [read tradition], and with
> the onslaught of the new, the social structure, values and lifeways of the
> 'happy' natives crumble. The anthropologist follows in the wake of the
> impacts caused by Western agents of change, and then tries to recover what
> might have been. The anthropologist searches for the elders with the richest
> memories of days gone by, assiduously records their ethnographic texts.…
> The people of anthropologyland, like all God's Children got shoes, got
> structure (Cohn 1980: 199).

In tune with this testimony, my discussion of the hegemonic worlds
created by missionary travels questions the privilege accorded to
Western origins of change and queries the primacy given to white agents

of transformation in non-Western arenas. Indeed, by emphasizing the contradictory location of the mission project in the creation of colonial cultures of rule, this chapter also challenges the imaginings of a singular West that simultaneously underwrites Euorocentric celebrations of a triumphant modernity and nativist laments for ravaged traditions. The dialectic of enlightenment and empire *negotiated* enduring bonds between colonial power and evangelical knowledge, but the key complicities here were accompanied and interrogated by reworkings of Western truths through the filters of the indigenous. In this chapter, my intervention traces quotidian cartographies defining spaces in time and places in history on the margins of the West, mappings that interrogate the bloated typologies and the spectacular reifications of Eurocentric imaginings of the metropole and the colonies (and beyond). The master languages of reason and race *contracted* lasting links between civilization and the Saviour, but the close connections in these arenas were equally attended and subverted by the recasting of European idioms through the grids of vernacular understandings. Elaborating and extending the critical spirit of Cohn, but also the combative concerns of other comrades and co-conspirators, this chapter further thinks through the shared complicities between the travels of missionaries (and similar mandarins) and the journeys of anthropologists (and like-minded academics). Hence to Heidelberg.

## In the Shadow of the Schloss

Heidelberg is a beautiful town with a character all its own. A place in history, it offers a rare site to discuss realms of knowledge and deliberate boundaries of disciplines. In the marvellously restored premises of the Wissenschaftsforum, located at a quiet end of the Haupstrasse, in the shadow of the Schloss (castle) that dominates the old town, overlooking the 'philosopher's way' on the other side of the river Neckar, scholars of the sciences and savants of the humanities gather together for colloquia and conferences several times a year. The early summer of 1997 was no different. Soon after the end of a workshop on plasticity in the physical sciences, in the third week of June, scholars and students from far and near converged to debate the contours, continuities, and changes in the study of state and society, religion and culture in eastern India.

The conference, I am happy to report, proceeded according to plan. Talks were delivered, presentations made, questions asked, points scored, and scores settled – in the seminar room but over the cold buffet at lunch too – and variously happy and disgruntled seminarians and speakers mingled together in separate groups in the evenings over beer and wine. Do not get me wrong. It was the stuff of most well-organized conferences. Why, then, do I discursively dilate on Heidelberg and the colloquium, since all that seems at stake are minor variations on a familiar theme? There is a purpose.

For the past five hundred years, the epiphany of the exotic, the memory of the other, and the longing(s) of the self running through voyages of discovery and journeys of Enlightenment to distant lands and curious cultures have been matters of violence. This violence has assumed multiple shapes and various guises, several hues and different colours. Its physical contours have been moulded by categorical imperatives, and its epistemic forms lie embodied in historical practice. Here is J. W. Shank, a pioneer Mennonite missionary in South America, a participant – as witting apprentice and hapless journeyman – in the ceaseless trek of a travelling West, writing on the missionary as a civilizing agent:

> He opposes slavery, polygamy, cannibalism, and infanticide. He teaches the boys to be honest, sober, and thrifty; the girls to be pure, intelligent, and industrious. He induces the natives to cover their nakedness, to build house.... It is hard to overthrow the long established heathenism, but slowly it yields to the new power and the beginning of civilised society gradually appears. In every country where mission work has been done we find that the first lasting changes for a higher social order began through missionary effort (Shank, cited in Lapp 1972:51).

The order of immanence and transcendence that shores this statement is a matter of temporality. This should not surprise us. At least since the Enlightenment, renderings of a universal history, cast in the image of a homogeneous Western civilization, rest upon a critical opposition between simple and sacral societies rooted in myth and ritual, on one hand, and dynamic and complex Western orders, grounded in history and reason, on the other. Here, the many modes of colonial domination – ideologies, hegemonies, varieties of epistemic and physical violence – are premised upon a temporal privilege, a franchise for the future accorded to Western arts of civilization by the blueprint(s) of a universal history. Yet most journeys outward from the West have *not* been endeavours to forget the past and the present of the places and the points of their departure. Rather, these trails lead us toward attempts at the immense monumentalisation of a spectacular memory. A singular mapping of Western civilization plots the past and future of other peoples. Such cartographies reveal that beyond (any)one is not just (an)other. Instead, these imaginary lines unravel hierarchies of otherness. Even as there is only one road to civilisation, different peoples have reached its different milestones. At the same time, it also follows that these varieties of otherness share a similar logic with the severalty of Western selves. The fantasy of the absorption of the other through the rigours of travel is a ruse (and more) for discovering an ever enchanted past of the self – erased from contemporary memory through the disenchantment of the Western world – in the timeless presence of the primitive. These memories and longings persist, and I will briefly touch upon their lingering seductions in the academy in the overture that follows before returning by way of a necessary coda to their many enchantments.

## Overture

There is a curious symmetry between the evangelical persuasion of those who would convert Hindoos and Heathens to Christianity in the last century and the sa(l)vage mind of others today who fetishize and freeze tradition to prevent the loss of a timeless primitive. This piece – like other chapters in this volume – discusses and interrogates the worlds created by the travels of the West. It focuses on the evangelical encounter in central India in the late nineteenth and early twentieth centuries. More specifically, it examines the missionary participation in the fashioning of colonial cultures of rule and explores the Indian converts' refraction of missionary authority in the construction of an indigenous Christianity in Chhattisgarh, a large linguistic and cultural region in central India. These particular moves – in their distinctive detail and their special singularity – also allow me to spread my net somewhat further and to cast my aspersions a little wider.

If we have to radically rethink dominant metageographies – 'the set of spatial structures through which people order their knowledge of the world' (Lewis and Wigen 1997: ix) – as a necessary condition toward reconceptualizing the world(s) of travel, it is imperative to endorse the perspectives drawn from margins. The patterns of the evangelical encounter in the dim and dusty land of Chhattisgarh are no less important than the designs of dominance in the smart and spruce sites of London and New Delhi for exploring the widest questions of meaning and power.[3] It follows too that margins invoke other mappings of the world. A story of the hegemonic worlds created by a travelling West that excludes the tales of the subordinate knowledges of subject peoples from the folds of its narrative runs the risk of reifying the very place and power of Western institutions and imaginings – ever incomplete, always questioned, already displaced in other realms – that it sets out to interrogate. Moving metaphors apart, this chapter elaborates the perspectives of an ethnographic history and articulates the 'everyday' as an analytical domain for exploring the production, transaction, and subversion of meaning and power (e.g., de Certeau 1984; Ludtke 1995; Sabean 1990).

The evangelical encounter in central India was located at a critical intersection of meaning and power. This involved two simultaneous and overlapping processes: on one hand, the engagement of the mission project with colonial cultures of rule; and, on the other hand, the interface of Protestant theology, evangelical beliefs and practices of missionaries with the principles of caste and sect and the institutions and dynamics of village life in the creation of an indigenous Christianity. The missionaries, indigenous catechists and helpers, native converts and congregations, and members of the local population were protagonists and players in dramas of divergent perceptions, actors and agents in plays of contending practices.

Tales about those worlds fashioned by missionary travels and every-day local interrogation of these realms, as rehearsed here, are not merely examples chosen at random from the diverse stories of a larger historical and ethnographic record. The fabric of the shared past of the evangelical entanglement was woven from the interlacing of various threads, different designs, and many motifs – stitches on time made by evangelical missionaries and indigenous converts. My effort is to untangle the weave of these threads in order to present the texture of the – far from seamless, often tattered – fabric of the evangelical encounter.

There is also something of a larger critical agenda here. I do not merely refer to the need to counter the responses emerging from professional anxieties of members of guilds of historians and corporations of anthropologists, ravings that persist in presenting history and anthropology as discrete and detached arenas of academic endeavour. The live legacies of Eurocentric imaginings – not only within the academic guilds but also far beyond – worry me rather more. As I have mentioned, the stark separation between unchanging and sacral non-Western societies rooted in myth and ritual, on one hand, and dynamic and complex Western orders grounded in history and reason, on the other, maintains its hold on the here and now.[4] Thus, a classic division of academic labour has separated the historical study of colonial rule in South Asia from contemporary anthropological analyses of indigenous society on the subcontinent (Dirks 1996). This chapter joins other critical exercises in the field to subvert the profoundly ideological division between the discrete desires of anthropology and the distinct longings of history.[5] It also goes a step further as the evangelical encounter, the metropole and the margins, the colonizers and the colonized, all form part of a single analytical field for untangling multiple strands of the shared past of evangelical entanglements and colonial cultures.[6]

## Early Encounters

In the summer of 1868 Oscar Lohr of the German Evangelical Mission Society initiated mission work in Chhattisgarh. His preliminary enquiries had drawn him to the region and revealed the Satnamis as heathens with a difference: they were a monotheistic group whose 'creed' was opposed to idolatry and caste.[7] To the missionary this was a providential connection. It was willed by the Lord. Would the flock not be delivered once it witnessed the Saviour? But the Satnamis did not accept the arrival of the millennium. The group declined its destiny. The missionaries continued to toil the field and to sow the seeds of faith. The halting enterprise of conversion gradually grew through ties of kinship and the prospects of a better life under the paternalist economy of mission stations. Over the next few decades the missionary enterprise in the region expanded. Members of the German Evangelical Mission Society were joined by missionaries of other denominations – the American and General Conference Mennonites, the Disciples of Christ, the Methodists, the Pentecostal Bands of the World – and there was a move to work with other communities. The converts continued to understand missionary injunctions and interpret Christian truths through the filters of local cultures. The 'harvest', never bountiful, was indeed more than a little curious. The missionaries tended. The missionaries reaped. If they made headway, they also had to retrace their steps.

In recent years, we have had forceful reminders that the white man did not always command the initiative in processes of cultural encounter (e.g., Apter 1993; Larson 1997; Prins 1980; Sahlins 1985; see also Obeysekere 1992 and Sahlins 1995). So in 1868 Lohr visited the Satnami guru at his home in Bhandar on the occasion of the community's 'annual festival'. The missionary describes in detail how he was seated next to the guru and served refreshments. He made the triumphant revelation to a 'great mass' of Satnamis that the real *satyanam* (true name) was Jesus Christ. Lohr was elated by the warm welcome. Inadvertently, the missionary also ventures into the realm of ethnographic representations and the pursuit of indigenous meanings when reporting that the Satnamis had stroked his beard to show him great honour and affection in their 'traditional way'.[8] Missionary hyperbole ordered the event as one of monumental 'historical significance'.[9] But was the stroking of Lohr's long flowing beard really the enactment of a timeless, mysterious and customary ritual? Or was it merely a display of Satnami curiosity? Was the serving of refreshments by the guru the extension of hospitality to a white *saheb*, a Western master? Or had Lohr's visit to Bhandar on the day of *gurupuja*, along with thousands of Satnamis, unwittingly signified his acceptance of a subordinate role within the domain of the guru's authority? Three months later the missionary unknowingly challenged a key principle of faith – the wearing of the sacred thread – within Satnampanth.[10] It followed that the curiosity of the Satnamis did not lead to their conversion to Christianity, and the hospitality of the community was replaced by its hostility. The millenarian hopes of Lohr lay in ruins. The Satnamis became wary of the missionary enterprise.[11]

## Missionary Idioms and Colonial Cultures

Recall here Bernard Cohn's remarkable rave on the missionary as the agent of change that frames the opening moments of this chapter. Implicitly, at the very least, the fragment compels us to reflect upon the plurality of Western travels for trade and treasure, evangelization and empire, and for souvenirs yielded by the hunt for distant bounty and the booty of saved souls. It also bids us to think through the mutual logic of the desires of the colonizers and the dreams of the colonized in the shaping of colonial cultures and evangelical entanglements. We need to pose anew that old question: what were the links between the mission project and colonialism? For long the question has translated itself all too easily into a rigid polemical divide: the rival caricatures of the crafty agent of imperialism versus the philanthropic apostle to the natives have dominated the debate (Ayandale 1966; Wilson 1969; see also Dachs 1972). This debate, Jean and John Comaroff (1986) have pointed out, has been confined to the issue of 'Whose side was the missionary really on?' and by extension 'Whose ends did he [or she] serve?' A complex historical problem has been turned into a crude question of cause and effect. The way out of this constricting impasse of competing instrumentalities, it seems to me, lies in a close analysis of the mutual imbrication of the cultural basis and the political implications of the mission project.

It was not often that evangelical missionaries in Chhattisgarh intervened in the arena that is conventionally designated as 'political', in this case the domain of institutionalized power relations between the colonial state and its subjects. The key links between the mission project and colonialism lay elsewhere. To understand these connections, it is imperative that we discard the profoundly disabling (mis)conception that turns the idioms of dominance embedded within colonial cultures of rule into mere reflections of the exercise of authority through the formal apparatuses of empire. In order to explore the myriad ways in which the constitution of colonial power, including the missionary participation in these arenas, often exceeded imperial institutions, I suggest three lines of inquiry here.

First, it is important to examine the missionary participation in the fashioning of authoritative discursive practices that lay at the heart of imperial inscriptions. A pernicious commonplace among historians and theorists of colonial discourse holds that the construction of powerful images of the non-Western other was carried out by a unified conquering colonial elite with a uniform Western mentality.[12] There is a need to focus instead on the complex location of the writings of missionaries within the field of colonial representations. For example, to the missionaries the converts, as Christians, were equals in the 'Kingdom of God'. At the same time, the missionaries also repeatedly emphasized the 'satanical travesties' and the 'savage customs' of these 'sons of wilderness'.[13] Within these mutually contradictory representations, the stock metaphors and routine images that structured missionary thought and writing, in inherently ambivalent ways, constituted and reinforced – but also questioned and subverted – powerful cultural idioms of colonial domination.

And what of the missionary rhetoric that often revealed a tacit approval of British rule? Time and again, until the 1930s, the missionaries and *sarkar bahadur* (colonial government), working in tandem, were depicted as the twin bearers of the light of the 'Western lamp.' It needs to be stressed once again, however, that this support cannot be seen to imply the existence of a seamless community of colonial interests made up of metropolitan policy makers, provincial practitioners, local administrators, members of the armed forces and missionaries. Rather, in order to understand the relation between the missionaries and the colonial regime, we need to turn to the tangled web of relations between the principles of mission work, the structure of Protestant beliefs and the policies of British administrators. In brief, there seems to have been a linkage between two sets of processes: the missionaries' stated commitment to the complementarity of the Church and the state, of spiritual and temporal power, and the post-Mutiny (rebellion of 1857) policy of British administration to effect a separation between religion and politics that critically served to strengthen colonial power (Dirks 1987).

Finally, another set of tensions at the heart of the missionary enterprise found its way into the wider field of colonial representations and imperial inscriptions. The missionaries invoked the precept of individual self-determination and the spiritual spectacle of the witnessing of Christ to argue for the religious freedom of the convert. At the same time, however, the missionaries regarded these converts as children, struggling to grasp rational objective thought.[14] The wards of the mission project had to be guided, nurtured and controlled within a paternalist enterprise.

Thus, within the interstices of these overlapping and tension-ridden movements, the missionaries participated, wittingly and unwittingly, in the construction of colonial mythologies of racial supremacy, the establishment of structures of paternalist authority, and the reinforcement of the legitimacy of bureaucratic colonial rule. All this came about without their formal entry into the institutionalized power relations centring on the colonial state. It is by looking beyond both the formal apparatuses of empire and a singular colonial discourse that we find the key manifestations of the political implications and colonial connections of the mission project.

## Home-Cooked Hegemonies

The missionaries, along with other members of the white population in central India, were agents in the creation of colonial cultures of rule. These cultures, Ann Stoler has argued, were not direct translations of European society planted in the colonies, but rather 'unique cultural configurations, homespun creations in which European food, dress, housing and morality were given new political meanings in the particular social order of colonial rule' (Stoler 1989). Close attention to the cultural forms borne and initiated by the mission project reveals intricate processes which need to be spelled out.

The missionaries participated in the new constructions of 'Westernness', embedded in distinct lifestyles, within the colonial order. J. A. Lapp, a Mennonite historian, has given us a detailed and sensitive description of missionary life styles in the late nineteenth and early twentieth centuries in Chhattisgarh.

> Missionary dwellings ... were large, one-storey houses of six to eight rooms....
> The ceilings were high (14-16ft.) with a punkah [fan]. In the pre-electricity days, servants operated these fans. Most of the stations were surrounded with ... glistening white walls..... Missionaries believed that their Western culture demanded a different approach to food, dress and houses from that of their Indian neighbours.... Dr. Esch [a Mennonite] reminded his fellow

missionaries of their need to adapt to India. 'The water isn't cold; the food isn't like American food; the people and especially the servants with whom one has to deal are not honest; the weather isn't pleasant – either too hot, too wet, or too dry'... [The missionary household] was operated by Indian servants ... [that often included] a *pandit* (tutor), a cook, *dhobi* (launderer), *ayah* (nurse), [two or] three *tonga wallahs* (drivers-gardeners), milkman, *chaprassi* (errand boy), *punka wallah*, *kotwal* (watchman), several sweepers, and coolies. Most were paid very nominally. Missionaries ... ordered canned foods and cereals from Calcutta and beef and pork when obtainable (Lapp 1972: 74–5).

All this involved the conscious creation and fashioning of the boundaries of the 'community' of white folk in Chhattisgarh. By emphasizing the similarities in lifestyles between the agents of the empire of Christ – the King of the World – and the imperial servants of Her Majesty – the Queen of England – these boundaries simultaneously served to under-play the internal differences among the white Europeans and Americans in central India.

At the same time, the missionary was also committed, as an integral part of the evangelical project, to civilizing the converts through the initiation of a set of key practices revolving around building, clothes, writing and the printed word. To briefly return to the statement rehearsed early in this chapter, J. W. Shank was speaking of the role of the missionary as a civilizing agent across the entire non-Western world, and his vision was profoundly shaped by the writings of his fellow missionaries in central India. These missionaries, in turn, saw the trans-formation of the world according to Shank as the doctrine that animated their labours in the wilderness of Chhattisgarh. The attempt of early evangelists was to rationalize the indigenous groups through the geo-metric grid of civilization.

We can find two simultaneous processes here, a double trajectory, to and fro, simultaneous processes that defy the exclusivist positions often embedded in discussions of travel and travel worlds. Thus, the mission-aries participated in the constitution of distinct lifestyles in the novel context of central India as a measure of the Anglo-European com-munity's distance from local cultures; and the missionaries used many of the same signs of Western culture to civilize the heathen. Arguably, it was within the interstices of these contradictory movements that the missionaries constructed a sense of belonging to a 'community' of white folk and reinforced the schemes of power that anchored the familiar symbols and signs of the cultural order of colonial rule.

These processes are best illustrated through practices centring on food, involving issues of gender that are embedded within the entire missionary archive – questions that at once bind the contradictions of colonialism and Christianity in the quotidian key, and the fashioning of colonial cultures of rule in everyday arenas. The preparation and preservation, the serving and distribution of food by wives of missionaries were central to the valorization of the home as the focal site of the civilizing process.[15] On one hand, this complex of practices centring on food brought together the metropole and the colony by serving as a model for the reproduction of gendered Christian personhood(s) among local Christian communities, particularly through its clear demarcations of the 'private' and the 'public'.[16] On the other hand, the relational idiom of food simultaneously drew the boundaries of the community of the white folk in central India through distinctions of race and class.

These differences were elaborated through alimentary divisions. During ceremonial feasts given by the converts to celebrate a wedding or the birth of a child, the missionaries presided over the occasion, eating rice and chicken curry, often using their hands, even sitting and squatting on the floor when chairs were not readily available. The native leaders – school teachers, catechists, and (later) pastors – among the Indian converts could be served tea when visiting the missionary bungalow. A few chosen converts could also be provided their first taste of ice-cream by the missionary family, often inviting the mirth of the white folk since the novel temperature and texture of ice-cream so confounded the taste buds of the Indians that they found this delicacy of the *sahebs* to be much too hot. But this is also where the lines stood clearly drawn. No Indian convert was asked to join the missionaries for hard-boiled eggs and cucumber sandwiches during Christian family picnics, a strictly white affair. At the formidable family table, covered with crisp white linen, no Indian pastor or church elder was invited to break bread with the missionary household, whether the meal was roast chicken and meat loaf or *dal* and rice.[17] This was not a mere tragedy of manners, where knives and forks were difficult to handle and indigenous belches were frowned upon. The distinctions of the civilizing process ran deeper. Indeed, we are in the face of a wider creation of home-cooked hegemonies – involving old recipes and novel ingredients, but also new blueprints and earlier elements – articulated through cooks and cutlets, meals and marmalade.

## Arts of Civilization, Signs of Enlightenment

The authority of the missionary was closely intertwined with civilization arts and enlightenment signs initiated by the mission project. But this too was not a one way process. For it was within the matrix of local cultures that the missionaries were fashioned as *sahebs*.[18] An early map of Bisrampur, the first mission station of the German Evangelical Mission Society, shows the imposing, square missionary bungalow in the centre. The other mission buildings were similarly neat square and rectangular structures, further emphasizing the symmetry of missionary designs and the clear demarcation of the area of their command.[19] A church, built opposite the missionary's house in 1873, completed the picture.[20] The geometrical precision of mission buildings was accompanied by the missionaries' close attention to the spatial organization of work. In September 1870 Oscar Lohr described the rhythms of his labour in running the mission station at Bisrampur, emphasizing the simultaneity between a close attention to time in labour and the spatial organisation of work:

| | |
|---|---|
| 9.00 a.m.: | Lesson in school |
| 9.45 a.m.: | Breakfast at home |
| 10.00 a.m.: | Dispensary |
| Afterwards till 2.00 p.m.: | Lessons in school |
| 2.00 p.m.: | Lesson in catechism |
| 3.00 p.m.: | Supervision of work in fields |
| 4.00 p.m.: | Lunch at home |
| 5.00 p.m.: | Garden[21] |

Clearly, the patterns of mission buildings and the spatial organization of work-discipline were imbricated in the everyday definition and reinforcement of missionary authority, the *saheb* who owned and regulated the fields, the (occasional) forest and the (ubiquitous) mission station that were placed at masterly discretion within his well-defined domain.

The missionary controlled the production of the printed word. This needs to be set in a twinned context: the importance that Protestantism attached to the convert's self-commitment to the Word and the Book as the mark of a true Christian; and the simultaneously symbolic and substantive power of writing within oral traditions. These overlapping emphases meant that the ability to inscribe and to engender print also served to underwrite missionary authority.[22] Moreover, the missionary healed bodies through Western medicine. A number of conversions to Christianity in Chhattisgarh came about after individuals recovered from prolonged illnesses, having been successfully treated by the missionaries.[23] Contemporary accounts suggest that these individual conversions could be prompted by an apprehension that the regenerative powers of missionary medicine and Christ the Saviour embodied greater efficacy than the healing powers of Hindu deities and local specialists. Indeed, the missionary knowledge of writing worked together with their power to heal: the primers they produced and the cures they conjured compounded these evangelists' command.

The missionary was the model in the moral discourse about Christian decency, bodily shame and physical modesty. Clothes became a distinctive sign of indigenous Christianity. The men wore pajamas, shirts, and some even had shoes; the women wore full five-yard sarees and blouses; and the little girls wore dresses sent by rich benefactors from across the seas. To be sure, these garments and accessories were not worn at all times. But to church and Sunday School, certainly. At other moments gestures of decency and modesty were enough. The days of loin cloths, *lugdas* (short sarees), uncovered breasts and naked children lay in the past. The missionaries with their shirts, jackets, trousers, solar hats and dresses – the insignia of the *saheb* and *memsaheb*'s power – presided over these public performances of propriety.[24] The gains for the converts were at once material and symbolic and they fashioned a distinctive understanding of missionary authority. A Satnami convert on being asked to perform a menial village duty, for instance, had replied, 'No, I have become a Christian and am one of the *Sahibs*; I shall do no more *begar* [forced labour].'[25] Indeed, the key social instruments of the mission project had contradictory consequences: the converts came to recognize these arts of civilization as attributes of the power of missionaries, but they were also to deploy these signs in their challenge to missionary authority.

## An Indigenous Christianity and Contestations of Missionary Authority

The converts' refraction of missionary messages through the lens of indigenous categories underlay their uses of Christianity and their interrogation of missionary authority. In Chhattisgarh, complications in the workings of hegemonies and the reworkings of power emerge in the ways that converts subverted the regulations laid down by the missionaries. We know that in Protestant ideology marriage is a sacred contract between individuals and the monogamous household is the basic unit for the conduct of a Christian life. In the colony, for civilization to flourish 'the holy family of the Christian cosmos' had to triumph over the moral murk and slothful chaos of the heathen world (Comaroff and Comaroff 1986). The missionaries' concern with monogamy and their fear of adultery, a snare and trap of Satan, meant that the converts were forbidden the practice of *churi* or secondary marriages.[26] This, however, was a critical arena in which the converts exercised considerable initiative and consistently challenged missionary authority to form what their masters designated as the 'adulterous' relationships of secondary marriages, time and time again leaving their earlier husband or wife to establish another union. If the missionaries, often unwittingly, participated in the creation of an indigenous Christianity, the converts defied missionary logic in fashioning their understanding of marriage and sexual transgression, finding their own uses for the 'truth' offered by their evangelical benefactors.

To illustrate this interplay in intimate arenas I turn to a conflict featuring converts and missionaries in the 1930s. The conflict had its apparent beginnings in adultery.[27] The villagers of Birampur claimed that Boas Purti had an adulterous relationship with Rebecca. Boas Purti, employed as the *lambardar* (man-in-charge) with the *malguzari* (owner proprietor) rights to the village held by the mission, was an 'outsider'; Rebecca was a 'virgin Christian girl' of Bisrampur. Boas Purti had ensnared Rebecca into his 'net of love'. Rebecca became pregnant. Boas Purti's guilt could be established by looking at the child. The inhabitants of Bisrampur were incensed. Boas Purti was seen as one among several 'outsiders' who did not belong to the community of Bisrampur but were employed at the mission station and 'violated the honour of virgin Christian sisters'. The converts invoked the threat to the honour and chastity of the women of community to question the presence and practices of these 'outsiders'. They brought into play the need for maintenance of the boundary of the community tied to rules of caste and sect *and* the Christian emphasis on adultery as sin in order to protest against all intrusions. The honour of women was at once turned into an evocative metaphor for order within the community and a symbol that constructed its boundary. Women had to be protected against acts of sexual transgression. The violation of their honour by an 'outsider' breached the boundary and disrupted the order of the community. Boas Purti's misdemeanour with Rebecca encapsulated the threat from the 'outsider' and evoked disruption and disorder within Bisrampur.

Bisrampur Mission had developed as a paternalist institution. From the late 1920s the missionaries sought to end the converts' reliance on the economy of the mission station in a bid to foster a self-dependent congregation infused with the ideas and principles of Christian charity and brotherhood. They clearly separated the functions of the *malguzar* and the pastor, and decreed that members of the Bisrampur church were to pay for their pastor, maintain the church, contribute towards public works, and donate for Christian causes. The missionaries also tightened controls to prevent the converts from grazing cattle and collecting wood and grass from the forest owned by the mission. Finally, the evangelists continued to appoint Christians who did not belong to Bisrampur as employees at the mission station.

Against these measures, the initiative of the converts centred on a pervasive 'us' versus 'them', 'community' versus 'outsider' divide. The community was formed around the converts of Bisrampur; all employees who did not belong to the mission station were 'outsiders'. The 'community' protested against the increasing intrusion of these 'outsiders' into the internal affairs of Bisrampur. Moreover, the efforts of the missionaries to dismantle the ties of dependence of the converts and to make the congregation self-dependent got entangled with their defence of these 'outsiders'. There was a disruption of the normative economy – the pattern of expectations and obligations – of the Christian community of Bisrampur. The figure of the missionary was transformed from the benevolent *ma-bap* (master, literally mother-father) of the past into a tyrannical *malguzar* who was in league with – indeed who had joined the ranks of – the 'outsider', the indefensible illegitimate intruder. Finally, the converts defended the paternalism that had bound them to the missionaries through complex ties of dependence and control: deference to the missionaries was one part self-preservation and one part the calculated extraction of land, employment and charity. This defence was inextricably bound to the converts' assertion of their self-dependence – an important constituent of missionary rhetoric – and their setting up of an independent and parallel congregation and Church with an honorary pastor who sent reports to the Home Board of the mission in the US, conducted Sunday service, baptized new members, and managed congregational matters. The converts seized the Christian signs of civilization and elements of missionary rhetoric and reworked them into their practice: their questioning of the missionaries – with its accent on truth and legality, faith and civilization – was constructed in an idiom and language of evangelical Christianity.

Examples such as these reveal the glimmers of a fluid world of subaltern discourse in popular practice where the meanings of a new faith were debated and contested through a reiteration and re-interpretation of the familiar, the novel and the old. Indeed, there was much at play in these worlds shaped by travel. A range of overlapping pasts underlay the construction of traditions and the making of modernities – accompanied by a simultaneous formation of anthropological objects and the constitution of truths of colonized subjects – so that Western travels became rather different journeys at the hands (and in the minds) of other peoples.

## Coda

The people of Bisrampur and Chhattisgarh were clearly – or always already – on the move, transforming Western worlds in quotidian arenas. These journeys involving local idioms and everyday spaces exceeded the travels of the more station-minded missionaries who imagined their movement as a profound civilizational transformation. All this has implications, I suggest, for the ways in which traveller-missionary-scholars see their work today. A sa(l)vage mentality is blind to movement. It erects fantasies around the forced thrust of a homogenizing civilisation, now mourned as the debilitating cost of progress. And so we return to Heidelberg.

On the afternoon of the second day of the colloquium on eastern India, in the course of two immaculately presented papers – the first on communication with ancestors among the *adivasi* group of Soaras and the other on ritual and reincarnation among the Gadabas, also of southern Orissa – I found myself returning to the enchantments of the epiphany of travel, the ends of memory, and the excess(es) of longings with which this chapter begins. Only in this case it was the anthropologist who was the pioneer and the traveller. More bluntly, in the first of these presentations, on Soara communication with ancestors (primarily) through the wall paintings in their huts, the invocation of the journey that carried the scholars – who actually walked for five hours through difficult terrain – to reach the highlanders of Orissa was all too reminiscent of the tropes that ordered Oscar Lohr's first-time travel through treacherous territory to arrive in the midst of the Satnamis of Chhattisgarh. If Lohr was served refreshments by the Satnami guru, our intrepid travelling scholars had to suffer the fate of sharing the local hooch – the liquor drunk with a small wince but with no major qualms, we were disarmingly told, all in the interest of ethnographic research – with the tribal folk. The pain evinced at the disappearing 'tradition' of wall-paintings among the Soaras evoked the paternalism – albeit in a different guise – that we have encountered in the missionary vision and practice in central India. The Soaras too were like children, far removed from the rational and objective thought of the West. Unlike the earlier missionary desire to guide, nurture, and control their wards within the confines of a paternalist enterprise, however, now the ethnographer's plea was to save the tradition of wall paintings of the guileless Soaras from the relentless march of modernity, represented acutely (if ironically) by the presence of Baptist missionaries in the region.

During the slide show mounted as part of this presentation, a tiny nod toward the crucial presence of cars and jeeps, planes and helicopters in the Soara wall paintings merely signified the adaptability of the aesthetics of tradition, as articulated by a juvenile sensibility to draw upon all objects of wonder from the West. The many ways in which these symbols of state power and significata of dominant local superordinates were at once creatively and critically reworked by the Soaras to (re)draw the relationship between life and death, the nether world and domains above in their wall paintings did not enter the picture. A participant brought up the bleak and grey landscape of Tarkovsky's *Sacrifice* in which a little child asks – not with the wonder of beginnings, but rather with the foreboding of ends – 'In the beginning was the Word. Why was that Father?' The participant persisted: did not the hills of southern Orissa serve also as a measure of distance, where the Word – carried to the lush landscape by Baptist missionaries in this instance – could be reinterpreted and transformed by the Soaras unto rather different beginnings and ends? (Or, as one of the editors of this volume present at the meeting put it more privately: what prevented the Soaras from smuggling a tiny image of baby Jesus into their wall paintings?) The answer was a studied and sardonic silence.

The other presentation of the afternoon followed a somewhat different course. The elaboration here of ritual and reincarnation among the *adivasi* group of the Gadabas of Koraput in southern Orissa was marked by a modulation of voice and a manner of writing that ceaselessly drew together nature and culture, collapsing the two in the act of description, even as these categories were set up as analytical oppositions in the formal framework of the paper. With the transcendental voice and immaculate vision of the ethnologist orchestrating the connected parts and disparate aspects of ritual and reincarnation, there was little in the description to distinguish between the manner of death of buffaloes as they were ceremonially sacrificed and the ways of life of the Gadabas as they negotiated an intrusive state and an alien ethnographer. Indeed, the ethnologist's writing and speech moved smoothly and seamlessly between a (ritual) description of drama and a (reincarnated) drama of description of the many moves and manoeuvres of the Gadabas, a community that was articulated as an individuated collectivity. Recall here the preliminary remarks that frame this chapter. If J. W. Shank implicated himself at the very least as a missionary in his immaculate conception of the missionary as a civilizing agent, now the place and the position of the ethnographer as author and witness stood erased from a landscape populated by groups of buffaloes and herds of men, where women merely oscillated as vectors of a masculinist logic of kinship defined by male bride givers and male bride takers. The circle stood fully drawn.

In both cases we are in the presence of versions of the timeless primitive, and there are many shared complicities between the missionaries in Chhattisgarh in 1868 and the scholars of Orissa 130 years later. But these missionaries and a few scholars are not mere exceptions. To retrace my first steps in this chapter regarding worlds of travel, the problem has deep roots. For very long now, mired as we have been in colonial, postcolonial and Western modernities, our thinking has been governed by a crucial set of oppositions and antinomies. I repeat myself once more. We have been conditioned in the academy and outside to separate dynamic and complex Western societies with history and modernity from simple and sacral non-Western communities grounded in myth and tradition. This mode of thinking is rather more persuasive and insidious than one wishfully imagines: it extends from conservative think-tanks, to left ideologues, to liberal thinkers, to radical NGOs, to contemporary primitivist and New Age alternatives. If one side celebrates modernity and Western reason, the other glorifies tradition and non-Western community. The two sides often mirror each other in their mutual underlying logic.

Here bloated images of a singular modernity suppress envisionings of the several chequered and contradictory modernities which have defined our pasts and continue to be a palpable presence. Reifications of tradition have little place for the ways in which traditions are continuously constructed, variously contested, and differentially elaborated over time. These renderings also often overlook that traditions and modernities are the products of the joint energies of superordinate and subordinate groups, of the pooled resources of the colonizers and colonized. But this is not all. The binary division between tradition and modernity both generates and is sustained by a series of other homologous oppositions that I have alluded to earlier, oppositions between myth and history, ritual and rationality, emotion and reason, magic and the modern, and indeed between those two fetishized concept-metaphors of community and state.

In questioning these overarching oppositions that hold sway in the academy in Western and non-Western contexts, my effort here is to highlight the necessity of elaborating another alternative beyond two dominant, competing conceptions. On one hand, it is critical to question authoritative Eurocentric imaginings, to interrogate the aggressive self-representations of post-Enlightenment traditions and Western modernities. After all, epistemic violence is very much a part of our here-and-now, defining the murky worlds we inhabit. On the other hand, we also need to guard against adopting and reproducing the several facile strains of anti-Enlightenment rhetoric that are on offer today. To reify and romanticize traditions or communities is not only to construct a new nativism – it is also to mock the subjects we study, to pillory the peoples who form the basis of our interventions, to stage *other* forms of epistemic violence.

There may also be another lesson to be drawn from the deliberations in the Wissenschaftsforum in Heidelberg that I have evoked earlier, particularly as we debate and question travel worlds from within academic arenas. We know that our intellectual discussions cannot proceed as though they are located outside realms and relationships of power, beyond the regimes of disciplinary truths. After all, today only puritanical positivists and endemic empiricists will deny that our academic work is conducted within wider contexts of power and politics. Yet, my point is less about these contexts as things out there, contexts as matters both in and out of place. In other words, my argument is directed against understanding contexts to academic work as those great overarching structures that we acknowledge with a perfunctory nod, only to banish them from our study and our seminar so that we can get on with our writing, thinking, and speaking. For in these familiar gestures of denial and affirmation – of denial in affirmation – contexts of power and politics hang outside. And thus we remain secure that these contexts will not come round uncomfortably knocking on the doors of our study, mercilessly messing up our lectures, upsetting all our well-laid plans. Yet, we only need to think about those horror films, of *Exorcist I* (and Linda Blair) and its sequel *Exorcist II* (and the big bad wolf). These films are reminders that to exorcise the devil is not to get rid of it. Moreover, the devil strikes by being within us. In tune with these testimonies from mass culture, the realms of power relations and the regimes of disciplinary truth that haunt the academy are also not merely contexts out there. Rather, they move through the capillaries of our bodies of knowledge, inhabiting the study and the seminar, stalking our lectures and talks, defining our articles and books.

All this is not to argue that we have arrived at that profoundly disabling moment when an undifferentiated notion of power freezes all activity, turning us into vectors and victims of power's singular dis-cursive and institutional force. Such is the stuff of which naïve, facile, tired and simplistic commentaries on Foucault are made. Instead, my advocacy of a critical recognition of the play of power at the heart of the academy refers to rather different realities. Eschewing elitism but also discarding populism, it is a call for making sense of the different and diverse modes of domination and authority – including geopolitical idioms and metageographies that shore travel worlds – at work in academia. It is a plea for an awareness of how we, as teachers, researchers and cultural activists, reproduce forms of hierarchy within intellectual arenas, in classrooms and bookshops, but over beer (and *bratwurst*) and coffee (and *kuchen*) too. Finally, it suggests moves to recognize at once the ways in which the realms of intellectual politics are complicit in wider cultures of power *and* the manner in which the sites of higher education engender and breed their own forms of pulpit-pounding politics.

At the end, we need to recognize the constant making of hegemonies and the ever-present possibility of fashioning counter-hegemonies within intellectual arenas (and of course, far beyond). Within these spaces of hegemonies and counter-hegemonies we rethink worlds of travel today.

## Notes

1 The light and baggage discussed here is that of the civilizing mission of God (and of the enlightened modernity of the Saviour), tying it up in different but similar ways to Banerjea's discussion of related themes in the previous chapter. I thank John Hutnyk, Leela Dube, David Lorenzen, Ishita Banerjee Dube, Raminder Kaur and Tico Taussig for discussion and criticism of earlier drafts. A grant (Gr. 5603) from the Wenner Gren Foundation of Anthropological Research made possible the archival and field work in central India and the United States in 1993 and 1994–1995, and a grant from the American Academy of Religion supported research in the United States in 1997. The paper uses the following abbreviations: AMC: Archives of the Mennonite Church, Goshen, Indiana; ARM: Annual Reports of Missionaries; *DDM: Der Deutsche Missionsfreund*; EAL: Eden Archives and Library, Webster Groves, Missouri. The archives that contain the records – written in English, German, Hindi, and Chhattisgarhi – on which this chapter is based is contained at the back of this book.

2 In this imagined interchange, it is possible to mark the reification of a heroic self – exorcised through its will to know, only to be reinstated later through its acquisition of betterment – losing and finding itself in travel. This construction continues to fuel the fantasies of alienated adventurisms on offer today. At the same time, it is equally possible to uncover from this fragment the importance of interrogating the self in order to make the familiar strange and to render the strange familiar. These are matters of readings, questions of emphases. My point is that the surplus of longing that underwrites travel in this passage informs both the fabulous fictions of the traveller's spectacular exorcism of the self through assiduous absorption of the other and the dark desires of the traveller's dominant construction of the other and singular celebration of the self.

3 Quite as Agreste (in Bahia in Brazil) may have rather more to offer than Lisbon (in Portugal) in terms of telling tales of passion and politics. I have in mind here the Brazilian writer Jorge Amado's quite spectacular *Tieta*, a novel that forces us to rethink various ways of travel (Amado 1979).

4 See Dube 1995b 1995c, 1996b, 1998, and n.d. (b).

5 Important studies here include Amin 1995; Appadurai 1981; Bayly 1989; Cohn 1987 and 1996; Dirks 1987; Van der Veer 1988.

6 It follows that this chapter also makes an incision on the body of writings on Christianity in South Asia. A large number of studies of the mission project in the region have been produced by church historians, providing detailed chronicles of actions and events (Von Tanner 1894; Lohr 1899; Seybold 1971; Lapp 1972; Juhnke 1979). Several other exercises in the field have been similarly guided by the simplistic assumption that Christian converts in India tended to replicate a modernized social order in the image of the missionaries (Whitehead 1913; Manor 1971; Oddie 1975; Forrester 1980). In recent years historians have explored the meanings of conversion and the articulation of Christianity with indigenous schemes of rank, honour, caste and sect, but this work has focused on Orthodox Churches in South India (Bayly 1989). Except for the interesting contributions by Eaton (1984) and Scott (1992), the evangelical encounter in the nineteenth and twentieth centuries remains a neglected area of study, an imbalance my work seeks to redress.

7 Satnampanth was initiated in the early nineteenth century, around 1820, by Ghasidas, a farm servant, primarily among the Chamars (leather workers) of Chhattisgarh. The Chamars, who collectively carried the stigma of death pollution of the sacred cow formed about one sixth of the population of Chhattisgarh. They either owned land or were sharecroppers and farm servants. Those Chamars – along with a few hundred members of other castes, largely Telis (oil-pressers) and Rawats (graziers) – who joined Satnampanth became Satnamis. They had to abstain from meat, liquor, tobacco, certain vegetables – tomatoes, chillies, aubergines – and red pulses. Satnampanth rejected the deities and idols of the Hindu pantheon and had no temples. The members were asked to believe only in a formless god, *satnam* (true name). There were to be no distinctions of caste within Satnampanth. With Ghasidas began a guru *parampara* (tradition) that was hereditary. Satnampanth developed a stock of myths, rituals and practices that were associated with the gurus. Over the nineteenth and twentieth centuries, the group negotiated the changing relations of power in the region, reworked the different efforts to regulate the internally differentiated community, and drew upon symbols of authority to question and challenge their subordination. The community continues to be a significant presence in Chhattisgarh. I construct a history of the Satnamis in my book on the subject (Dube 1998).

8 *Der Friedensbote*, 79, 20 (1928), pp. 309–5.

9 Thus the missionary Notrott in the manuscript of the first history of the German Evangelical Mission Society. The manuscript was written in 1892; Nottrot revised and typed the history in 1936. Both copies are in German. Notrott, 'Typescript history of Mission', p. 5, EAL.

10 On the sacred thread among the Satnamis see Dube 1992a and 1998.

11 This is one tale. There are other stories. They are elaborated in Dube 1995a.

12 Rather more than an explicitly stated agenda, such conceptions appear as implicit assumptions that then guide the analyses of what is framed as a singular colonial discourse. Take as an example an exciting intervention by a fine historian of the subaltern, Gyanendra Pandey 1989. The work of Homi Bhabha (1994) skilfully,

strikingly and usefully opens up the different registers of colonial discourse, but here too the 'pluralities' remain internal to a binding colonial discourse.

13 Examples taken from DDM, 1875–90; Von Tanner 1894.

14 Annual Reports of the Chuttesgurh Mission, 1872–79, ARM, EAL; Bisrampur Malguzari File [1925–1955], EAL.

15 See, for example, Correspondence of Missionaries, Menzel, E. W. and Ida, 82-16b MIS 69, EAL; Hist Mss 1–117, J. A. and Lina Zook Ressler Correspondence – Lina 1887-1903 (Box 1), AMC.

16 Hist Mss 1-117, J. A. and Lina Zook Ressler Correspondence – J. A. (Box 2), AMC.

17 Correspondence of Missionaries, Menzel, E. W. and Ida, 82–16b MIS 69, EAL.

18 A longer treatment of the themes discussed over the next three paragraphs is contained in Dube 1995a.

19 DDM, 9, 7 (July 1873), p. 48.

20 DDM, 10, 8 (August 1874), p. 57; 8, 4 (April 1872), p. 26.

21 The account is incomplete. *DDM*, 6, 12 (December 1870), pp. 89–90.

22 *DDM*, 6, 4 (April 1870), p. 3; *DDM*, 8, 11 (November 1872), p. 82; *DDM*, 13, 2 (February 1877), p. 11; *DDM*, 10, 10 (October 1874), p. 74; *DDM*, 11, 2 (February 1875), p. 13; Annual Report of the Chuttesgurh Mission, 1874–75, pp. 10–14, ARM, EAL.

23 Annual Reports of the Chuttesgurh Mission, 1874–9, ARM, EAL.

24 *DDM*, 8, 7 (July 1872), p. 50; *DDM*, 8, 11 (November 1872), p. 85; *DDM*, 9, 8 (August 1873), p. 58; See also the photographs of missionaries and converts in Lohr 1899.

25 *C.P.Ethnographic Survey XVII, Draft Articles on Hindustani Castes*, First Series (Nagpur, 1914), p. 57.

26 *Churi* has been a widely prevalent form of remarriage among all but the highest castes – Brahmans, Rajputs and Baniyas – in Chhattisgarh. Under the *churi* form of marriage a married woman could marry another man if he gave her *churis* (bangles). Questions of gender and kinship involving *churi* are discussed in Dube 1993a, 1993b, 1996a, and 1996b.

27 This is elaborated in Dube 1995a.

# 4

## ANTHEM

### Joyoti Grech

St George's Day has been commemorated in England since 23 April 1222. The ensuing poem was written after a walk down Chapel Market, Islington on St George's Day in 1997. Red-on-white George crosses were hanging from stalls the whole length of the market. Just up the road is the Bemerton Estate where Somalis have been the target of racist attack and have repeatedly had BNP propaganda pushed through their letter boxes. 'Anthem' was written with these images in mind, in order to explode the use of the Saint George myth for nationalist or fascist ends, and to spotlight the blatant inaccuracies of a nationalism based on racial purity.

According to archive material at the British Museum, George was of aristocratic Arab-Christian parentage, born somewhere in the Levant region, possibly in Ramleh. He was a high-ranking soldier, invoked as a saintly inspiration by Richard Lionheart in his imperial crusades, and died around 303 AD. In addition to his travels in his own lifetime, George's body parts continue to travel even after his death, with his relics scattered around the Christian topography. The irony of an Arab saint-soldier being taken both as the patron saint of England and a figurehead of anti-Islamic imperialism is striking. If we place an Arab man, whose family had been Christian for some generations, as the crusading converter of heathen Britons, then stock images of the 'native', 'savage', 'pagan', 'colonizer' and 'migrant' called up by imperialist or orientalist ideologies are turned on their heads.

At the same time, the poem is an anthem to a migrant experience which, contradictorily, in this case, is also a colonizing mission. Nationalist mythology is essentially a remaking and mistelling of extant archetypes. By unpeeling the layers, we can expose the complexities of contradiction, until the truth is left vulnerable and multiple, so that we can make up our own minds rather than accept wholesale the agendas and mythologies passed down to us.

## Anthem

the marketplace awash with red on white /cross barbed no-go zone for all us not
those minds mistake who hung them there : George was Arab / born of noble blood
high in mountains of Lebanon / proud and sure / deep in family
messengers of fire tore him by the roots / explaining nothing / tossed him
skin to sea

long nights across the ocean: he lands on dark shores / life
hiding in the black earth / not forgot without the death
of fish and unborn children
Streams spew chemical fumes / strange buildings spunk poison
into frozen future air
Wind back the suited men! Undo their wrong lineage!

George of Lebanon
far from his beloved /
homeland / his beloved /
beloved / beloved

sunrise on sprawls of sex / the heart of George disturbed /
at peace for he has found the terror faith taught him
to expect

Above the huts of straw / the heathen homes /
the great green he has been sent to vanquish

the natives rub blue stuff on their bellies because
it feels good yes

George heard the voice of god
sleepless / confused / tripping
on loneliness
in a strange land of stained
bodies he flings his sword
deep into the heart of
that which has no shame

he might have loved the dragon / could have known the fuck /
the subversive nature of love in any language
leaves the statepolice trembling in their hightop shiny boots

Rename the day / and fuck and know
the god in you in all of us for george's sake
of lebanon

# 5

## THE STRUT OF THE PEACOCKS
### Partition, Travel and the Indo-Pak Border

### VIRINDER S. KALRA AND NAVTEJ K. PUREWAL

Nineteen ninety-seven marked the fiftieth anniversary of the withdrawal of British colonizing forces from South Asia. Much has been written celebrating this moment of so-called 'independence'; less has been articulated about the ongoing battles of the people for independence and freedom in South Asia. While not belittling the struggles and sacrifices of those who fought for independence from the British, it is worth remembering, as Prashad notes, that '*Azaadi* means both freedom and partition' (Prashad 1997: 56–7). Independence from direct colonial rule and the partition of British India into two nation states, India and Pakistan, occurred simultaneously, making the recollection of 1947 a bittersweet memory. The communalization of identities through the divisive erosion of relations between the Sikh, Muslim and Hindu communities has marked partition as a permanent element of both individual and collective memory (Menon and Bhasin 1996). It is the aftermath of partition which concerns us here, though not on the large scale that has often been talked about, nor on the totally human level which has also attracted considerable attention.[1] Rather, we take a sideways glance, towards a specific location on the border dividing India and Pakistan, through the lens of travel and the focus of history.

The routes and paths open to travel in Panjab were blocked by the partition in 1947. Panjab had once been a region symbolizing religious coexistence, cultural and linguistic cohesiveness and traditions of social and spiritual reflection. The border, which was created in order to divide east Panjab and west Panjab between India and Pakistan, resulted in an unprecedented remapping of geography and demography. Each half of the landscape of the divided Panjab suffered an amputation by the knife cut of constitutional arrangement. Never before had the region experienced such a catastrophic crisis, with millions of people displaced and several hundreds of thousands killed during the 'exchange of populations' (Butalia 1994). Amritsar and Lahore, which had grown to be twin cities prior to British colonization of Panjab, now became strategic border towns of the two new rival nations. The border posts in Panjab are a lasting legacy of the exodus of partition and the division of people. The sole crossing between modern-day India and Pakistan, by foot or vehicle, is at Waggah, only a few miles from the train station border at Attari. It is at these sites that one of the symbolic remnants of partition, as division, is played out in the maintenance and fencing of 'international borders' restricting people's communication and movement.

## Border Theory

Recent theoretical interventions in cultural studies have taken the notion of 'border' as a metaphor for describing and illuminating several contemporary phenomena. Notions of diaspora, exile and travel have all come to intersect with what has been called 'border theory'. The Chicano author, Gloria Anzaldua, is often cited as a main impetus behind the development of theorizing the border. Taking the US/ Mexican border as her starting point, Anzaldua (1987) creates and depicts the various borders that construct her identity. A border does not therefore simply relate to a physical boundary but becomes a metaphor to describe situations where a whole range of differences of, for instance, gender, race or class coalesce or are forced together.

> Borders are set up to define the places that are safe ãnd unsafe.... A border is a dividing line, a narrow strip along a steep edge. A borderland is a vague and undetermined place created by the emotional residue of an unnatural boundary. It is in a constant state of transition (Anzaldua 1987: 3).

Anzaldua's work has been taken up by a range of contemporary theorists (Chambers 1990, Giroux 1992), placing emphasis on the border, or more accurately the borderland, as a site for cultural creativity. Border crossing in this view is seen as a radical act. People who engage in this process are therefore attempting to overcome the limitations imposed by hegemonic and dominant forces that construct and maintain socially congealed 'difference'.

One aspect of Anzaldua's work which has not been as widely taken up is her evocation of the violence and policing which maintain and enforce divisions and differentiations at the border. In the opening chapter of her book *La Frontera*, we are presented with a powerful historical/poetical narrative relating the construction of the US/Mexican

line. This extract from one of Anzaldua's poems (1987: 2–3) resonates
with similarities to the Indo-Pak border in Panjab:

> 1,950 mile-long open wound
> dividing a *pueblo,* a culture,
> running down the length of my body,
> staking fence rods in my flesh,
> splits me splits me
> *me raja me raja*
>
> This is my home
> this thin edge of
> barbwire
>
> But the skin of the earth is seamless
> The sea cannot be fenced
> *el mar* does not stop at borders
> To show the white man what she thought of his
> arrogance
> *Yemaya* blew that wire fence down.

This is a new approach to the theory of borders in cultural studies. The
poem starkly calls for the removal of the border rather than its
maintenance for the elaboration of cultural critique. Crossing a border
may cause shifts in its boundaries, but this does not necessarily result in
its removal. To address problems such as the legitimacy of the border
we require a different set of questions than those hitherto posed by
'border theory'.

Our focus on the Indo-Pak border involves a number of such sharp
questions: How did the border come into formation? Is it legitimate?
Who represents the power that created and maintains it? How do efforts
to overcome the border continue to defy the processes it symbolizes?
Is the crossing of a border inherently a radical act or does it depend on
who is engaged in the process? Put another way, for whom is border
crossing an act of transgression ('illegal' Mexican workers in California)
and for whom an act of transition (day tourists with American passports
visiting Tiajuana)? Whereas transgression involves actual fear of death
and prosecution, transition can be a playful moment, a liminal stage at
which identity travelling and actual travelling are blurred. At the Indo-
Pak border this contrast, between transition and transgression, is demon-
strated in the free travels of Western tourists and the imposed restrictions on travel for locals on both sides of the wire. Before considering

these border crossings, we will explore the potent question of how the Indo-Pak border came into being.

## Lines in the Sand

The lines which currently carve and pattern the map of the globe are often part of the treacherous legacy of colonial withdrawal. Local elites along with colonial bureaucrats scribble lines on pieces of paper with little regard for the demands and needs of the populace. The wrenching of India and Pakistan, therefore, cannot be seen in isolation. Just after the Second World War, the British people elected a government which, unlike Churchill's regime, was less wedded to the Empire. The new regime was interested in rebuilding a shattered Britain through the development of a social welfare state. Meanwhile, the massive peasant and working-class uprisings across the subcontinent, including the Royal Indian Navy Mutiny in 1946, the Telengana, Tebhaga and Punnapra-Vayalar rebellions, as well as in West Asia (notably with the formation of the Arab League in March 1945), crippled the British military and forced them to seek a 'hasty finish' to the imperial project (Hubel 1996). The British drew up swift plans to leave.

Partitioned states carved out of imperial territories became the logic of the British withdrawal. In India alone, the territories of Bengal, Kashmir and Panjab were brutally dissected. The destabilizing effects of these lines scored by overworked British jurists would allow the former imperial power to maintain influence and hinder stable development in the region. History bears witness to the conspiratorial nature of the British departure. Insurgency in Kashmir began at the moment of partition in 1947, which was followed by uprisings in Nagaland. In 1973, Bangladesh split off from Pakistan and in the 1980s the 'Khalistani' movement in Panjab demanded partition from India. It was not only in South Asia that the British created such hot spots: perhaps the most striking parallel is with the creation of the Israeli state in 1948 at the expense of the Palestinians, a dispute which continues today.[2]

These map marks are an enduring legacy of a colonial history whose long-term effects have been a cartography of violence, destruction and loss of life. On 15 July 1947 the British India government had appointed a boundary commission under Sir Cyril Radcliffe in order to decide the shape of the nation states that were to be formed when the British left. Radcliffe was chosen for the mad reason that he had no prior knowledge of India (in fact, he had never set foot in India) and it was believed he would therefore give an objective and impartial view (Wolpert 1989).[3]

Commenting on this process, fine artists Iftikhar Dadi and Nalini Malini have produced a map of the subcontinent which merely shows the border lines, drawn as dividers, on golden-brown rectangles. The texture of the material used, and the shapes created by only representing the international boundaries, evokes an alien landscape, signifying the fact that Radcliffe may as well have been on Mars – the red planet of war – when constructing his dividing lines.[4]

## Border Posts

Setting out as a line drawn on a departing imperial power's map, the Indo-Pak border now takes the form of a mesh fence topped with barbed wire, electrified in many places, and guarded by armed security. It is an extensive land border, running for some 1500 miles yet offering only two places to those who wish to cross it, the pedestrian and vehicle crossing at Waggah and, a few miles south at Attari, a train track. Both are located in Panjab, even though the border runs through the provinces of Sindh (Pakistan) and Rajasthan (India), and touches on Gujarat (India). Indeed, for the peoples of India and Pakistan who may wish to traverse the border, only one crossing at the rail frontier is open. The privilege of road crossing is conferred only on international tourists.

The road border is a blockade denying travel to the people of Panjab. It is patrolled on either side by army personnel who attempt to uphold the created 'difference' between the Indian and Pakistani sides of Panjab. The army personnel themselves, however, have more in common than sets them apart: men who look alike, speak the same language, often eat the same sort of food – but wear different uniforms. On one side are the Pakistani Rangers, on the other the Indian Border Security Force. The line between them, and so dividing these two multi-nation states, is called 'Zero', and it is literally a line which cuts through the Grand Trunk (GT) Road. Here is a border which for the most part has no borderland, no shape, only the guards, and an open space 25 metres in width, backed up by two hostile governments and their militaries. The gulf of separation which that gap displays is so great that it duly marks its own time zone. Once you cross from India to Pakistan the time changes, with clocks in west Panjab ahead of those in the east, as though people on either side of the minuscule line will witness the sunrise and sunset a half-hour apart.

Zero Line is presented by a white strand running through the GT Road, not much wider than the shroud of a coffin, but it is a gulf of immeasurable distance for people on both sides of the border: 'I was born in Amritsar. I now live in Lahore. How far is Amritsar from Lahore? Barely thirty-two miles. For me it feels like thirty-two million miles.'[5] It is difficult to appreciate the extent of this psychological distance. A journalist wrote of an encounter he had just before crossing from East to West Panjab:

> Though Amritsar and Lahore are geographically very close, the psychological distance between the two is enormous. When I was about to leave for Lahore from Amritsar a young woman asked as to whether I would arrive in Lahore on the same day of my journey from Amritsar and if the weather would be the same there. (Mehmood, *The News* 26 August 1995).

The question asked here about arriving in Lahore on the same day reflects the power of borders to erase the memory of what goes before. This is clearly illustrated in the history of the GT Road, upon which the Waggah border post, so crudely, marks the separation between East and West Panjab.

Prior to the arrival of the British, the GT Road was known as the Sher Shah Suri Marg, named after the Moghul ruler who originally constructed the route. Sher Shah Suri reigned in the subcontinent for only five years, 1540–5, but during this period he established an administrative and communications system which lasted until the coming of British colonial rule. He constructed highways connecting the capital (Delhi) to other parts of his kingdom. The most famous road he constructed was the Sher Shah Suri Marg, which ran from Sonargaon in Bengal to Peshawar in the north-west of Pakistan. The road became the main route for getting from the east of the sub-continent to the west via the major urban centres. Wayside *dharamsalas* were built for the convenience of the travellers along the route.

With the advent of British colonialism the road was renamed the Grand Trunk Road, and entered popular Panjabi folklore and musical culture as 'GT Road'. During the period of British rule, it was developed and enhanced as one of the main routes between the summer (Simla) and winter (Delhi) capitals. Imagine the 1940s when the GT Road was bustling with people traveling in *tongas* (horse-drawn carriages) from Delhi to Lahore, Jalandhar to Jhelum, Peshawar to Patiala. An occasional bus or other motor vehicle would be surrounded by a cacophony of other forms of transport making local and long-distance journeys. At the time of partition, the usual hustle and bustle of life on the road became a stampede. GT Road was a lifeline during the exchanging of populations, a crescendo of movement before a deafening silence.[6] In contemporary South Asia it is no longer possible for the inheritors of the road to cross its full length without visa stamps and border passes.

## Tourist Sites

Borders mark what belongs and what does not, and in this case the border has erased the presence of what can be seen geographically and perceived as continuous. The total lack of any geospatial logic to this border is highlighted by the areas on either side where fields have been cut in two, villages halved and houses divided with a line running through the courtyard. There is no borderland or site of cultural hybridity at the Indo-Pak border, but instead a sense of something unknown, something dangerous. The actions of, and tensions between, the governments of these two nation states are represented microcosmically in the ceremonies that take place each day at the Waggah border post.

Every evening, each side engages in a ritual marking of the border. A flag lowering ceremony, mimicking the British penchant for boundary marking, and attracting tourists on both sides, is the highlight of the show. Pomp and circumstance surround the lowering of the flags of both nation states. Each army forwards its tallest *jawaan* (soldier), with the bushiest moustache, straightest turban, best-creased uniform and shiniest gun. These two men stomp up to the Zero Line, their legs rising and falling, boots crunching in an obscene dance of aggression. Each man gets close enough to the other to share the same breath of air (still marked as Pakistani and Indian we presume), almost touching at the climax of their peacock ritual. Guns are raised and lowered as this violent maintenance of the border re-enacts, relives and recalls the crass and inhumane slaughter of partition that is at the foundation of this line.

There are other spectacles, not so noticeable but equally significant, that take place at Waggah. It is important to note the sluggish flow of people across the border. A contrast is immediately struck, between the back-packing, sunglass-wearing British, Australian, German and North American tourists, who are the only people allowed to pass through the border on foot and the gaunt *coolies* by their side. Each man carries goods from one side of the Zero Line and deposits his cargo on to the back of another *coolie*, earning an equal pittance, who then carries the goods to an overladen, old and dilapidated truck. Like the soldiers, the *coolies* on either side of the border wear different colour uniforms, but otherwise share the same poor conditions of work. Underneath the spectacle of monumental nationalism and vicious rivalry between states, the movements and conditions of the *coolies* highlight how little the basic conditions of the mass of people have changed.

Streams of coolies and the spectacle of the strutting peacocks are the actors on the stage that makes up the border. This play is framed, however, by the signs which greet you as you enter the states of India or Pakistan – chilling signs which express continuities with the past and pointing to a predictable future. On both sides arches symbolizing entry greet the border-crosser. These square constructions, built of wood, awkwardly straddling the GT Road, present a porthole into the new time zone. On the Indian side, the top of the arch bears the sign, 'Bharat Welcomes You', which is only marginally more visible than the Pepsi symbols and colours that flag its other side. The colours are the globally familiar ones of blue and red, resembling the former servility to the Union Jack and the more contemporary allegiances of both states to the American-style multinational corporations. For the international tourist this sign may be as warm and welcoming as the border is open to them. For Indian passport holders who wish to pass through the Pepsi gate, however, the border looms large and omnipotent. On the Pakistan side, the sign that greets you reads 'Tootie Frootie', a soft drink owned by Nestlé. Another multinational in local guise, it welcomes Western tourists (and a few diasporized returnees), but keeps out the local populace. As the British once patrolled, guarded and colonized the masses of South Asia, the new guardians of the social order come in the form of soft drinks and structural adjustment programmes. Here is the logic of capitalism as neocolonialism, maintaining borders that allow Western tourists to travel, in the same way that the *coolies* maintain the minuscule trade that travels across the border. Indian and Pakistani goods cross the Zero Line every day, but the *coolies* who handle them cannot. The flow of capital continues where the flow of the masses is stopped.

Waggah border is a premier site of tourism on both of its sides. Those on the Amritsar *yatra* from other parts of India make the trip (up to, but not over, the 'crossing') as a part of the worship of gods, this time the god of nationalism. Hastier pilgrims – Americans, Australians, Germans and other Europeans – do not notice the border beyond its snapshot significance, nor do they stop to engage in ritual nation-affirming pursuits beyond a flash of their passports. Their freedom is guaranteed by the Pepsi symbol: 'Welcome to India'. There are also other travellers on this land route: the occasional group of religious travellers from Saudi Arabia or other parts of the world, the few British and American Sikh pilgrims on their way to Nankana Sahib, the birthplace of Guru Nanak. A few travellers each day cross what essentially has become a back post on what used to be the busiest road in South Asia. For those who have relatives or who wish to visit the land of their birth, the land border is an insurmountable mountain.

As we have stated, these restrictions do not apply to Western travellers. Indeed, as the following quote from a *Washington Post* journalist illustrates, the GT Road has taken on a symbolic value of 'freedom' in the US-dominated New World Order.

> Today the Grand Trunk is a channel for the changes coursing through post-colonial, post-socialist, post-Cold War Indian and Pakistani society. For more than four decades after independence, these societies were built by bequeathed colonial elites and subsidized by foreign superpowers..... Now the state is broke and withdrawing from its paternal role. This means those on the Grand Trunk Road are increasingly *free* to sort things out for themselves. (Coll 1998, our emphasis)

Coll places the contemporary GT Road at the centre of a narrative of social change, one that is in contrast to 'Nehruvian socialism' and symbolizes the ascendancy of the 'commercially-minded, socially ambitious, newly self confident middle and lower middle classes'. In a similar way to the signs at the border, the GT Road is also appropriated as a positive symbol for the intrusion and extension of multinational capital. In Coll's narrative the demise of the state gives 'freedom' rather than domination by multinational capitalism: a freedom similar to the 'freedom' to cross the border, one that privileges the West and extends the reach of libertarian ideals, but restricts the movement of the peoples of India and Pakistan. This latest intrusion of capitalist development has precedents in history. It points to a century earlier when the British invested in the railway network to ensure penetration of their goods into all parts of the subcontinent.

## Seven Hours of Separation

While the border across the GT Road is closed to Indian and Pakistani nationals, the train crossing at Attari is nominally open. A tired, rickety Northern Railways train departs, once a day, from Amritsar in the early morning and euphemistically is called the 'Samjota Express'.[7] It arrives by 10 a.m. at the Attari station and meets another train from Delhi, carrying other travellers. These people are not the back-packing brigade, nor pilgrims from the diaspora, but ordinary citizens of both countries. Most are on the way to meet family, separated by bureaucratic mayhem which ensures that obtaining a visa takes many months and then is often revoked at the hint of poor relationships between the two countries. Visas for both countries can only be obtained in their respective capitals, which requires a journey, of an even longer distance, to either Delhi or Islamabad. Indian and Pakistani nationals have to specify which city they are intending to visit and then register at the local police station once they arrive at their destination. Their visits are limited to only a few locations, and they tend to be subject to scrutiny by security forces.

Despite the bureaucratic obstacles, many persevere, only to be greeted by more intransigence at the train crossing. Once both trains have arrived at Attari, the tortuous wait begins. Customs and immigration clearance personnel take an eternity in searching each bag and interrogating each person: *What is your reason for travel, why are you going to the land of our 'enemy'?* These are brutal questions underscoring once again the violent maintenance of a border.[8] Once the train is under way, it soon reaches the other side of the border, but all the passengers are taken off the train, along with their luggage and goods, and again scrutinized and searched by customs and immigration on the Pakistani side. A half-hour journey is stretched into seven hours by the deliberate machinations of both national security forces. The 32-mile distance between Amritsar and Lahore suddenly seems further than a flight from either Delhi or Islamabad to London.

Trains are powerful symbols at this border. The history of the development of the railways in the subcontinent stands as a metaphor for the expansion of capitalism into the region. For the apologists of colonialism, the train network and the establishment of the railways was a lasting gift of the British to the Indian subcontinent. Perhaps it is most poignant that these were the very vehicles which became carriages of death with the departure of the British in 1947.[9] The recurring images of partition are of massive lines of humanity moving in a slow disbelieving chain towards the unknown. The stories of brutal massacres, of trains full of people arriving at stations with only the driver surviving, are spread throughout narratives of partition. Train stations became impromptu graveyards, and the sounds of whistles were the only mourners to signal the passing of life. Those trains that bore witness to such violence no longer run on any tracks between India and Pakistan. The Samjota Express, however, reflects the current intransigence of international relations, built on the back of partition, as a symbolic reminder of the historical experience shared by the people, through British colonialism, communal violence and partition.

## Crossings

No border is impermeable. Many things flow through the most guarded and tightly sealed of boundaries. The following extract from an interview with Hazara, a man whose family is divided between East and West

Panjab, evokes the sense of longing that the border has created but also
illustrates that it can be crossed:

> He could only look skywards at a flock of birds crossing over and, voice
> quivering, say, '*Hum se to yeh parindey achhe hain, koi border nahin in ke liye*' (These
> birds are better off than us, there are no borders for them) (*India Today* 1997:
> 45).

It is not only in the flight of birds that the fence is overcome. For those
who dare to make the journey across, the border is not so formidable.
As with the survival equipment taken by adventurous mountain climbers
to the Himalayas, simplicity is all: a border-crossing kit includes a strong
horse to jump the double barbed wire and a bottle of whisky to bribe
guards met on the way. For others, particularly those who cannot afford
such a kit, the routes come by knowing every groove and crevice of the
border. Scaling the wall or climbing under the fence can become part
of the journey to see loved ones.

Routes across the border are often carved out and mapped by
smugglers who have well-established ties with the Border Security Force
and local police in securing the trade route. Smuggling of goods over
the border takes place continually – tea, Bollywood videos, cigarettes,
cloth and electrical goods make up the standard hauls.[10] Goods that are
illegal or hard to purchase in either country, constitute the bulk of items
bought and sold. Whisky flows from India to Pakistan in exchange for
dry fruits. *Choraan* Bazaar (thieves market) in Amritsar is the place where
goods coming over the border from Pakistan make their first stop. The
market is conveniently located next to the train station. It is the place
where Urdu writing is displayed on shop fronts, where smugglers meet
and rest, and money is exchanged.

Illegal movements of the kind described are small in scale and make
little impact on the general atmosphere of hostility. More broadly,
organizations such as the Pakistan-India People's Forum for Peace and
Democracy, established in 1995, have begun a 'people's dialogue'.
Central to their aim of normalizing relations between the two countries
is the establishment of a free flow of information and peoples:

> The most important step towards confidence building is the creation of
> facilities for the people of India and Pakistan to freely meet with each other
> and exchange information, views and experiences. Restrictions on travel and
> on exchange of newspapers, books, magazines etc. must be lifted. Both
> governments should adopt open policies for issuing visas. Railway travel
> should be made easy. Road links need to be re-established (PIPFPD 1998).

The critical nature of this demand is clearly shown in the difficulty of
sending letters and photographs across the border. At the best of times,

these arrive months after being sent and, at times of conflict and tension, they are subject to confiscation and censorship. Perhaps, most poignant is the fact that a telephone call from Amritsar to Lahore costs more than a call from Amritsar to London. A line between the two cities is usually crackly and difficult to obtain, with constant interruptions by operators and unknown listeners.

There are many such political borders which separate communities and families from one another. Cubans settled in America must communicate with their relatives on the island routing their telephone calls via Canada. It is communication technologies, nevertheless, which are facilitating the freest exchanges across the Indo-Pak border. For many years radio broadcasts were the most direct form of media communication, surpassed in the 1980s by television programming. PTV (Pakistan Television) from Pakistan and Doordarshan (Jalandhar) from India are received on both sides of the border. In recent times, satellite technologies have brought an exponential increase in the amount of broadcasting that crosses the border. Television software in this new medium is often dominated by multinational corporations in an Indian guise, however, and their interests lie less in bringing people together than in the establishment of regional markets for consumption. Of the new communication technologies, it is perhaps the Internet, the favoured medium of organizations such as the Pakistan-India People's Forum for Peace and Democracy, which has the best chance of increasing actual communication and cooperation between the two peoples.

## Redrawing the Lines

Drawing a line on a map is child's play unless it is backed by military and political power. To some extent the departing colonial powers were indulging in a mischievous prank, telling themselves self-serving stories about how they should have stayed on, how they were the best thing for India, etc. They could look on in the comfort of the imperial motherland while millions suffered the consequences of their actions. But the blood of partition also indelibly marked and created two nation states, which in that wake have been struggling, unsuccessfully, to shake off the violence of an unnatural birth. Partition is virtually the paramount metaphor by which to describe the subsequent histories of India and Pakistan, each disavowing and oppressing its peoples in the name of the spurious enemy over the border – a border which retains a symbolic magnitude of inverse proportion to the scale of its physical presence. Waggah and Attari, the land and rail borders, are small openings in a seemingly endless fence.

Borders, boundaries and the 'national' entities which they represent are sustained by the violence required for their maintenance. Free border crossers, rather than initiating or developing a radical cultural critique, are often carriers of Western superiority, tourists for whom international border crossings are not acts of transgression but more akin to transitions. This is not to represent the border as insurmountable for local people; as we have shown, the flow of goods, people and ideas does overcome the Indo-Pak border with the help of local ingenuity and transnational technological communications. The fundamental question remains, however, with regard to the difficulties and obstacles that lie in the way of this border crossing. Ultimately the extent to which these obstacles undermine or reinforce border maintenance is something still beyond the frontiers of today's border theorizing.

Historically, nation states and border formation have been subjected to shift and change. The Indo-Pak border has survived for 50 years, bolstering the elites of both countries and suppressing regional aspirants for nationhood.[11] In post-liberalization South Asia, there are new forces upholding the regimes that have increasingly become mere tools of repression. The multinational corporations bolstering the arches at Waggah have become the chief strategists of the nationalist war between India and Pakistan, and the allegiance of the elites of each nation state to capitalist development sheds a subtle light upon the unlikely heroes of the war – those who continue to defy the border and all that it represents, and those who work to overcome it by any means necessary.

## Notes

1 Mushiral Hasan (1997) examines the trauma that partition inflicted through personal histories and literature. See also Kirpal Singh (1990) for a description of the macro-events of partition and Urvashi Butalia (1994) and Susie Tharu (1994) for voices of people who suffered from the consequences of the event.

2 It could be argued that this thirst for partition began with the division of Ireland in 1922.

3 Ahmed further illustrates Radcliffe's lack of experience: 'As he had never been east of Suez before, had only been in India for six weeks and knew practically nothing about India, Sir Cyril was totally out of his depth' (Ahmed 1997: 124).

4 The work by Dadi and Malini referred to here is an important example of collaboration across the border. Dadi is based in Pakistan and Malini in India. Both artists wished to work together on the project, but Dadi was unable to come to Britain. The work was jointly composed by the use of faxes for descriptions

and the telephone to explain the substance of the work. A collaboration across the border, the line on a golden ruffled background, abstracted in this way, throws into sharp relief the bizarre fact of the very construction of the border in the first place.

5 This is an extract from an interview in the Channel Four documentary, *Division of Hearts*, 1997.

6 Most of the population exchange during partition took place along the GT Road and this proved to be far safer than the trains.

7 *Samjota* means conciliation.

8 The insanity of such questions also resounds in the story 'Toba Tek Singh' by the renowned Urdu/Panjabi writer Saadat Hasan Manto (1950–90) in which the inmates of a mental asylum in Panjab at the time of partition are asked the similar question of which side they belonged to, Pakistan or India. Manto's depiction of the delusionary effects of border making and the separation that it entails leads one to ask who were the insane ones: the inmates or the exiting empire and its collaborating politicians and elites. The mental asylum in Manto's 'Toba Tek Singh' reappears in a carriage of the Samjota Express. Today, the inmates of this cross-border train, once released, experience a sense of helplessness and disillusionment.

9 Ahmed (1997) argues that a good deal of the uncontrollable and spiralling violence could have been avoided with better management of the situation by Mountbatten. This of course begs the question as to whether the latter was capable or motivated. His later experience in regard to British colonialism in Ireland ended with his being blown out of the water.

10 Bollywood is the affectionate name given to the Bombay film industry which produces the most Hindi films.

11 The independence movement in Kashmir is perhaps the best example of the brutal suppression by the Indian state. The recent denial of the renaming of the North West Frontier Province in Pakistan to Pukhtoonistan is an example of Pakistan's fear of separatist national consciousness developing amongst its peoples.

# 6

## BORDERCROSSING

### JOYOTI GRECH

The Jumma people have resisted more than two decades of military occupation by the Bangladesh state.[1] Partition, based as it was on the imposition of religiously defined identities, created Pakistan – both East and West – as a majority Muslim state. The Jumma people of the Hill Tracts – being Buddhist, Hindu, Christian, animist or non-religious – expected to be included in the self-proclaimed secular Indian nation. Inclusion in the majority Muslim East Pakistan, however, marked them out as a community of difference and resistance to hegemonic forces. In the early 1970s, the Jumma people of the Chittagong Hill Tracts (CHT) in the south-eastern parts of Bangladesh elected a JSS (People's Solidarity Party) representative to parliament. Shortly afterwards the party was outlawed by the state for its perceived secessionism. In the early 1970s, an armed wing, the Shanti Bahini or Peace Force, turned to armed struggle as a means of bringing about a political solution to the violent erosion of basic human rights by the state.

The next twenty years saw an intensification of village destruction and massacres, military rape, forced conversion to Islam, arbitrary arrests and executions by the state and state-sponsored agencies, including settlers from the plains who were brought into the hills in order to change the demographic make-up of the CHT from the majority indigenous populace to the now almost fifty-fifty Bengali to Jumma ratio that has been created in parts of the region. Settlers were organized into paramilitary Village Defence Parties and handed weapons by the military at dusk – the very time when Jumma farmers were obliged to hand in their *daos* (large-bladed knives) and other farming tools. Jumma languages were outlawed in schools and all syllabus subjects had to be taught in Bengali. At the core of this struggle for self-determination is the violent imposition of national boundaries which carved up a continent and divided peoples according to historical colonial manipulations of ethnicity and community. In addition, central to the propaganda that denied the Jumma people the right to self-determination is the hierarchical dichotomy between nation and tribe which privileges a political system based on territory over a political system based on kinship structure. In December 1997 the Bangladesh state closed a five-year process of negotiations with the JSS. The peace accord has been fêted by the state as an end to the crisis which has taken so many lives in the CHT, but there are many people in the Jumma, Bengali and international communities who are wary of the accord's conditions and commitment to peace. People's lives have been damaged and fractured materially and spiritually by 20 years of warfare. It will take more than a piece of paper to repair them.

Centrally, the following poem recites an incident among many which happened during the struggle for self-determination. A cadre of Jumma youth workers who were travelling in the region to work with villagers in the interior was attacked by the Bangladesh military, and either killed outright or captured. The poem follows a fictionalized character who managed to escape that raid, taking refuge in the one place not searched by the military – the nurses' home at the top of the hill. From this hiding place, the cadre member cannot escape the screams of his comrades as they are tortured to death in the valley below. In the years that follow, he continues to work as part of the movement for self-determination and travels to the interior as he would have done with his comrades.

The poem joins him at the point where it is no longer safe for him to stay in his own country. He is about to cross the national border, but to do so he must take on the trappings of the state. The love that he shares with his partner of more than ten years must be formalized with a marriage certificate. He must also take on a new identity, recreating himself as someone ten years younger than he really is, less likely to have accrued years of experience and knowledge and, therefore, seemingly less dangerous to the state. Double-sided imagery refers to the dual identity of his new, false life – one face for the state and one for the people who share life in the underground. Crucial to this new identity is 'the loyalty of new friends' who stand witness to him in the courts in the spirit of collective support. The poem explores the couple's lives, flashing before them on their journey away from home, into a new life of both danger and precarious safety, enough safety to continue to live and fight. Some scenes illustrate the richness of the life they are fighting to protect for their people, if not themselves as individuals. Others hint at the continuance of surveillance by the state, and the need and reality of collective organization for change and self-determination. Yet others paint the continuation of life, and the birth of a new generation. The poem ends on an open note, locating it within the continuing struggle.

## Bordercrossing

He met her at the border
in the waiting space between two lives
before them, a future without signposts,
roots naked of earth
language is all they carry
across the line
there is nothing to declare / safely
the Wasteland air too spare
to nurture truth

silence sharp as
double-headed arrows
protects the history
that they dress in foreign clothes
of the new country they inhabit

they turn their faces
blank as the pages
of forged ID

in the courts their lives are stamped
a decade lost as the falsehoods of the law
Erase / negate / obliterate
ten years of toil
struggle / flight / the underground
create birthdays, marital ink,
an absence of experience
whose memories remain /
tattooed on the nightmares that
do not recognize
the boundaries of the state

and the loyalty
of new friends
bears witness:
their love a twin-braid
wedding gift
granting existence /
denying
every pain and joy that

brought them here
a feast of two servings
hollow gourd
filled with green rice
for those in uniform
and for the family
twice-brewed
*dochoyani*
toasting both
celebration and loss

The sampan pushes
from the river bank
through the pre-dawn mist
behind them parents become his own
cannot tell if they are cutting through
or swallowed by the floating wreaths

Along the passing slopes of the interior
scenes blur
future past unclear:
the khaki lightning raid
no sight / white flash
the cadre codes / recodes quick
scatter / hide for yr life
continuance the only possibility
the steep / leap
locked inside the nurses' hostel room
back to brick
knees to heart
hands to ears
in the valley below
screams of comrades
rise over days and nights,
weakening to final
silence
one life / paid for by death
border crosses into
second skin

the *tang ghar* of his childhood
*chula* smoke funnelling from the
cookroom doorway.
beneath its stilts
chickens peck and cluck

and in the waters beyond
fish jump thick with life
she weaves new *khadi* for *bizu*
going house to house with
*pita*, fragrant coconut, banana,
good wishes and joy for the new year

a dark room in the city
time adds colour to its walls,
brings comrades in
the same cause /
the same word
in different states / one language

the passage empties out to leave
the two of them
until he is taken also
for how long they cannot see
nor in what order these absences occur
and the dark room is empty

blood on the washroom walls
death or birth
the landlady / old
with no family,
brings *sandesh, kola*
the day the Wife returns
– the word stickles sideways
crabs scuttling over paper
permits travel
legalizes birth
irrelevant to the soul
– what do I care
for the state's approval
of my love?

Carrying the son she named for sun
someone holds her *jholabag*
full of labour linen that
she will have to wash
The watchers from the sampan search
for recognition
in the shadowy features / of the holder's face
the river flows faster than the scene

—

## Notes

1 Jumma is the collective name for the ten nations indigenous to the region all sharing the Jum method of slash and burn cultivation.

2 Glossary:

*Dochoyani* – Jumma rice wine distilled twice in bamboo tubes dug into the ground.

Sampan – open-topped river rowing boat.

*Tang ghar* – bamboo house raised high off the ground on stilts, typical of the interior of the Hill tracts.

*Chula* – clay oven.

*Bizu* – New Year's festival.

*Pita* – cakes steamed in banana leaves, a Jumma sweetmeat.

*Sandesh* – a Benglai sweetmeat made of milk, typically given or eaten with friends and relatives at celebrations.

*Kola* – a small and sweet banana.

*Jhola* – a woven shoulder bag.

# 7

## TOURISTS, TERRORISTS, DEATH AND VALUE

### PETER PHIPPS

## Tourorists

The news that a Norwegian backpacker was beheaded by members of Al-Faran at an unidentified Himalayan hideaway in October 1995 had a powerful resonance in the Euro-American media. Journalist accounts of the execution portray an extremist, Islamic, Kashmiri-separatist terrorist group transgressing all bounds of decency, law and order by beheading the very pinnacle of international innocence and neutrality: a Norwegian backpacker trekking through the Himalayas. This incident, and the threat to the four surviving foreign hostages, has held the continued attention of the Western media as an attack on the assumed right of First World citizen tourists to penetrate all corners of a world 'made safe for tourism'.[1] The indignity of this act is further compounded by the common-sense assumption that tourists are, by definition, innocent of the implications of global geopolitics. Anthropologist Valene Smith gives this truism a twist when she describes tourism as 'the single largest peaceful movement of people across cultural boundaries in the history of the world' (Smith 1989: 12). A militarized consciousness unfolds where tourism becomes noteworthy for being 'non-war' while sharing some of the symptoms and anxieties of war: massive population movements, the crossing of cultural boundaries; a cheerful invasion.

That violent incident in Kashmir is just one among a litany of mishaps, murders and hostage crises involving tourists which suggest that a sustained consideration of the interrelations between the categories tourist and terrorist, and between tourism and violence more broadly, is in order. In the course of this project, originally just on tourist discourses, tourists have kept cropping up in the news media as victims of acts of anti-state (and less clearly explicable), terror. This chapter is a tentative exploration of the connections between those two things: tourist discourse and tourist death, and the logics which make the

representations of those events meaningful. I argue that tourist ideologies are implicated in the structuring of the violent times in which we
dwell. Mentioning tourists and terrorists in the same tenor unsettles
already-tenuous notions of guilt and innocence, citizen and criminal,
consumer and killer, victim and perpetrator. While Said and others have
challenged the discursive effects and political deployments of the loaded
term 'terrorist' as opposed to '[our] freedom-fighting allies', tourists,
their unassuming doppelgänger, have escaped sustained attention while
being at least as politically and morally charged a category. 'Dead
tourists' are a more significant trope than one might ever have
expected.[2]

Interviews with backpackers and other tourists, their correspondence
and photography, articulate a system of thought which could be
characterized as extremist in its commitment to notions of authenticity
and experience. The stridency with which many tourists have been
willing to assert, or just assume, their right to experience the Other at
any time and place resonates with an imperiousness that is almost
militant. The underbelly of this logic, ironically, is expressed in a
'discourse of touristic shame' (Frow 1991); a general condemnation of
tourists by tourists for ruining that authentic otherness which they have
travelled so far to experience. Just as the supposed terrorist comes armed
with extreme ideological commitments and powerful connections, so
does the tourist; just as the ultra-nationalist/religious fanatic detests
tourists, so do tourists; just as the terrorist craves anonymity in the
crowd, so does the tourist. These strange equivalences are captured in
a mainstream popular Hindi film by Mani Ratnam. Set in a Kashmir torn
apart by insurgency, the local Kashmiri guide asks the hero and his
girlfriend, *'Tum tourist ho ya terrorist ho?'* ('Are you tourists or terrorists?'),
concluding that only the latter come here now.[3] The differences between
tourists and terrorists, war and peace, may well be less than imagined.

Every traveller who has passed through the security cordon of an
airport and been subject to the technologies of luggage x-ray and metal
detectors, sniffer dogs and customs interrogation, security cameras, and
the ubiquitous question 'Did anybody else pack for you?' should know
something of the connection between tourism and terrorism. Indeed
these features of travel have become so common as to pass almost
without question, a naturalized artifact of the tenuous relationship
between travel and violence. These concentrated technologies of
transition are designed largely to regulate the flow of travellers under the
scopic control of the state, represented by its functionaries: customs,
immigration, police. This is the point at which the state attempts to
regulate the flow of citizens, aliens, commodities, narcotics, biological

materials, firearms and other prohibited substances: symbolic or potential violations against its authority. These places are also the site of enormous potential damage directed against that authority by acts of terrorist violence, both directly and by extension in an attack on 'the people' whose protection is the official rationale for intrusive regulation.

Security cameras, x-rays and random searches are designed to screen out these potential incendiary threats. Ironically, while the state is officially acting to protect mobility through this intense surveillance, it is simultaneously structurally threatened by mobility, even as it is bound to protect its sanctity and is utterly dependent on it. Governments express enormous anxiety about illegal aliens and immigration, smuggling, contraband ideas, diseases, politics and so on. Ironically the 'freedom to travel' was one of the key, and most seductive, distinguishing features of the 'free world' in the Cold War propaganda battles, and features as one of those much-ignored articles of the Universal Declaration of Human Rights. Deleuze and Guattari's 'nomadology' thesis articulates the structure of state ambivalence towards movement, equated here with the tireless movement of the 'war machine', exemplified for them by (somewhat dehistoricized) Mongol hordes.

> One of the fundamental tasks of the State is to striate the space over which it reigns, or to utilise smooth spaces as a means of communication in the service of striated space. It is a vital concern of every State not only to vanquish nomadism, but to control migrations and, more generally, to establish a zone of rights over an entire 'exterior', over all of the flows traversing the ecumenon (Deleuze and Guattari 1986: 59–60).[4]

Airports, train stations and border crossing points are crucial markers of regulatory attempts to control movement. These are sites where the discipline and authorization of movement – stamping passports, searching bags and so on – are always possibly about to be attacked in radical transgressions directed against that very logic of regulation: blowing up aeroplanes, taking hostages, smuggling contraband. The aim of the tourist, or legitimated traveller, is to pass through these points of surveillance and control as quickly and smoothly as possible with the authorization of all the authorities concerned. In a dark parallel, the terrorist or other illegitimates in transit (smugglers, illegal aliens) attempt to slip around or through this regulatory authority in the dis-guise of tourists; in the case of the terrorist, to deliver to such legitimacy and omnipotence a mocking blow. Diller and Scofidio quote Freud: 'A great part of the pleasure of travel lies in the fulfilment of early wishes to escape the family and especially the father' (1994: 41). At this end of the twentieth century, it is perhaps a great deal harder to 'escape the father' as his capacity to police has become ever more sophisticated and insistent (though of course Deleuze and Gauttari warn us, in the tome mentioned above, against such Oedipal reductions!).

The ever-expanding list of incidents involving dead tourists, most recently in Egypt, is a mark of the strategic importance of tourism in global and regional warfare and terror.[5] This significance extends beyond the fact that tourism has become the biggest single trade item in the global economy, but is located in the very logics at the heart of tourism itself. Tourists, particularly from the United States, have become acutely aware of their status as privileged targets of terror attacks, and the US overseas travel industry is extremely sensitive to dramatic international conflicts. This was illustrated most clearly in the Gulf War when travel from Europe, but more especially the US, came to a virtual standstill from a widespread fear of 'terrorist' reprisals against First World soft targets. In this context it is little wonder that a Wexco publication, *The Complete Travellers Guide*, which has such chapters as 'Executive Targets', 'Surviving a Hijacking' and 'Fill the Bath; It's a Civil War' has been consistently reprinted from 1980 to 1994. Peter Savage's *The Safe Travel Book* recommends the following precautions when in countries with a 'security problem':

> In public spaces, such as a restaurant, sit where you cannot be seen from the outside and try to sit on the far side of a column, a wall, or other structure, away from the entrance. You want to be inconspicuous, out of the line of fire and protected from any bomb blast. The same precautions should be taken at hotels, at clubs, and even sitting on the deck of a yacht in the harbour (Savage 1993).

While something of a cliché, the construction and loathing of the loud, stupid, gringo stereotype (or Australians in Bali, Brits in Majorca, etc.) carries a different nuance in the light of the 'savage' advice above. The loud and obvious tourist gives away the undercover operation of the 'sensitive' cultural tourist (the fantasy of being invisible or undisturbing), reducing both of them to crass consumer. While this is often expressed as a nationality cliché, the issue is more one of class, which harks back to Wordsworth's condemnation of Cook's tours and the railway which brought working-class people tramping into his precious Lake District. It would be interesting to know if there was a similarly resentful response on the part of colonial officials at the instigation of Cook's tours to the Orient from the late 1860s (Mitchell 1991: 21). It is reassuring for self-conscious tourists to displace their self-loathing, or at least their vague intuition of local hostilities, onto their 'othered' fellow travellers. Kaplan (1996: 62) quotes Kincaid describing her expatriate Antiguan perceptions and memories of tourists which confirm the very worst touristic anxieties of being 'uncovered' by the perceptions of local people:

> An ugly thing, that is what you become when you become a tourist, an ugly, empty thing, a stupid thing, a piece of rubbish pausing here and there to gaze at this and taste that, and it will never occur to you that the people who inhabit the place in which you have just paused cannot stand you.... That the native does not like the tourist is not hard to explain. For every native of every place is a potential tourist, and every tourist is a native of somewhere.... But some natives – most natives in the world – cannot go anywhere.... They are too poor to escape the reality of their lives; and they are too poor to live properly in the place where they live, which is the very place you, the tourist, want to go (Kincaid 1988:17–19).

As the ideal operative works under cover, so too should the ideal tourist. Drawing attention to the presence of tourists, blowing their cover, can itself be an invitation to danger for tourist operations. The danger is in the very literal sense of making tourists a more obvious target for overcharging, intimidation, pick-pocketing and, at the more extreme end of the spectrum, attack, murder or hostage-taking. Just as immediate, though less obviously dramatic, is the danger that being conspicuous presents to the tourist fantasy of invisibility. The tourist mission of penetrating the everyday life of the Other to observe and record their difference is disrupted when the tourist operative is uncovered: an army of touts selling souvenirs, offering everything from taxis to prostitutes, moves in to end the illusion of invisibility in an episode that causes tourists grief, confusion, anger and, very often, acute embarrassment.

> Camouflage can be as tactical for the tourist as it is for the soldier. This is all the more difficult, however, in that the tourist and the soldier alike are marked bodies, unable to blend into the crowd.... These excluded figures – the tourist and the soldier – assume a similar representational role on foreign soil: they are both living symbols of another nationalism. Each one is seen as a performative body, measured against the image of its national stereotype (Diller and Scofidio 1994: 24).

As 'a living symbol of another nationalism' tourists are perhaps more like an intelligence agent than an invading soldier. The 'good' tourist who blends as much as possible with the crowd has a mission as firmly etched on the mind as any intelligence operative: seek the authentically Other, record it as experience, photography, souvenir and written word, and return home to file a report as anecdote, recollection, and the personal transformation of having 'been there'. Like the intelligence operative or the foreign soldier, the tourist has passed out of the security of the relatively fixed identity of home and into a far less clearly defined liminal zone. 'To leave home and journey to distant places as a tourist is to enter a symbolic limbo: not at home and yet partly still there; elsewhere but only passing through on an always-returning-home trajectory. The tourist in transit, and the tourist is always in transit, is at once nobody nowhere, as well as the bearer of certain nationalities, credit cards and currencies. Just as the individual identity of the travelling subject is unsettled, a different set of more anonymous identifications come into play. Tourists become value in motion, both in their regular operation as consumers, and in their more rarefied symbolic values as exchange objects embodying another nationalism, for example as 'normalizers of relations' (US visitors to China post-Nixon), or as hostages, such as in the Kashmir situation.

## Experience and the Real

'I went to get an authentic experience of another culture, to get away from my own usual experiences of Western life, things and tastes' (Backpacker in interview).[7] 'Experience' is an elusive quality which, regardless of its intangibility, is a powerful rationale for some of the otherwise inexplicably strange and dangerous pursuits of contemporary tourism, from bungie jumping to 'disaster tours'. Experience can refer to an event of a particular kind, and can also be communicated as an air adhering to a particularly 'experienced' individual. Bruce Robbins provides a critique of the 'epistemological privilege of experience' as a 'domain of direct truth', 'a kind of pristine contact between the subject and the reality in which this subject is immersed' (Robbins 1986: 148). Tourism is one of modernity's great compensations; it is the space where the fantasy of reforging that connection between the self and the world still tenuously hangs on.

For the most part, First World tourists share the modernist concern about the loss of a realm of authentic experience beleaguered by the extension of the market to touch the most basic aspects of social life. This 'loss of innocence' is a familiar Romantic trope for representing the experience of other cultures, deployed by everyone from novelists to anthropologists and other travel writers. The astute tourist is constantly on guard to protect his or her travels, particularly their documentation in letters, postcards, journal reminiscences and the photographs which accompany them, from the taint of 'inauthenticity' which invariably threatens where modern tourism is present. The primary fear here is that the tourist experience is fundamentally and irretrievably inauthentic. This is what cultural tourists, backpackers in particular, are concerned to avoid above all else in making the distinction between their own search for, and access to, 'authentic' experience and 'those other tourists', characterized as unable to pursue anything but the most banal and artificial forms of experience. The following quote illustrates this sense of 'communion' or authentic experience of one backpacker in India:

> In Varanasi I would just sit by the Ganges, near the burning *ghats*, near a *sadhu* or a monk, or someone playing flute.... I went into the Ganges for a bath and visited the temples there. Things were just so real there; life, death, pilgrims from the villages dressed in traditional clothes. I didn't feel like a tourist, I felt like another pilgrim. Nobody was hassling me or trying to get things.... It was the India I came to experience, less artificial.

This fixation on the pursuit of authenticity finds expression in a slightly different form in discursive accounts of the 'purity', or loss of it, of nature on the one hand, and cultures on the other. This notion of purity is set in opposition to that which is modern, capitalist, bureaucratized and developed. Nature and folk culture were added to the tourist's multiple interests and motivations, which had already included notions of high culture, history, education and physical rest and recreation, with the fashionable 1920s interest in nature and the authentically 'ethnic' as repositories of the non-modern (Graburn 1989: 30–4). This theme crops up from time to time as the 'untouched' tribe or village, or the hidden land, always on the verge of destruction by contact with modern, industrial societies and their values.

This concern with an authentic experience of the Other, untainted by the 'modern' themes of alienation, mobility and money, is not limited to the conceptual framework of backpackers alone. Professional travel writers, photographers and social scientists are not immune to the allure of the possibility of 'authentic' experiences of other cultures; indeed, much anthropology is predicated on such assumptions. In her 'Third World Landscapes', a discussion of tourism in India, Barbara Weightman assumes that an 'authentic experience' of India is waiting to be uncovered: 'communion with the ambience of Indian life worlds' (1988: 232). She asserts that mass tourists miss out on these 'real' experiences by being encapsulated in a 'cultural bubble' in which they are shielded from any meaningful or spontaneous contact with local people. Weightman believes there is a 'zone of authenticity' (1988: 235) to be found in cities and villages. In Varanasi this zone is the Ganges and the Ghats, in Jaipur the pink city, in Delhi the old city. Her 'zones' correspond remarkably closely to those depicted by travel brochures and guidebooks, uncritically reproducing the banalities of the romanticist travelogue.

## Death and Danger

> What gives value to travel is fear. It breaks down a kind of internal structure ... stripped of all our crutches, deprived of our masks ... we are completely on the surface of ourselves.... This is the most obvious benefit of travel (Camus 1962: 26).

The main feature which distinguishes backpackers from other tourists is the disproportionate value they place on the physical sufferings and dangers of travel on the cheap as a marker of value.[8] There is an extensive vocabulary of renunciative strategies and gestures which attach enormous status to poverty, hardship and illness as signifiers of the authenticity of an experience. Backpackers engage in a competitive recounting of austerities undertaken and survived, be it a three-day train trip without a seat or a bout of typhoid. Every suffering is valuable because it can be reconstituted later in a powerful narrative strategy adding to a sense of true connection with alterity. This focus on the austerities of 'authentic' travel (also described in Teas 1974), often leading backpackers to absurd extremes, is highlighted in this comment from the letter of a backpacker in India:

> You would not believe what an image trip the younger ones (travellers) are on. People going out of their way to check you out, to see if you're scumming it enough, or if you're staying at the 'right' cheapie hotels, etc.... We mentioned to some people that we were flying from Varanasi to Kathmandu and you should have seen their faces, all snooty, looking down their noses at us. How dare we avoid the gruelling thirty-hour bus trip!

The emphasis on self-testing can be seen as an example of voluntarily undergoing a 'rite of passage', acting out a ritual space signifying a break from one life stage to another, or proving to themselves that they have the strength to deal with a major crisis in their lives. Graburn takes up Van Gennep's *Rites of Passage*, suggesting that his general framework of rites of separation from the ordinary, a period of marginality and rites of reincorporation, 'is applicable to all forms of tourism' (Graburn 1983: 13). By his account those most likely to engage in 'rite of passage tourism' include young people deferring the responsibilities of adulthood, often in an intermediate stage between completing further education and embarking on a career or making commitments to a family, those recently divorced, widowed, or making major career changes. It is characterized by prolonged absences from home, and often arduous travels and activities involving some form of self-testing, attributes which Graburn compares to the spirit quest of pre-invasion, North American indigenous societies.[9] This could be seen in a postcolonial context as a 'Kiplingesque' quest to test the mettle of one's independence (whiteness) in the fire of the exotic, or one's national self in a space other than that nation.[10]

One of the sites of this distancing from ordinary life is the more conscious awareness of encounters with dangers or the possibility of some danger in exploring the unknown. In India the prime danger the traveller perceives is the risk of contracting some debilitating or even fatal disease. Most of the backpackers I have interviewed had experienced either fevers or diarrhoea.[11] One claims to have been close to death from a serious infection and another from typhoid, despite the precautions available to the Westerner in the form of immunization (an activity that could be seen as a metaphorical blessing, protection or granting of power by the home culture to the travelling individual). Travellers in India constantly discuss illnesses, symptoms, cures and so on. These range from the frequent jokes, 'When the bottom falls out of your world, come to Calcutta and watch the world fall out through your bottom' (reported in Hutnyk 1996: 54), to discussions of the most appropriate forms of medication and treatment for particular ailments. Status is attached to those who have suffered the worst or most gruesome afflictions, lost the most weight or come the closest to death. It is as if the very ill person has succeeded in moving as far as possible away from our everyday world which includes health as normal and a civic (bourgeois) duty. Eschewing the 'closed' hygienic environments of mass tourists, backpackers valorize an openness to the environments they travel through, including the microbial.

This logic meets its penultimate expression in the significatory power of death. There is, ultimately, nothing more indisputably 'real' than the fact of death experienced either close at hand or personally. Hutnyk (1996: 63–4) confirms that in the early 1990s, a rumour spread like wildfire on the backpacker circuit that Tony Wheeler, editor and publisher of the ubiquitous *Lonely Planet* travel guide empire, had died violently in transit, either crushed by an elephant or in a bus crash. The rumour took hold on a collective imaginative theme: as his guides so meticulously reproduce backpacker ideologies and mark the limits of possibility, his imagined death confirmed the authenticating power of his gritty guidebooks. There is a cult quality to these books, commonly referred to as 'the Bible', which demands a sacrificial saviour in the great Judeo-Christian tradition. Wheeler remains alive, well, and very rich.

Death itself becomes a macabre and fascinating tourist site. No trip to India is complete without a ghoulish visit to the burning *ghats* at sites along the Ganges river (in Irian Jaya/West Papua it is the preserved bodies of ancestors, in Borneo dried heads, etc.). This fascination is due in part to the state-regulated segregation and professionalization of death and dying in the overdeveloped world, which adds further fuel to the notion that death, or in this case the dead, are the ultimate signifier of the real. Ian Catanach (1997) describes a collection of nineteenth-century British postcards sent from India during an outbreak of plague which show piles of corpses in one image, while another shows patients dying in a more orderly fashion in a specially constructed plague hospital.[12] While such a postcard would probably be regarded as in poor taste today, it does demonstrate a certain continuity of interest in 'death elsewhere', which was far more likely actually to visit nineteenth-century travellers than today's.

In 1992 Italian travel agent Massimo Beyerle was offering clients visits to an unspecified (due to the obvious contingencies) 'October war zone' (Diller and Scofidio 1994: 136). He was offering to take tourists to the ultimate reality, 'places shown on the television news' for US$25,000 per person. His services included armed guards, a doctor, flak jackets and other necessities for visiting 'the edge zones of combat'. Possible sites included 'the south of Lebanon, Dubrovnik or Vukovar; as close as possible to the places shown on the television news, so that our clients can see and speak with the people, and see for themselves the damages caused by the war'. This is not a new phenomenon. Mitchell (1991: 57) describes how, in 1830, entrepreneurs from Marseilles took tourists to Algiers to watch the colourful spectacle of the ongoing French bombardment of that city from the comfort of a large barge at sea.

The themes of death, the destructive forces of modern warfare and the dangers of the road are an inescapable part of tourist thought. A recent edition of the women's magazine *Marie Claire* features three stories of luckless tourists who died on holiday. Titled 'Trouble in Paradise', the article warns, 'that long-planned trip to paradise can turn into a holiday in hell' (1995: 55–8). Ironically, as Camus reminds us (see above), this threat of death and danger is something that tourism relishes so as to retain its imaginative power as a space for reconnection with that 'real' which remains so elusive, and thoroughly denied, in the order of highly stratified, regulated and abstracted capitalist postmodern society.

## Tourists and Commodities: on Exchange

For backpackers, their highly contested in-group status on the road is determined by a checklist of factors. High on the list are contact with the 'authentic' Other, one's nonchalant relationship to time and disciplined work, the ability to live on very little money, distance from Western values and culture, a lack of materialism, and length of travels and stay in one place. Backpackers value those factors which can be seen to set them apart from the conventional experiences of tourism: their lack of availability to the mass tourist, their relative danger or lack of certainty of outcome and the sincerely non-commercial nature of the exchange (this last being something that the backpacker is never quite at ease about yet determined to assert). These are themes of the utmost importance in the backpacker status game; they authenticate experience. Ironically, experiences then become a kind of commodity, exchangeable for status in the travel sub-culture.

The language of exchange is an appropriate one for this encounter as it so much underlies the anxieties of tourists about being exploited in their ignorance of local conditions and values. Many tourists/ backpackers complain of never feeling they had contact with locals outside of these commercial boundaries, some even feeling outright hostility towards all local hospitality workers as 'exploitative rip-off merchants'. The small army of touts, competitive rickshaw-wallahs and salesmen with which most tourists have to contend at some point, can leave those who perceive themselves as having come for more personal and 'meaningful' interactions with locals (that is, outside the market) a little frustrated with the consistency of their hosts' capacity to see them primarily as the source of lucrative transactions (more so where tourism is one of the only means of supplementing local economies). Even where non-commercial motives are assumed in an interaction with locals, backpackers tend to remain wary of any suggestions of a commercial or financial nature as a threat to her or his sense of engagement in an 'authentic' friendship. Conversely, the market can be one of the main measures of authenticity, and the struggle to only pay the 'local price' for a commodity or service can be seen as an achievement of the 'real'.

The relations of exchange are reversed somewhat in the situation where tourists are taken hostage, such as the European backpackers in Kashmir. It is precisely because of their high exchange value, in the image economy of the media and in the public relations economy of international diplomatic relations, that they are captured in the first place. Ironically the quest of these backpackers to add maximum value to their adventures, by travelling way off the beaten track and even into 'dangerous' territory, sees their own bodies converted into a form of exchange value, in this case held by the militants against the Indian Government.[13] The high anxiety of national governments, underwritten by national media attention in such instances, illustrates the significant resources that back up the itineraries of most backpackers. While they may often carry little money, holding certain passports has a real value on the ground that mostly confers an assumed protection; that harm done to a foreigner from a powerful country will make for terrible trouble.[14] This logic, of course, is reversed in the hostage situation, where the citizens of the most powerful nation, the USA, seem to carry the highest exchange value.[15]

In the recent case of the three backpacker hostages in Cambodia, it may well have been the fact of their national composition that caused their final demise. After a Khmer Rouge attack on a train travelling to a coastal town, the guerrillas rounded up all the foreign nationals on board. The Vietnamese passengers were summarily shot on the spot, one can only surmise, on the assumption that they were agents of the anti-Khmer Rouge Vietnamese government. The remaining foreigners, three unsuspecting male backpackers who had been headed south for famed marijuana and adventure on the frontier of anarchy, comprised an Australian, a Frenchman and an Englishman. Consistent with backpacker logic, they had ignored the advice of their expatriates that it was too dangerous to travel where they planned. The first two carried particular value as subjects of neocolonial players in Cambodian politics: Australia and the country's former colonial ruler, France. Both countries were sponsors of the Cambodian peace accord, and were major sponsors of the Hun Sen administration after the breakdown of relations with the Khmer Rouge, supplying aid, weapons, and military training for government forces. The hostages were potentially powerful bargaining tools with the Cambodian government, which could be expected to pay dearly for the return of the citizens of its sponsor states. As it so happened they became pawns in a complex geopolitical game and were ultimately executed, arguably because elements of the Cambodian government thought they could extract more value from them dead than alive.[16]

Occasionally tourists are targets of terrorist attacks and kidnappings primarily because they are available. There is, however, a more complex dynamic at work as well. The media value of tourists as hostages is not only based on their coming from a powerful or wealthy country, but is also fed by common perceptions in media-saturated cultures of their apparent innocence. The tourist is almost by definition an innocent abroad; a consumer suckling infant-like at the great breast of the world. At the same time by turning everything around them into exchange value tourists are necessarily guilty and undeserving in the terms of their own discourses of authentic and uncorrupted otherness. Tourists are caught in a dialectic of innocence, whereby their very innocence as consumers propels them into being guilty participants, even agents, of global exploitation and corruption. This clearly seems to have been the combination that served as justification for the killing of tourists at Luxor, Egypt at the end of 1997.[17]

My interviews with tourists suggest that at least my youthful sample group travelling in Asia feel trapped within this dialectic. I suspect by imputation that tourists of all sorts feel guilty and anxious at some level about being tourists. Hostage taking and murder confirm this dramatic anxiety in a real and deadly way.

## Tourist Shame, or Dealing with Homicide: a Conclusion

MacCannell (1976) analysed the structure of tourist semiotics over two decades ago. Primarily, tourists are engaged in a quest for the real or authentic site. He pointed to the simple fact that this real could not be found without convenient markers to present it as such. He argued that the astute observer (theorist) would notice a productive apparatus behind this staging of the authentic which was in fact the 'really real'. This apparatus would in many cases become itself a tourist site in turn: the sewers of Paris tour, tours of Hollywood studio lots, tours of 'real working life', and so on. The subsequent critiques of MacCannell's work have of course pointed to the privileged position he accords to the theorist (himself) who can somehow escape the world of artifice and show, and delve straight into reality itself: tourists are dupes and theorists are smarter than tourists.[18] The greatest irony is that Mac-Cannell's theory repeats one of the primary motifs of late twentieth-century tourism: the claim of privileged access to the real shored up with the assertion of being different from the mass of other tourists. Obviously intellectuals, acutely status-conscious bourgeois creatures that we tend to be, suffer far more severely from this painful delusion than do those tourists more resigned to, or even celebratory of, or maybe even, as MacCannell would have it, oblivious to, their status as consumers of a staged authenticity.

Not surprisingly, it is the former, bourgeois intellectual, touristic sensibility that predominates in representations of tourist activity and consciousness: travel books, ethnographies, documentaries, postcards and other technologies of dissemination. Two strategies are almost universal in these technologies:

1 Deny the presence of mass, or any other tourists, in the visited locale. This is most commonly practised in photography where frequent attempts are made to erase other tourists, and any other signs of capitalist modernity, from the frame; a symbolic destruction of the signs of the self and its possible multiplication. Any challenge to the claim that being here in this place is a unique, unrepeatable event, any rupture that might shatter the aura of the real, must be denied, erased and refused.

2 In those moments when the presence of other tourists is an undeniable and inescapable fact, the primary strategy is that of removal by distinction. Other tourists become 'them': the uncouth, despised, insensitive, problematic, simplistic tourist, who threatens to give the whole game away and blow the 'real traveller's' cover (he or she in search of the real, the intelligence officer of romanticism). This is a common strategy of travel writers from Paul Theroux through the more playful Pico Iyer or the ruggedly adventurist Robyn David-son (1981). Indeed, the claim to be more than a tourist, to see that which could otherwise not be seen, to travel with the purpose of gathering intelligence to write a report is the very currency of travel writing.

Continuous with this logic, the ultimate tourist fantasy is to visit lands and people free from the blight of other tourists and modernity. Backpackers carry this theme with particular vigour and enthusiasm as the first wave of tourists to visit a region newly opened to touristic exploitation. These travellers tend to have an awareness of themselves as the vanguard of the hordes of tourists who would be responsible for the commercialization, and for their demise, of the very things which drew them there. As a consequence of this constant need for a touristic frontier, each few years a new country, beach, mountain or desert place is reified in the travel pages of *The Times* and other petit-bourgeois news-papers, as the little-visited authentic place for the non-tourist traveller to explore. As its whereabouts and popularity spreads on the extensive word-of-mouth traveller's information network, the place becomes more and more touristed. By the time a small, well-institutionalized tourist industry has been established by locals or entrepreneurial outsiders the place will be 'ruined' in the terms of the discourse which made it so popular. Bali has a particularly developed history of being subject to this discourse; it has been declared to be on the edge of devastation by crass tourists since the 1930s. In each case the declarations have been made by its self-appointed guardians of good taste and tradition.

All this leads to the conclusion that there is an underside of abject self-loathing, almost to the point of homicidal fantasy, in tourist ideologies. Tourist discourses consistently return to themes which deny, negate or obliterate the presence of other tourists where this conflicts with their commitment to contact with the authentic Other. Erik Cohen (1982) has a brilliant illustration of this in his account of beach and hill tourism in Thailand. He describes how foreign tourists in Thailand go to the hills of the 'Golden Triangle' to observe, photograph and experience the tribal peoples, cultures and costumes of the region. Cohen observes that when these same tourists go to the beach islands of southern Thailand they express and demonstrate almost complete indifference to the existence of 'exotic' and vibrant village life a hundred metres inland from the beaches which so captivate them. In the first situation, discovering authentic cultural difference is the tourist's inspired mission; in the second, the experience of 'nature' obliterates the local inhabitants as anything but service personnel. Cohen records a near-homicidal encounter between a tourist and a taxi driver on the island of Koh Sammui in southern Thailand. He saw this explosive conflict as a result of the consistent indifference to local sensibilities by tourists in the region, and predicted the inevitability of more such dangerous encounters.

This argument is not attempting to explain the motivations for the kinds of individual psychotic violence directed against tourists from the Port Arthur massacre (Tasmania 1996) to the Miami serial killer (Florida 1997) or the Luxor massacre (1997).[19] It is, however perversely, suggesting that these acts resonate so powerfully in the Western media, at least in part, because they confirm the worst fears, anxieties and fascination of tourists with their own destruction. Tourist ideologies include the notion that tourists are a scourge on the earth, and the fact that other people actually do violence to our fellow-tourists merely serves to confirm this half-submerged anxiety. The deaths of our fellow tourists brings us face to face with the ambivalent and death-driven horror of those formations which make us homo-touristus. As American Express advertising reminds us: 'Don't forget to pack your peace of mind.'

## Notes

Thanks to the editors John and Raminder, and to Michael Dutton, William Mazzarella, Claudia Chambers and David Martin for reading versions of this chapter and providing suggestions and corrections.

1 This is a rephrasing of a cartoon strip theme by Chris Francis and John Hutnyk, Australia, 1991–3, which itself was quoting Fussel (1980: 390). The cartoon strip extended this theme: 'Making the World Safe for Bureaucracy', 'Making the World Safe for Soft Drinks' and 'Making the World Safe for Banks'. Learn to Like It. Thanks also to the Gnocci Club.

2 In many ways this project is perverse: it is after all an analysis of the structural significance of the murders, executions and abductions of tourists. This assessment was vindicated and intensified when, a few days after this chapter was proposed, a young white man in Tasmania, Australia, walked into a tourist kiosk at the former prison/concentration camp, now tourist site at Port Arthur, and said, 'Not many Japs here today, mostly WASPS', before opening fire and killing large numbers of tourists and employees of the tourist facility. In the perverse logic of media-mediated violence, news consumers were constantly reminded that it was some kind of numerical record of deaths of this kind, setting a challenge that one assumes some other man crazed with the fantasies of power on which capitalist modernity runs in panic will soon feel moved to surpass. Besides feeding a sense of guilty implication in the deaths of tourists everywhere, the repulsive coincidence of this writing and that violence made thinking about dead tourists (and the living over whom they cast their shadows) all the more serious a proposition. This writing has been pressed by its uncanny timing to take some responsibility for these deaths, or take some account for them in a different (cash/knowledge) register than the media's hyper-numeracy. The chapter is an attempt to speak of these horrors as if they were just another passing strangeness in the world; with some abstraction. I hope not to offend those who have known and loved 'dead tourists', but only to offend assumptions about innocence and guilt, rationality and irrationality. While making no claim to explain the excess of violence in the world, aspects of it speak in a language that might be heard from a certain distance.

3 Quote taken from Tejaswini Niranjana's critique of *Roja* (1994: 81). Thanks to Raminder Kaur for bringing this article and film to my attention.

4 The quotation continues: 'If it can help it, the State does not dissociate itself from a process of capture of flows of all kinds, populations, commodities or commerce, money or capital, etc. There is still a need for fixed paths in well-defined directions, which restrict speed, regulate circulation, relativize movement, and measure in detail the relative movements of subjects and objects. That is why Paul Virilio's thesis is important, when he shows that "the political power of the State is polis, police, that is, management of the public ways," and that "the gates of the city, its levies and duties are barriers, filters against the fluidity of the masses, against the penetration power of migratory packs," people, animals and goods. Gravity, gravitas, such is the essence of the State. It is not at all that the State knows nothing of speed; but it requires that movement, even the fastest, cease to be the absolute state of a body occupying a smooth space, to become the relative characteristic of a "moved body" going from one point to another in striated space. In this sense the State never ceases to decompose, recompose and transform movement, or to regulate speed.' (Deleuze and Guattari 1986: 59–60). The real border-crossing threat to the power of the state has been identified by

one of the world's main currency speculators, George Soros, as the movement of finance capital, both as investment, and the much shorter-term movements of currency dealing and exchange rate fluctuation which hold governments to ransom. Why not follow calls of the Left to allow labour the same freedom as capital and let us all go where we please?

5  The following list of sites and incidents of violence directed specifically against tourists or tourist destinations is a random, and far from exhaustive accounting of the ongoing litany of violence: Aqile Lauro: hijacking ... Beirut: 'playground of the rich' to civil war.... Tokyo: subway gassing ... TWA: mysterious explosion and crash ... Lockerbie: bombing ... Manchester: bombing ... Cambodia: hostages ... London Docklands: bombing ... Irian Jaya (West Papua): hostages ... Egypt: random attacks on foreign nationals ... Charles Sobraj: 1970s tourist serial killing ... Algeria: random attacks on foreign nationals ... Gulf War: travel angst ... Uffizi Gallery Florence: bombing ... Dubrovnic, World Heritage listed city: destruction by shelling in Balkan war ... Balangalow State Forest, New South Wales: backpacker serial murders ... Port Arthur, Tasmania: mass murder ... World Trade Building New York: bombing ... Jerusalem tunnel: riots/civil war ... Sri Lanka: repeated hotel bombings and Temple of the Tooth bombing ... Miami: tourist serial murders ... Empire State Building: mass murder ... Kashmir: Al-Faran hostages ... Luxor, Egypt: massacre of tourists.

6  The Hollywood science fiction film, *Total Recall*, runs a nice parallel to this idea of the tourist as secret agent. The hero, played by Arnold Schwarzenegger, takes a hi-tech holiday package with Rekal Incorporated 'where you can buy the memory of your ideal vacation cheaper, safer and better than the real thing'. On this mind trip, or in reality, the plot obscures; Quail discovers he is not an ordinary tourist, but in fact a secret agent who must now turn on his evil, double-crossing Corporate-State employers (and his wife) and liberate the residents of Mars from their oppressors while posing as an ordinary tourist. As undercover agent and tourist Quail becomes deeply confused about his true identity, and ultimately has to make a leap of faith to identify who and what he really is in the unstable reality of his holiday to Mars.

7  All backpacker quotes are taken from interviews with international backpackers in Calcutta 1989, Melbourne 1990 and Delhi 1996, unless otherwise specified.

8  For a more detailed account of the tourist/backpacker distinction see Phipps (1991). Even the apparently straightforward category 'tourist' remains a troubled one in the social science of tourism. To revert to a moment of legalism, tourists are defined under the definition of the UN International Travel and Tourism meeting in Rome in 1963 as: 'temporary visitors staying at least 24 hours in the country visited and the purpose of whose journey can be classified under one of the following headings: i) Leisure (recreation, holiday, health, study, religion, sport); ii) Business, family, mission, meeting.' (quoted in Cohen 1974: 530). Obviously these categories are extremely general and permeable.

9  Diller and Scofidio (1994: 80) cite a wonderful demographic survey by S. Plog:

> Travellers can be categorized according to psychographic segments distributed along a spectrum extending, at one pole, from the 'psychocentric' (inhibited, nonadventurous travellers) to the 'allocentric' traveller demanding change and adventure. The bulk of travellers fit into the intermediate area, the 'mid-

centric'. There are five basic motivations for leisure travel, with the following distribution: life is too short 35%, adds interest to life 30%, the need to unwind 29%, ego support 4%, sense of self-discovery 4%.

10 Thanks to Michael Dutton for this observation.

11 Hutnyk notes that while most budget travellers suffer from bowel-related problems, and reports regular discussions of this over breakfast; they are less likely to suffer from serious afflictions than the 'poor' whom they go to visit (Hutnyk 1996: 40).

12 Visvanathan cites an occasion on which a terrible plague was promoted by British medical wisdom, testing a vaccine and forcibly preventing other measures to sour the experiment: 'Haffkine's plague resulted in thousands dead and lasted 12 years, and it is not clear that his vaccine did much more than hurry along a declining epidemic in any case. Yet Haffkine is remembered as hero' (Visvanathan 1988: 264–5). Thanks to John Hutnyk for finding this text.

13 I would like to thank Raminder Kaur for making these fascinating connections for me. Much of this paragraph is a simple paraphrase of an e-mail she sent me.

14 Most passports carry a variation upon the following statement, this particular one being from an Australian passport and so bearing marks of that country's ongoing colonial legacy: 'The Governor-General of the Commonwealth of Australia, being the representative of Her Majesty Queen Elizabeth the Second, requests all those whom it may concern to allow the bearer to pass freely without let or hindrance and to afford him or her every assistance and protection of which he or she may stand in need'. Such documents have long played a role in the travel-emissary diplomacy-threat gambit.

15 Recent events in Peru are a brilliant variation on this theme, where the Tupac Amaru Revolutionary Army bypassed all symbolic intermediaries (such as tourists) and kidnapped the diplomats and ruling elite themselves. They wagered – in the end at some cost to themselves – on the fair assumption that the diplomats with whom they would be negotiating would have enormous concern for the welfare of diplomats. Similarly, they bypassed all media intermediaries by publishing their plans, objectives and press releases on an internet site on the same day as their raid on the Japanese embassy: http://users.cybercity.dk/~ccc17427/

16 The complexity of power in Cambodia, however – a country where the military had over 1,000 generals at the time, some of whom operated as semi-independent warlords or on behalf of differing government factions – ensured that the hostages were to become part of a still more complicated game. Over the months of isolated reports of the hostages whereabouts, some photos and tape recordings were smuggled (or sent as part of a media-savvy strategy) out of the jungle. In Australia the media ran the story as front-page news each time new information emerged. They were particularly responsive to the release of images of the hostages and their recorded voices, and from the start of the crisis developed a portrait of the Australian hostage, David Wilson, as an embodiment of the virtues of spirited Australian youth: independent, suspicious of authority and brave. These representations reached a climax when images and recordings of the hostages became available which were interpreted to show Wilson as the leader and spokesperson for the group, as much by national as personal strength. Just as Australia had led the Cambodian peace process, and was the apparent leader

of diplomatic efforts to free the hostages, the Australian national held hostage became the leader of the hostages in a poignant moment of symmetry. This image had still more emotive depth because of its association with Australia's official drive to 'become part of Asia' on the one hand, and its resonance with deeply rooted memories of Australians as prisoners of war under the Japanese Imperial Army.

After months of intense confusion over the whereabouts of the hostages, their welfare and who was conducting the negotiations for their release, a breakthrough appeared to be immanent. The Khmer Rouge base where they were being held was identified and approached by government military forces. A price for the release of the hostages was negotiated, and as they were being brought towards the government forces, and being approached by the negotiator, the military opened fire on the Khmer Rouge in an intense bombardment and brought an immediate end to the exchange of money for hostages and weeks of careful negotiation.

It has since been surmised that there were elements in the Cambodian government who concluded that it would be more advantageous to fail to secure the return of the hostages than to succeed. If the hostages could not be returned, or were killed, it would increase Australian, French and possibly British support for the government's war against the Khmer Rouge. This view was further encouraged in Australia by the extreme obfuscation by the Australian Foreign Affairs Ministry over the exact process of negotiations, what had gone wrong, who was responsible, and so on. In the months that followed, confused and contradictory reports emerged about the hostages' location and welfare, until finally their bodies were found by Cambodian soldiers led there by a Khmer Rouge defector. They had been killed in the method characteristic of the Khmer Rouge in their genocidal phase, with a blow to the back of the head by a mattock. In this instance it was the particular value of the national affiliation of the hostages that had determined their ultimate fate through such a complex chain of values and strategies. Had they been Indian, Kenyan or Dutch, they may have been released without mishap, or perhaps have more rapidly met the fate of the Vietnamese nationals.

17 Sheik Abdel-Rahman, an inspiration for Islamic militants in Egypt, was quoted in 1993 as saying of tourists, 'They go to Egypt for transgressions such as fornication, drinking, intoxicants, gambling and usury. They transmit diseases such as AIDS to our land. To those lamenting what has happened to tourism, I say it is sinful ... the lands of Muslims will not become bordellos for sinners of every race and color'. (*The Age*, Melbourne, Australia, 22 November 1997: 19)

18 See also van den Abeele (1980), Morris (1988), Frow (1991) for ongoing discussion of this problematic.

19 A similar phenomenon to that identified by Cohen occurs where Egypt is always prefigured as 'ancient', absenting contemporary Islam and Arabs from this European fantasy. The pyramids are known as a tourist site primarily for monumentalizing the dead. In the face of this the living can perhaps only pale into insignificance, though in the case of Egypt, tourist accounts are inclined to inscribe the local people as a kind of pestilence! This absenting hostility has ironically, and in some cases fatally, been returned recently by Islamic militants

who find foreign tourists a disturbance of their reality, or as useful targets in a campaign to destabilize the 'moderate' government of Egypt which generates substantial foreign exchange from tourism to its pre-Islamic monuments. These overdetermined relations of tourists to place and people are widely varied, but for the most part revolve around the well-worn themes of nature, culture, history and nation. The theme which is perceived to hold the key to the authenticity of a place may vary over time, but the commitment to its pursuit remains militantly persistent. (This paragraph was written before the Luxor massacre, which unfortunately confirms its significance as a site of tension.)

# 8

## MAGICAL MYSTICAL TOURISM[1]

### JOHN HUTNYK

'White' appropriations of African-American culture, sentimentalising images of 'disappearing' Native Americans, condescending caricatures of 'inscrutable' Asians or 'hot-blooded' Mexicans have a long and disreputable history.... Their consequences are no less poisonous when well-intentioned ... identification with otherness has become an essential element in the construction of 'whiteness' (Lipsitz 1994: 53).

### Kula Shaker Tourist Tales

In 1997, on MTV Europe, a young white male pop star stood outside a Hindu temple in India and looked into the camera to say: 'Did you ever get the feeling you were in a Star Wars movie?' His comment on the project of filming in India: 'What happens here is about what you feel, you can't necessarily show that on camera'. When filming local musicians he explains: 'This is the tribal stuff, everyone has a good heart and they put it into the music ... they are just happy ... them living their culture just seems completely natural' (Crispian Mills, *Kula Shaker in India*, MTV 1997).

If our project is to argue for a transnational perspective, it is crucially important that it is not one which becomes the ideology of a new universalist liberalism.[2] The transnational here cannot be merely some form of touristic culture appreciation society (slide shows of the most boring kind imaginable, sanctified by the new editing facilities of documentary television and staged authenticity). Instead what must come to attention are the international networks and interrelations that are the coordinates of contemporary culture and politics, the integrations and disjunctures of the inter-state and inter-commercial systems, from the disproportionate distribution of benefit from production, to the concerted global effort to push through a new geo-media satellite hegemony via CNN and the new telecommunications world systems.[3] Within these processes tourism also has a place, since tourists are in large measure engaged in the very processes that bring the transnational to attention, but only as one kind of process amongst others such as migration, media, warfare or liberalization.[4]

This chapter is a reflection on the politics of music and travel which places theoretical and political concerns alongside the popular culture visibility of 'Asia' in the work of white male pop groups like Kula Shaker. Clearly South Asian musical and cultural forms can be appropriated by global commercial interests even at the point of claims to 'radical alternatives'. Kula Shaker's lead singer and guitarist Crispian Mills makes souvenirs of 'real experiences, man' by meeting *sadhus* and priests at Indian temples and buying trinket versions of cosmic harmony, singing dirge-like versions of devotional tunes while strumming his six-string guitar. Of course this souveniring of sound and culture is only possible on the basis of a long history of colonial power and theft (and nostalgia for that idealized exotic India – one that is other and which was resilient despite, or even because of, the British visitors). I also want to tie in the ways in which this nostalgia and souveniring travels now to the UK and Europe, not just with MTV, but the general population flocking to curry houses to dine out on twisted appropriations of colonialism brought here in new packets; the red-hot 'fuckin' vindaloo' (Banerjea and Banerjea 1996: 111) as England's national dish; white women wearing *bindi* and nose-rings; world music festivals and the popularity of the 'new' Asian dance music at fashionable nightclubs. All this follows the economic structure of the souvenir – exotica deliciously snapped up at prices that are cheap because the 'tourists' won't pay the full price and because the workers and producers of the exotic are underpaid. Synchronously, this underpayment applies also to both the cut-rate club prices and the low remuneration of the curry house workers in England.

In this chapter, tourism is singled out for the very reason that the form exhibits the kinds of reification and appropriations that I want to examine in other media as well – especially, for example, that of the importance of authenticity, the status of representation and the 'authority' to report back from the local to the transnational, wherever this 'local' might be (after all the local is often a code word for the attribution of unsophisticated or uncivilized status). Is it worth focusing upon the touristic practice of the pop star Crispian Mills? Kula Shaker's orthodox rock singer-guitarist-frontman has considerable opportunity, and resources, to expound his views to the world. Here, music cross-cuts travel and the media in ways that are useful, at least from the transnationalist point of view of the critique I want to make, as illustration of the processes and structures of the current cultural conjuncture of contemporary capitalism. This chapter also attempts to take up hard political questions about culture and feed these into a transformatory project that is interested in changing the world. Some may squirm at the recalcitrant optimism of this, but instead of fashionable ready-to-wear cultural cynicism, I want to extend a reading of tourism, television and music into an active political domain.

What is political about tourism and music? There is much that can be (and has been) said here: tourism as the largest truly transnational industry; its massive infrastructural investment; its astonishing integration of sectors, from transport and banking, to the building industry, guidebook production and suntan oil manufacture. Music as the soundtrack: satellites float in the sky, strange noises stream through the hotel window, performances travel and tunes dominate the landscape.[5] The entire apparatus encircles the globe. Both tourism's and music's most esoteric aspects are wholly political as well: be it the sun-seeking break from the rigours of bourgeois life or the unabashed romanticism of Western campaigns against Third World poverty – from Concert for Bangladesh to 'Do They Know it's Christmas?' (and why should they care?).[6] In the former case the leisure industry works as refuelling time for the clapped-out office workers of the First World, serviced by the underpaid service workers of the Third; in the second, performative catharsis assuages the guilt born of media intrusions upon complacency, as stray images of poverty are transmitted across the international wealth and labour divide. While music exists in a more aural and temporal dimension, the political quality of tourism is easy to spot. World domination takes monumental forms, as Kaplan writes:

> Imperialism has left its edifices and markers of itself the world over, and tourism seeks these markers out, whether they consist of actual monuments to field marshals or the altered economies of former colonies. Tourism, then, arises out of the economic disasters of other countries that make them 'affordable' (Kaplan 1996: 63).

Donald Horne's description deserves repeating, where he saw tourism as walking among 'monuments to the wreckage of Europe's greatest ambition – to rule the world' (Horne 1984: 211). Today, such visits are accompanied by a 'shrunken music' soundtrack (Chow 1993: 142) provided via Sony Walkman.[7] To speak of tourism, then, is to speak of the politics of those who conquer, and in this context it is important to listen with a critical ear to the travel tales of megalomaniacs. We have long learnt that authentic histories are not clearly audible in the official record.

In the search for authenticity it has become fairly commonplace to acknowledge that authenticity is a sham. Indeed, the more sophisticated poses available in the theory and tourist marketplace, not to mention in the popular music scene, hold that the conscious recognition of the staged character of 'authentic' performance does not compromise, but can in effect enhance, authenticity. It would be enough here to consider the carefully crafted and annually remodelled identities of Bowie, Madonna or even the Spice Girls – in recent times all three took an 'Asian' turn, with the Spice appearing dressed in saris for a performance in Delhi, and both Bowie and Madonna doing Asian-influenced dance tracks on their latest albums – the material girl displacing Asian group Cornershop at the top of the charts with the track 'Frozen' from her album *Ray of Light* and her performance videos now include decontextualised symbols of Hinduism and tawdry imitations of *Bharatanatyam* dance moves (*MTV Madonna Special*, March 1998). Dean MacCannell, in an early work called simply *The Tourist*, suggested that the search for authenticity is born of an anxiety in the face of the disorienting experience of capitalist modernity (MacCannell 1976: 14). Disorienting or not,[8] it has become more common now to note that such anxiety can also be repackaged and sold as touristic manna. Among others, John Urry (1990, 1995) is probably the most prominent commentator on this complexity, with his notion of the 'post-tourist' (for which, deservedly, he has been criticized for succumbing more to the need to coin new terms, than to the presentation of argument or content). Against this post-tourist sham consciousness, souvenirs – the trinket, the photograph, the jingle, the local sample samba, tabla, Rumba, and of course the travel anecdote – have not lost, but have rather regained, status as markers of authenticity. Seemingly impervious to the onslaught of deconstruction (as if deconstruction was only about destroying so as to find ultimate hidden truths or nothing at all), the souvenir gains, and the holder of the souvenir deploys authority and cultural credibility.[19] Once again, with a family similarity to the astonishing capacity of the commodity form to manifest in so many endless shapes and sizes, the global reach and interchangeability of the souvenir suggests an imperialist ambition – never more so, I will argue, as when Crispian goes to India.

## Crispian Who?

So there is an important cultural politics at stake in the touristic practice of Crispian Mills. Son of Hayley Mills, Hare Krishna devotee and film actress star of Disney's *Pollyanna* and much later *Whistle Down the Wind*, both his estranged father Roy Boulting and maternal grandfather Sir John Mills were also film stars in their own right (Grandpa Mills won an Oscar for his role as the village idiot in David Lean's *Ryan's Daughter*). Crispian's travel adventure is another version of the old pop star goes to see the gurus routine. Best of luck to the temple touts who manage to redistribute a few of the pop star's royalty monies, but in terms of influence, media visibility and contribution to international under-standing (and/or the flipside of this, prejudice), his pronouncements on India are fundamentally dangerous: for example when he says that 'India is the Ibiza of concepts' (Mills, MTV 1997). Obviously many people who might hear such a comment will laugh, and know that shit still smells like shit when it's dished out undisguised like this. But at the risk of picking on a soft target, there is an element which prides itself on its ethnic cosmopolitanism and will accept such statements with the lack of irony intended. Much more than 'enthusiasms' for temples or for 'India' are required to escape prejudicial patronizing and garden-variety orientalism – how many Indologists reading Sanskrit and quoting Vedic verse were also co-conspirators in imperial rule? Slave traders were proto-'Africanists', taking 'native' wives and learning local languages long before anthropologists arrived and realized the practice was good for business.[10] The first arrivees of the British East India Company bought land with silver earned in the slave trade,[11] and they also 'went native' – before the arrival of white wives and 'clubs' and the strict social demarcation that was then enacted (at least in public). Clearly, enthusiasm for 'concepts' is not enough to undermine imperialist incursions, however much it may seem preferable to the racisms of hate. Kula Shaker's Crispian may fancy himself as Luke Skywalker in a Star Wars adventure, but India is not a fantasy planet and political issues might still be canvassed through the music-travel frame in a way that does not rely upon a simplifying stupidity. MTV, however, does not appear inclined to pursue this because it works within the old orientalist paradigm. While Star TV, despite the Murdoch Empire controlling stake, can manage a 24-hour election news coverage channel interviewing leaders and candidates of the competing Communist, Congress and right-wing BJP parties, and satellite modernity delivers 43 channels and more to even the TVs of urban *bustee* dwellers and rural *sarpanch* households, MTV Asia still beams only a *Lonely Planet* kind of India to the screens of its viewers. MTV's India was pre-programmed by videographic preconceptions ranging from Louis Malle to *Heat and Dust* and never seems able to step aside from these choreographed, cinematic old-school conventions. Similarly, in Attenborough's *Gandhi* a mainly

Western film score accepted only samples of Ravi Shankar's sitar in a way that confirmed continuity with previous trinketizing appreciations of even this 'most accessible' of South Asian musicians – it is useful to remember how at the Concert for Bangladesh the audience applauded enthusiastically after Shankar had tuned his sitar, and after thanking them for their appreciation the 'maestro' said he would now play them a raga....[12]

Let us consider some other possible passages into this adventure. Cool Kula Crispian's search for the alterity of Asia through music, like that trek of George Harrison thirty years ago today, means we could also be talking about 'whiteness in crisis' here.[13] I agree there is a crisis to be examined but crucially the discussion needs to avoid a cul-de-sac of political options and self-indulgent brow-beating.[14] Even leaving aside for the moment the anxieties and limited horizons of mainstream commercial actors, the political capability of the white Left, and the political role of popular culture, too often anti-racism today tends towards conservative introspection that alibis power. Discussion of such crisis should go on in tandem with recognition of how such a crisis is only possible on the back of the old colonial game, how, in the context of anti-Asian racism, it posits a nostalgic regret for an imaginary India that was not plundered by British imperialism but which cannot ever really admit to that history, and so now warbles on – in song, from The Beatles to Kula Shaker's forthcoming *Holy River and Golden Avatar* – about cosmic temple tolerance. It is this kind of displacement we do need to examine.

If the desert was the white space inside the dark continent which provided another chance for the heroic European invention of self (Lawrence 'of Arabia' through to Bertolucci's *Sheltering Sky*),[15] then the populated, history-laden, olfactory, sensuous abundance of India for Crispian can be seen as another site of reinvention based on the power to do what you like to the planet – here, the reinvention of self goes by way of a lament and longing for what is missing inside. He has said, in what amounts to a commonplace Western backpacker truism about India, that 'It's a place you go to when you are looking for something, and you will usually find it' and 'that's what it's for, it's a place for changing your life' (*Popview Live* interview 1997). In this routine India becomes the biological/genetic/conceptual repository and archive for values, concepts, styles and 'life essences' considered absent in the individualistic 'developed' West. As if India were not also subject to development, and as if loss (this feeling of inadequacy, or at best alienation) could be eased by yet another round of plunder and pilfering. This time the theft is spiritual, but yet again by way of gross miscomprehension. What seems perhaps at first to be 'something completely different' becomes a comic parody of even whatever degree of counter-establishment sentiment the notion of 'alternative' might once have held. 'Alternative' becomes just one, rather empty, safe and non-threatening lifestyle choice among others, and ends up affirming only a return to the heyday of commerce and more of the same. MTV programming and Kula Shaker's psychedelic India offers not even a substantial chance for the teenage ritual of rebellion anymore; not the pursuit of experimental mind-expanding chemical experience, nor wild creative forays into communal living, nor even the licentious practice of multiple relationships and polyvalently perverse sexualities. What is on sale is a safe rehash of tame Victorian morality glitzed up in gaudy out-of-date fashions and third-rate replays of sounds better done elsewhere. Everything, it seems, can be taken to market second time around, but the more significant factor might be how this reveals a sense of cultural anxiety and collapse, and an incapacity to do anything much about it, which is Crispian's middle-class affliction. Rehearsing the parable of alienation and failing to see any scope for action to improve his lot at home, such a figure looks towards the (fantasy) horizon jealously. Caught in the self-obsessed dead-end of appreciative cultural relativism, he can take no responsibility, has no ambition, no confidence and no capability to do anything but moan about the horrors of self-abuse and the end of the world. Crispian's conspiracy theories and his mysticism are not some form of solidarity with the marginal, esoteric, or with minority religion, but are instead an opportunist cashing in that steers dangerously close to madness alongside support for a quite pernicious form of Hindutva right-wing cultural politics.[16] Relativism and cultural sensitivity sometimes play with such fire.

Even though urban demographics – and therefore many from MTV's audience – provided much of the Bharatiya Janata Party's electoral base, there is not a great danger of the BJP's fortunes being furthered by the support they get from bands like Kula Shaker. Yet the effect of the 'anthropological' gesture of relativist understanding without judgement is somewhat similar to the role played by ethnographers in revitalising Brahmanical ritual traditions without consideration of the context of a resurgent Hindu chauvinism and the contemporary ascendancy of such politics. The self-ish project of temple tourism played out by Crispian on the influential media circuits of satellite imperialism cannot be wholly separated from this context.

Crispian's musical search for the alterity of Asia celebrates an 'India' that is almost entirely in his mind. Supreme irony, then, that Madonna's Sanskritized single lyric repeats: 'You only see what your eyes want to see' (*Frozen* 1998). Crispian and the MTV film crew went to India to explore the 'Eastern influences' of the band. Embarrassing travelogue this: in one scene the singer faces up to a Brahmin priest who mixes and applies red paste to Crispian's brow. Crispian says he doesn't know why it's done or why the Brahmin says he needs it, but afterwards – well, after an edit cut away to Crispian on his own outside the temple – he explains it is a 'third eye' and that it is the sun, just set, on his forehead. This process of moving from incomprehension to explanation, from letting something happen to explaining it to camera, from participation to observation (and later dissemination to the MTV audience world-wide) is the typical structure of ethnographic storytelling and the way exotica is always coded and consumed, irrespective of local significance. Collecting cultural experiences and displaying them provides the pattern for intercultural engagement that relentlessly produces meaning and text (and videotape) in the global tourism apparatus.

The violence of this appropriation is that an already violently marked scene becomes an object for consumption in a traffic of ideas barely understood: be it of the imperialist history which allows Crispian to be there in the first place, the authority of the roving camera eye which can go everywhere – without even stopping to remove shoes – or the sinister echoes of communalism and the unacknowledged project of the Hindu far right. The *bindi* becomes a free-floating universal fashion item, and is recruited as an icon of display signifying experience, otherness and understanding at the very moment when it is none of these things (is it ever just a fashion item?). The spiritual souvenir here is just another example of the flexibility of market appropriation and the ongoing subsumption of all things in all corners of the globe – the capacity to find, in even the most esoteric, aural or spiritual realms, material to enhance the sale of commodities. The plunder of such realms for profit means that the simple *bindi* is rarely innocent of some play of power, whatever its originary significances.

But fashion saves: according to Crispian, it is by paying attention to the supposedly 'timeless' spiritual message in the music that the contemporary ills of the planet can be cured. To a journalist who asked him if all this India pose wasn't just a bit 'out of fashion' and kitsch, he insisted that it is not some

> incense burning, talking philosophy bollocks. It is always relevant, it always means something. India is the source of all, they hold a lot of secrets.... We are in a civilization about to destroy the planet. Everything is destroying itself ... and so where is the rescue mission gonna come from ... we have something to learn from India ... it's just about keeping a door open in the back

of your head ... for some people it's just a fashion, but for others it is timeless (*Popview Live* interview 1997).

The moral certainty is presented as instruction, the music is the message, the planet must be liberated (such is his missionary zeal). Indeed, most of Kula Shaker's public relations repertoire is moral and ethical (why, for example, does Crispian need to tell us he isn't into drugs anymore? How does he cope?). To understand the marketing of the band in this register it is important to remember that cure-alls for alienation and moral-epistemological crisis have long been sold in mystic bottles. Call this the snake-oil medicine man gambit of the cultural frontier.

## Pothead Pixie Jaya Jaya

Too many *bhang lassis* Crispian? Could it really be that he thinks mumbling conspiracy theories about an imminent apocalypse out of Asia is funny? Important by self-decree and MTV/Sony publicity, such amusing speculations from the youthful oracle of things mystic are too sorry for words. The accusation that Kula Shaker are racists and 'racist by ignorance' (*Time Out,* various issues 1996–7) was always going to be controversial, however substantiated by actually and really offensive comments (Crispian says rap isn't music, it's attitude; and so buys into the complaint rock explanation routine of the right-wing reactionaries). No matter how well-intentioned and multicultural the lead singer might claim to be with his studies of Eastern scripture, the consequences of commercial appropriation and decontextualized decorative aesthetics were always going to offend. Gross ignorance is confirmed in slide shows at live gigs which superimpose Lord Horatio Kitchener (the butcher of the Transvaal) over Radha (Krishna's consort), as well as in the imperious arrogance of planning a concert at the Great Pyramid of Cheops on 31 December 1999. This big gig is to go ahead presumably only if the promised Armageddon which Crispian believes will begin with conflict in Pakistan, India and China can be averted by the saviour St George arriving from a place of spiritualism destined to free the world – that is, from England.

Further evidence for the unacknowledged but ever up-front persistence of colonial nostalgia is the reproductions on the first Kula Shaker album cover. Imitating the Fab Four and Sgt Pepper's Lonely Hearts with a collage, including Rudyard Kipling, Kitchener again (this time towering imperiously over the image of Jomo Kenyatta) and Ben Kingsley (Attenborough's imported Gandhi), with arch-imperialist JFK and (for balance?) Martin Luther King, as well as Clark Kent and Captain Kirk to remind us of contemporary US fantasy imperialisms in the sky (all K's, but tactfully no Klu Klux Klan, yet no KC and the Sunshine Band either. Old Beardo Uncle Karl is included as fashion statement, alongside Kruschev). Finally, among others such as Boris Karloff and Katherine Hepburn, an image of Kali and the centrepiece of Krishna and Radha (the only three non-Western representations of things Indian) which confirms that orientalism also thrives in the days of desktop publishing.[17]

That Crispian is covertly rehearsing a grand epic nostalgia for the days of the British Raj must be taken seriously. Although family participation in the imperialist venture of England would not figure in the consciousness of many of his generation, when forced to consider the variety of likely connections, most can recall some immediate family link to the implementation of global political, economic and ideological power. For example, a grandfather who taught at a mission school on the Zambezi, a great grandmother tending to the administration of a club in Shimla, a father or uncle in the forces during the war, and not demobbed in 1945, perhaps even participating in the pre- and post-war anti-Communist police actions in South and South-east Asia....[18] Or, in Crispian's case, his thespian relatives worked in the ideological division, grandfather John portraying the heroic deeds of such as that same slide-show Lord Kitchener (in the film *Young Winston*).

Salman Rushdie famously commented that the trouble with the British is that their history happened overseas and they remain unaware of it (Rushdie 1981). I would argue that they are well aware, only that they are in severe denial born of the continuing project, and this denial has been repackaged for commercial gain by Kula Shaker and bands of their ilk, circulating through the new international circuits of satellite television, international distribution and mediatized tourism. Given that the project of capitalist development and restructuring is, on the face of it, incompatible with the tranquil temple romance of Crispian's dreams, perhaps his representations of Indian mysticism can be read as a kind of guilty rehearsal, parallel to the paradoxical – or hypocritical – structure of imperialist nostalgia recognised by Rosaldo: 'A person kills somebody, and then mourns the victim.'[19] Rosaldo goes on with contemporary resonances: 'In a more attenuated form, somebody deliberately alters a form of life, and then regrets that things have not remained as they were prior to intervention. At one remove, people destroy their environment, and then they worship nature. In any of its versions, imperialist nostalgia uses a pose of 'innocent yearning' both to capture people's imaginations and to conceal its complicity with often brutal domination' (Rosaldo

1989: 69–70). Kaplan, following Rosaldo and indeed quoting the same passage, adds that: 'Imperialist nostalgia erases collective or personal responsibility, replacing accountability with powerful discursive practices [or in Crispian's case, loopy ones]: the vanquished or vanished ones are eulogized (thereby represented) by the victor.' Kaplan includes 'the recent rash of 'Raj' nostalgia' as an example in narrations of the Euro-American past as 'another country' (Kaplan 1996: 34), although her focus on history does not necessarily mean that the history that is denied here is so long past. Indeed, India does still exist, if never in the benign forms beloved of orientalist desire and fantasized by the Raj and by the likes of Kula Shaker. This India is subject to ongoing participation in capitalist production, structural adjustment programmes, tourist and service industry expansion, satellite installation, and so on: neither vanquished nor yet vanished, except in Crispian's addled mind.

In some ways imperialist nostalgia requires flexible adaptation to suit the practice of those present-day 'mystics' who find that through the mechanisms of the tourism industry and telecommunications, that which is feared lost in the West (spiritualism, meaning and harmony), can be sought out on the temple trails of the subcontinent and broadcast again. Another parallel denial process is necessary for this nostalgia to work – contemporary India must be completely ignored, kept off-screen. The extent of this process is profound and codified into a budget traveller's experience of India from the word go – even the *Lonely Planet* set find Delhi to be only a starting point for travels to 'real' India.[20] In the MTV special, Crispian repeats this denial of Delhi, adapting half-understood snippets of Vedic philosophy to sweep industrial development and urban culture aside as an illusion – if only it were true that years of imperial plunder were just so much Maya. There is another dimension to this temple tourism that can be read in the code of anxiety. The crisis of guilt for the brutality of colonialism alongside the lost honour and glory of strong Empire is resolved by Crispian's visit. On MTV, as global witness and tribunal, the white boy-knight can demonstrate that the temple was not desecrated, that the traditional remains intact: the contemporary sensitivities of a caring, sharing world sigh with relief that the violence of the past can now be safely ignored along with any recognition of current political contexts – for example, structural adjustment and ascendant Hindutva. If the temple was not desecrated, as evidenced by the presence of Crispian in the temple, then by extension this opens the possibility of temple visits for all other Western tourists, and horror stories of imperialisms now past can be reassuringly erased from the current guidebooks. This kind of fantasy nostalgia fits India up again as a site for more than simple touristic consumption, a nostalgia directed at, and intrinsically part of, the politics of the present.

Kula Shaker plays at a struggling rerun of the psychedelic late 1960s because that was the last moment of excitement before the post-imperial crisis really hit home (yet even the '60s UK music scene fascination with an 'otherworldly' India of peace and good vibes was in large part in denial of, and even counter to, a sharp and strident world-wide political movement – eclectic and disorganized in some ways, but with serious student politics and worker alliances in Chicago, Paris, Algeria, Japan and, in different ways, China). Today's tamed psychedelics operates without the counter-establishment threat – neither Crispian nor Clinton inhale these days. In retro '60s nostalgia, opportunities to extend the parallels to political issues are never taken. Whatever the tactical incoherence of the Situationist International at the Sorbonne in 1968 or of Abbie Hoffman and Jerry Rubin's exuberant Youth International Party (Yippies) in Chicago, it was at least possible for the vehicle of music to convey concerns about Western imperialist aggression in Vietnam and racist exclusion and white supremacy at home. This is not matched in the rerun of the 1960s sold to us today (what is Crispian's view on direct foreign investment in India? On the bombing of Baghdad or Sudan? On anti-Muslim sentiment in the media? On racist violence and murder on the streets of Britain? On import/export quotas? Or must we remain in trivial fanzine land and only ask him about Rajasthani mirrorwork vests, the Knights of the Round Table, his horoscope and his star sign?).

## Asian Sounds, Sounds Asian?[21]

The Kula Shaker sound is blind to the circumstances of its own pro-duction even at the point where it tries to claim some sort of heritage. That K-S sitarism can place itself on the eastern end of British pop in seeming ignorance of the myriad presence of Asian musics in the UK is not only naïve, but a wilful failure of Sony's signed stars to recognize the full heritage of Asian musics in their own country – at precisely the time when Sony was attempting to market those very musics (through a temporary alliance with Birmingham turntable stalwart Bally Sagoo, and the release of a double LP sampler of other 'new' Asian artists).[22]

What does Kula Shaker know of how Asian musics have travelled to Britain? They trace their interest in 'Eastern' sounds to white 'innovators' in the West: the Byrds, the Incredible String Band, Donovan and later Quintessence (Shiva Jones), Gong (Daevid Allen), Magic Carpet (Clem Alford) and the Teardrop Explodes, right on up to Paul

Weller's Parisian sitar experiments on 'Wild Wood'. Yet theirs is only the white Britpop side of British Asia (Are Kula Shaker Britpop like Oasis? – What does Oasis signify if not T. E. Lawrence's mirage desire for a green and pleasant island in an inhospitable desert?).[23]

There is of course much more going on in British music than the market hype of guitar bands. It would be plausible to think of groups like Fun-Da-Mental and Asian Dub Foundation (ADF) as the avant-garde of a well-pedigreed sound only now becoming saccharinised for commercial purposes in the Sony production sampler and in popular mixed club nights like Anokha in London. This does not mean that outfits like Fun-Da-Mental and ADF have not also sought commercial success, nor were the efforts of Bhangra, Qawwali and playback singers before them without commercial desire. But as much as the publicity machine was cranked up around the Fun-Da-Mental videos produced for MTV, financial success was secondary and in any case not readily forthcoming[24] – the Nation Records posse directed their efforts to using the media space, and all their time and energy, in projects like bringing Pakistani Qawaal Aziz Mian to British audiences, campaigning against the removal of asylum rights from British law and against the draconian Criminal Justice and Public Order Act (see Sharma, Hutnyk and Sharma 1996).

The political aspects of these antecedents of the so-called 'Asian Underground' are in danger of being lost in the attempt by Sony to claim mainstream sales through High Street marketing of artists such as Bally Sagoo. Sony have woken up to the size of the Asian market, but failed thus far to find a way to capture the sales, with Sagoo and Sony parting company after a year, citing 'mutual agreement' but also with rumours of bootleg sales controversy and 'artistic differences'. Sony's next attempt to break into the Asian dance arena was 'Eastern Uprising: Dance Music from the Asian Underground', a sampler which does include tracks by some of the best Asian dance music practitioners, including ADF, Black Star Liner and respected Bengali outfit Joi, but the album's four sides fail to deliver a sense of the diversity and sophistication of the 'underground' sounds, or of the political context out of which Asian dance music comes. Instead, the liner notes read like the script of one of those awful package curry dinner advertisements from the telly: 'Cor blimey! Strike a light. By 'eck ... What the f**k is going on' (Sony's asterix). 'The embers of the empire shimmer like a distant blood-soaked sunset as the urban subtopias of downtown blighty rumble to the rhythms of a brand new internationalism'. The cover mocks a serious politics and instead proposes that the listener 'take a stroll' [good old English pastime this] through inner city Britain and you will be bombarded.... The cab drivers are all clued up and glued down to Bhangra FM.... BMW nightriders cruise the streets issuing menace with bruising drum'n'bass and the cornershops echo to the shrill syncopation of the Bollywood thriller.' This language is in fear of muggers and drug addicts; the respective code words are menace and BMW nightriders (at one point the text refers to 'safe European streets'), while it is also orientalist romanticism; 'the lustre, melodrama and breathless panorama of Asiatic culture and tradition ... Top! Wicked! Safe! Who? Where? Why?' (Sony Corp 1997 *Eastern Uprising*). A reader who mistook this mockery as a report 'from the streets' would be seriously misled.

## So what does Karl Marx think about Sony Corp?

The Sony liner notes wax lyrical and corny in ways only cheap advertising can. But perhaps every word is not a total loss in a text written most likely by more than one hand. It would be plausible to distinguish the 'cor blimey' and 'safe' citations from knowledgeable sentences about the scene in Brick Lane and the pernicious effects of boom and decline in British manufacturing and its ravenous need to chew up and then spit out the 'legions of Norjawan'. Nevertheless, the unintended irony of a sentence that describes the music as the sound of a new breed of urban Asianite 'Freed from the dead end of industrial employment, liberated from convention and able to juggle duality and pluralism with more skill than a pre-coke Maradona' is striking. Leaving aside the overdetermined designations that Asians are dextrous and hybrid ('juggling' between two cultures yet again),[25] I would like to take up this contradiction – 'freed' from employment – on another, quite different, level of analysis. The point here is to establish the basis for arguing that cultural appropriations such as those by Kula Shaker in regard to 'India' are not innocent, but rather do ideological work for a basically exploitative project – the inexorable logic of value misappropriation, prejudicial division of labour, inequitable distribution of resources and homogenization of social relations throughout the world. The homogenization of the world under capitalist relations proceeds by bringing all differences to the HMV bargain bin and it indeed 'thrives' on 'cultural' content where differences can be equated through abstract equivalencies: all this so well foreseen by Marx, not Madonna.

Can the Sony copywriters have been quoting intentionally Marx's famous passage about the transition from feudalism to capitalism as a sly commentary on the consequences of post-industrial Britain in

decline? Since 'freedom' did not come to India/Pakistan at 'decoloniza-
tion',[26] perhaps Sony are repackaging it today with a deeply subtle play?
The allegory at least deserves a closer reading. In the Economic
Notebooks of 1887–8 (*Grundrisse*), Marx sets out his moment in a vivid,
if abstract, passage:

> when the great English landowners dismissed their retainers, who had
> consumed with them the surplus produce of their land; when their tenant
> farmers drove out the small cottagers, etc., then a mass of living labour
> power was thrown on to the labour market, a mass which was *free in a double
> sense*: free from the old client or bondage relationships and any obligatory
> services, and free also from all goods and chattels, from every objective and
> material form of being, free of all property [eine Masse, die in doppeltem
> Sinn frei war]. It was reduced either to the sale of its labour capacity or to
> beggary, vagabondage or robbery as its only source of income. History
> records that it tried the latter first, but was driven off this road and on to
> the narrow path which led to the labour market, by means of gallows,
> pillory and whip (Marx 1857/1987: 431 my italics, trans. from 1857/1974:
> 406).

The goods that previously had been consumed by the feudal lords and
their retainers, and the released produce of the land, are thrown on to
the exchange market, as are those who henceforth would be known as
labourers. The sale of labour power instilled by discipline – the gallows,
the workhouse, the prison – becomes the only choice.[27] Even the
poorhouses and their charity instil the discipline of work (only Dickens's
Oliver dares ask for 'more' it seems). That this was conceived by Marx
as part and parcel of capitalist development can be confirmed from other
(re)writings of almost the same paragraph.

In *Capital* Marx returns more than once[28] to this scene:

> Thus were the agricultural people, first forcibly expropriated from the soil,
> driven from their homes, turned into vagabonds, and then whipped,
> branded, tortured by laws grotesquely terrible, into the discipline necessary
> for the wage system (Marx 1867/1967: 737).

Over and over Sony and Marx 'free us from employment'.[29] One is
ironic, the other obscene: the obscenity is from Sony, because here the
way out of the ghetto is the old, often repeated trick/panacea of pop
stardom or forced wage slavery. That MTV and the music industry can
market this lottery dream as a vehicle for selling ever more records is
no longer a surprising point (you can't actually be the popstar with the
escape clause, but buy the album and you feel like it could be you). The
trick is that we are free to endure this, we volunteer to be retold the
improbable tale over and over, we walk willingly into the record store:

For the conversion of his money into capital, therefore, the owner of money must meet in the market with the free labourer, *free in the double sense,* that as a free man he can dispose of his labour-power as his own commodity, and that on the other hand he has no other commodity for sale, is short of everything necessary for the realisation of his labour-power (Marx 1867/1967: 169 my italics, Marx's gendered language).

That this, too, is no equal exchange is of course the biggest trick of capitalist appropriation. Though it would seem that in the marketplace the capitalist offers a 'fair' price – money for labour, wages – and that the entire history of reformist unions has been to ensure the 'fair trade' of this exchange, the capitalist does not, in fact, pay for every hour that the labourer works (nor for every cost of reproducing labour power). Here, at the crucial point of the labour theory of value, the expansion of the trick of the market is played out. This moment is exported universally. It would be worth reading the history of Asian labour in Britain as a variation on the dynamics of this market trick. Here it is helpful to draw again upon the work of Virinder Kalra (1997).[30] Disciplined by the inequities of the international division of labour, workers from the colonies are brought to the UK to work the mills in shifts. Irregular employment means they do not benefit from the welfare net of superannuation and pensions, and with the decline of the mills, they are 'freed' into unemployment, taxi-driving (the Sony text again) and service work (kebab shops and the like).

Again towards the end of *Capital* labourers are 'free workers in a double sense':

> The capitalist system presupposes the complete separation of the labourers from all property in the means by which they can realise their labour. As soon as capitalist production is once on its own legs, it not only maintains this separation, but reproduces it on a continually extending scale (Marx 1867/1967: 714).

The extending scale of this process as we see it today seems well anticipated, but this was only a 'sketch'. In a letter to the editors of the paper *Otechestvennye Zapiski* in the last years of his life, Marx warned that the chapter of *Capital* which set this out in the most detail – Chapter 27 – should not be 'transformed' from a historical sketch of the genesis of capitalism in Western Europe to a 'theory of the general course fatally imposed upon all peoples, whatever the historical circumstances in which they find themselves placed' (Marx 1878 in Shanin 1983: 136). Far too often the technical abstractions necessary in setting out Marx's *Capital,* which begins with commodities and expands in complexity to encompass trade, circulation of capital, rent and so on, lead to orthodox fixities and dogma. Nevertheless, the general point of the expansion of the logic of market exchange and the creation of 'a "free" and outlawed proletariat' (Marx 1867/1967: 731) can be illustrated thus and it makes sense to use it to understand the circumstances in which the politics of the Asian dance musics might be elided by a commercial outfit like Sony Corp. The history of this expropriation is written 'in letters of blood and fire' (Marx 1867/1967: 715).

There is little need to go further into the hagiographic mode of repeating Marx as oracle, particularly when we have Crispian. There are sufficient other examples, too – Felix Guattari: 'it is clear that the third world does not really "exchange" its labour and its riches for crates of Coca-Cola.... It is aggressed and bled to death by the intrusion of dominant economies' (Guattari 1996: 238). Harry Cleaver, summarizing, quotes Marx pointing out that 'the veiled slavery of the wage-workers in Europe needed, for its pedestal, slavery pure and simple in the new world' (in Cleaver 1979: 76). Marx there adds a footnote to make it clear that he is talking about the global cotton trade (Marx 1867/1967: 759–60) which again makes it relevant now to link this section to Asian workers in British mills. In any study of the ways colonialism 'had to use force to make the indigenous populations accept the commodity form at all', Cleaver continues, the various examples would range from slavery and death to persuasion (Cleaver 1979: 77) and, especially today, cooptions of all kinds. Though it might not have been their (worthy) intention, and though the outcome is not guaranteed, the ambition of Kula Shaker belongs to the wider propensity of capital always to insist on being *free* to take whatever it chooses to market. This trick is nowadays articulated through the rhetoric of the 'open market', the 'level playing field' and 'a fair day's work for a fair day's pay' (and equal access to the pop star dream for all) necessarily subservient to the master trope of the direct equivalence of exchange values mediated through the universal standard money form. Not everyone has the same resources to bring things to market, so what is it that enables Crispian to appropriate India as the 'Ibiza of concepts' and take this booty to Sony for a multi-million deal, while the *Sadhu* and Brahmin custodians of the concepts barter *bindi* for rupees?[31] The rough discipline of inequality and colonial (white) supremacy. Why is it that the trick of the market is not ready to pay out in the same ways for those South Asian practitioners in the UK such as Fun^Da^Mental, ADF or MC Mushtaq who have been working with the community for many years without corporate support? Why does culture defer to Crispian's grasp? Cleaver lists 'massacre, money taxes, or displacement to poor land' as the ways that capital dealt with resistance and refusal to be put to work. We could add cultural appropriations and the repetitive drone of a Britpop mono-culture that absorbs all into its pre-packaged grip. On the basis of this comes the 'civilizing' mission of the West, that would teach 'backward' peoples the values of thrift, discipline, saving and a snappy melody.[32] In a contemporary extension of this, we could read Sony's wayward attempt to capture the Asian music market from the corner shops and the boot-leggers as an institutional instance of pretty much the same missionary zeal run aground once again on the rocks of the foreign.

Freedom in the double sense can also refer to the double bind of this trickery. Some are free of chattels and possessions, and may ever so freely choose when to sell their labour if they ever want to eat. Some, though, are free to travel the world in search of trinkets. The old colonial adventure is performed with Lord Kitchener as overseer. Capital drives hard to subsume precapitalist, non-capitalist (and even postcapitalist retro reruns) into its cannibalizing orifice.[33] The 'free flow of ideas', the free operation of the market, the freedom train. In a mercifully brief psychedelic moment of their career The Rolling Stones sang: 'I'm free, to do what I want, any old time'. This arrogant freedom is now in crisis, but Britpop wants to defend it. 'Cor blimey'. The posturing moralism, holier-than-thou spiritualism, and good-ethics-guide preachery of Mills is a still more zealous example of the same righteous sermon.

So when Sony and Kula Shaker present themselves as a 'rediscovery' of the Asian sound and its crossover into popular music they ignore the significance of political and musical histories that paradoxically they must also acknowledge, if only to appropriate and convert. This is nothing more than the operation of a business-as-usual colonial project. It is still about wanting to rule the world.

## Traveller's Souvenir India for Show and Display

The 1996 single *Govinda* is a dirge which has Crispian singing semi-obscure *bhajans* in Sanskrit. The accompanying video deploys a clichéd narrative of fire and brimstone followed by redemption, placing the band in the symbolic space of a monotheised Krishna. The versions of Krishna often deployed in Western tourist renditions of India rely on the translation of three major Hindu deities – Shiva, Vishnu, Krishna – into a Christian-style triumvirate, which then allocates Krishna a Jesus-like position. The popularity of cartoon versions of this part of the *Mahabharata* among travellers has been documented (Hutnyk 1996) and is especially appealing to those of the banana-pancake trail, backpacker, *bhang lassi* set just where Krishna seems to bestow a psychedelic experience on his follower Arjuna. This popularity was reinvested on a Kula Shaker CD release (*Hey Dude*) which featured the dulcet tones of Crispian reading from the *Mahabharata*.

How such 'translations' and associations appeal to backpackers can be clearly heard in the Kula Shaker repackaging of souvenired knick-knack mysticism in tracks like *Tattva* and *Govinda*. When, in the MTV travelogue, Crispian was faced with an unscheduled performance at a conveniently 'found' Hindu 'party' at a Roadside Hotel stop, the most uncomfortable and awkward moment of 'intercultural relations' is shown in full glorious colour. The mix of pop star prima donna and nervous pre-stage appearance tension, the embarrassing, halting, jangling, acoustic and discordant – though mercifully short – performance, and the attempt to authorize this difficult moment as the culmination of Crispian's India pilgrimage illuminates the hypocrisy. The disturbing spectacle of consumable India presented to audiences in this version at least has the merit of being too transparent for most viewers and fans to swallow whole – though it may be feared that even this could some-times be taken as representative of a real and available India. The only image that conveys the possibility that there is also a political domain in India is a split-second still of a red protest banner declaring 'Coke-Pepsi Quit India' – but you need a dextrous hand on the pause button to read it. Music industry reception of the band has in large measure been sceptical,[34] but tourist package promotionals on MTV travel far. Sales suggest something big is going on in the marketplace, and in any case, any degree of scepticism and cynicism from the music press (or academic commentators) is insufficient to undo the ideological stereo-typing achieved by the new media orientalisms that Kula Shaker, Madonna, Bowie and Sony Corp are able to deploy. The post-tourist, post-guru, post-psychedelic revival has the air of sanctimonious and righteous truth.

## Trinkets and Tablas

In the end we are left with an apocalyptic vision of a scary alternative universe: what should we make of Crispian's interest in Arthurian legends, the flag of St George pasted onto his guitar (ironically?) along-side the Sanskrit Om? The eulogy for empire in his display of both Kitchener and that flag evokes a nostalgia for the East (nostalgia as a career, to paraphrase Disraeli?)[35] that omits the oppression, violence and struggle of history, as if a different outcome to the Raj can be imagined into being through Crispian's mystical trip. The high visibility of trinket Asian sound bites on the media circuits of popular culture are souvenired baubles in an ongoing Raj power play – a sitar-strumming, tabla-thumping, temple-touring, nick-knack, grab-bag philosophy of distortion and remix of the past.

Can the subaltern dance?[36] I know this is a conceit, Crispian is no subaltern, but in the 'post'-empire the struggle to retain a faded glory now appears as a parody of the old psychedelic appropriations. Of course the serious side of this is the Sony empire that finds contingent convenience in marketing this nostalgia (since it can't yet find the code to market Asian musics to Asians). But can Crispian keep to a different beat, or will the Mosley–Thatcher anxiety of swamping require a reversal back to orthodox Fortress Oasis Britpop? So much of cultural life in the UK today is marked by South Asian influences.[37] Further incursions into South Asian cultural production for general sale is the almost inevitable outcome of Sony's initial forays into the zone. Although hegemonically, institutionally and in all significant class, gender, race and socio-economic categories Anglo-Saxon dominance remains; it has done so increasingly only on the basis of nostalgia (both Britpop and Kula Shaker trade on the 1960s revival, white flight glosses urban abandon as a return to old rural values). Dining out still on the benefits of empire, dining out in the curry corridor of urban England, welcome to the last feast of colonial power. It comes as no surprise that Brick Lane in London has been designated an 'Official Tourist Zone'.[38]

Rather than the global jukebox which Kula Shaker and so many others seem to imagine as the perfect multicultural soundtrack to the feast of Eastern dining, an engagement with political issues, exclusions and the co-constitution of racism and imperialism would be a far better project. Indigestion in the face of deportations, police attack and repressive force may seem unsavoury, but an injunction to 'shut up and dance' to the *bhajans* of Crispian or the sitars of Sony is just not an adequate response to the expansive gluttony of the capitalist project today.

## Notes

1 Thanks for comments on this writing go to: Raminder Kaur, Saurabh Dube, Peter Phipps, Sanjay Sharma, Virinder Kalra, Gerard Goggin, Liz van Dort, Josie Berry, Hari Kunzru@Mute, and Ashwani Sharma.
2 The project of a transnational cultural studies correlates dangerously close to the market niche agendas of the media empires of Murdoch, Time/Warner and MTV.

The notion of a shared 'electronic community' celebrated by audience studies 'ethnographers' like Ien Ang (1996) fits all too neatly with the target audiences of specialized satellite television provision and the theoretical arabesques of 'diasporic' cultural studies in eloquent personnel such as James Clifford (1997) and even Paul Gilroy (1993) (see my discussion in Hutnyk 1997). The transnational does not mean the economics of the capitalist nation has gone away, rather, insofar as it may have been displaced to some degree by new cross-border markets, the nation-like economic and demographic scope of these markets remains the same. No, the nation has not disappeared, it's just sometimes a cross-border frequency and a corporate sponsored timeslot. As Saurabh Dube reminds me, the IMF and World Bank still seem to think (discourse, ideology, practice, police) in terms of nation and flag/logo.

3 On this the work of Armand and Michelle Mattelart is exemplary (1986/1992 and Mattelart 1996). It would be possible to question Mattelart's claim that the 'historic turning point of the deregulation of communication networks' is responsible for 'the move to worldwide economic integration' (Mattelart 1996: 303), but it is certainly the case that 'The integration of everyone into the material benefits of modernity reserved up to now for the few has become more and more problematic' (Mattelart 1996: 305).

4 Appadurai's famous essay gives a useful code already (Appadurai 1990), but see also Mattelart who begins his *Mapping World Communication: War, Progress, Culture* with the sentence: 'The nineteenth century saw the slow emergence of a new mode of exchange and circulation of goods, messages and persons, as well as a new mode of organizing production' (1991/1994: 3).

5 My one and only self-reflexive bit: the first two or three times I visited the Indian countryside it seemed strangely empty until I realized the soundtrack I'd been preprogrammed to expect from so many films and documentaries wasn't playing the same tracks 'in the real'. Of course this critique of Kula Shaker is also autobiographical, but I would contend that this is relevant only in a minor register. See Note 19.

6 At a Kula Shaker performance in 1996 I found graffiti, obviously written on the venue walls on an earlier occasion, which captured the sentiment of the point I want to make here with wit and economy: 'Christmas Teaches Kids to Love Capitalism'.

7 See du Gay *et al.* (1997) for a very accessible introduction to cultural studies via the famous personal music system of Sony.

8 In *Dis-Orienting Rhythms: the Politics of the New Asian Dance Music*, we began by noting how the voracious appetite of the market had turned all manner of 'Asian' markings into exotic objects of value – sarees, vindaloo and Ravi Shankar being the least offensive items – but we also noted that this was concurrent with increased racist violence and murder on the streets, police persecution and deportation by the government, and a purulent voyeuristic interest in 'culture' on the part of much of academia. See Sharma, Hutnyk and Sharma 1996.

9 Some folks even look forward to Madonna's next incarnation of self.

10 See the film *Ill-Gotten Gains* 1997 (directed by Joel Marsden, Spat Films 1997) for a recent uncompromising take on this theme, far and away better than any moment of Spielberg's *Amistad*.

11 See my discussion of this in 'Capital Calcutta: Coins, Maps and Monuments' (Hutnyk forthcoming).

12 This is a paraphrase of a comment by Philip Hayward at the Globalisation and Music conference, Centre for the Studies in Social Science, Calcutta, 1998, and I thank him for the reminder. See his *Music at the Borders: Not Drowning Waving and their Engagement with Papua New Guinean Culture* for a very different version of cultural engagement on the part of white rock (Hayward 1997).

13 This formulation was originally written in discussion with Ashwani Sharma. Thanks Ash.

14 I would share Liz Fekete's (1998: 77-82) critique of a therapy model for anti-racism which would approach white masculinity looking for latent causes and reified Oedipal complexes within 'identity' formation rather than pursuing racisms politically.

15 See the chapter in this volume by Koushik Banerjea.

16 Hindutva, especially in its Mumbai Shiv Sena form under Bal Thackeray, has been explained as a consequence of Hindu nationalism mixed with 'casino capitalist' black market speculation and Green Revolution pay-offs enjoyed by the landed Maratha elites. There may be resources within Hinduisms that would not lead to support for the far right, but ignorant participation in the 'natural' celebration of Brahmanical and fascist Hindutva populism by white pop stars cannot pass unacknowledged.

17 It might be a little hard-line to claim that the repressive nostalgia of this imperialism is structured into every cup of tea drunk in the British Isles, but the teapot also features on the Kula Shaker cover, K is for kettle – here to the Ks I'd also add Khatam, the war word of the Naxalites from the foothills of Darjeeling – recently celebrated by Asian Dub Foundation, and also the name of a Manchester South Asian club night. The possibility of underlining so many of these congruous links does seem overwhelming, although it must be left to another occasion to address the omission of this kind of politics from the growing recognition and international travel of South Asian dance musics (Kalra and Hutnyk, forthcoming article in *Theory, Culture and Society*).

18 British (as well as US and Australian) soldiers in the South-east Asian theatre were kept on after the second (imperialist) World War to fight various communist insurrections. In Malaysia many communists were slaughtered, and this was just a part of a concerted effort to 'cleanse' the world of the 'Red' threat. A useful, if harrowing, documentation of the millions killed for the crime of wanting the best possible world for all is Kovel (1994).

19 Nostalgia and guilt operate in travel and in ethnography (see the chapter in this volume by Peter Phipps). The doyen of ethnographic fieldwork himself is complicit, and arrives with the cops: Malinowski admits, in a revealing confession: 'The discipline of Ethnology finds itself in a ludicrous situation.... For ethnology to live, its object must die'. Malinowski arrives in his South Sea Island village in the company of the police, with the begrudging support of the District Governor and the approval – for the reason that his research might help in native affairs – of the Australian Government (Atlee Hunt in Mulvaney and Calaby 1985: 453n). The opening words of the premier text of the fieldworker's method, *Argonauts of the Western Pacific* (1922) begins with a confession, and indeed this is the house

style of the discipline. Today, more than ever, the confessional tone characterizes the reflexive turn, the postmodern fashion, the postcolonial angst, and this has now been universalized and exported as prerequisite for all. A pale mimicry of criticism-self-criticism continues even into the recent family resemblances which can be traced into cultural studies and, for example, the work of Jean Baudrillard, who in similar words, even 'the same' words as Malinowski [without citation], writes about the discovery of the Tasaday people in the Philippines: 'For ethnology to live, its object must die. But the latter revenges itself by dying for having been 'discovered', and defies by its death the science that wants to take hold of it' (Baudrillard 1983: 13) [Curiouser and curiouser, the Tasaday seem to have been an invented 'lost tribe' set up as a touristic publicity stunt – a simulation that would not disturb Baudrillard's schema much at all. Who were these people? Who were they fronting for? Who 'disappeared' them? Who took the cut?].

20 Credit for directing travellers first into the pit of the Pahar Ganj tourist strip, and thence onto trains and buses out of Delhi in the direction of Rajasthani forts, the Taj Mahal or Varanasi's burning *ghats* (again see the chapter in this volume by Peter Phipps) is due to Tony Wheeler, publisher of the *Lonely Planet* 'survival' guides. It was Wheeler who wrote that 'real India is on the trains' (Lonely Planet 1984, 1991, 1997 etc.).

21 This heading is an adaptation of Sanjay Sharma's chapter title 'Noisy Asians or Asian Noise?' (Sharma, Hutnyk and Sharma 1996). In that chapter Sanjay carefully catalogues the emergence of South Asian dance musics in the UK, from Bhangra to the present.

22 It could be objected that Sony Corp is after all an 'Asian' company – but I think in this case the reification of Japanese business practices tends towards another mode of exoticization – I would argue that the capitalist 'identity' of Sony overrides any corporate 'ethnicity' which might be deployed. Elsewhere I will discuss the question of Sony TV's South Asian satellite channel offerings.

23 Of course the Gallagher brothers cannot be blamed for getting it while they can. Thankfully they don't really go in for identity therapy except maybe in relation to the uneven fortunes of their Maine Road football team, Manchester City. To return to the issue of masculinity, one of the more tragic aspects of the rise of identity politics is the articulation among hegemonic white Euro-Americans of a sense of not having any 'ethnicity' at all, and of experiencing this as a kind of loss. Worrying about this should not lead to a defence of the old invisibility of white supremacy of the pre-identity politics phase, but the desire for ethnic character – manifest in moves as diverse as wannabee wiggas through tribal Celtic nostalgias to ultra-Aryan fascisms – is no excuse for another round of Britpop celebratory national cheesiness.

24 Recently Nation Records released a double CD compilation of the label's best-known and memorable tracks, entitled *And Still No Hits*....

25 See the chapter in this volume by Seán McLoughlin and Virinder Kalra.

26 See the chapter in this volume by Virinder Kalra and Navtej Purewal.

27 Michel Foucault's somewhat reluctant Marxist inheritance in his inspiring and influential work on asylums, clinics, punishments etc., emerges from these insights, although it is important to remember that labour itself is a major mode of disciplinary formation.

28 Also: 'They were turned *en masse* into beggars, robbers, vagabonds, partly from inclination, in most cases from stress of circumstances. Hence at the end of the 15th and during the whole of the 16th century, throughout Western Europe a bloody legislation against vagabondage. The fathers of the present working-class were chastised for their enforced transformation into vagabonds and paupers. Legislation treated them as 'voluntary' criminals, and assumed that it depended on their own good will to go on working under the old conditions that no longer existed' (Marx 1867/1967: 734).

29 There is, of course, an extensive literature on freedom in this context. For a beginning see Marx's famed 'Paris Manuscripts of 1844' (1844/1979). Marcuse spoke of freedom in the 'sixties' in ways that would require Crispian to do more than sing about revolutions of the mind: 'Marxism must risk defining freedom in such a way that people become conscious of and recognize it as something that is nowhere already in existence' (Marcuse 1970: 32) Another recent reworking which draws upon Luxemburg, the existentialists, Mao Zedong and Hegel is found in the writings of Raya Dunayevskaya: *Rosa Luxemburg: Women's Liberation, and Marx's Philosophy of Revolution* (1981/1991) as well as her *Philosophy and Revolution* (1973). Today we might want to ask how the struggle for freedom seems to have turned into the struggle for the extension of free trade (the freedom of a free fox among free chickens as Rosa Luxemburg might have said). In general terms, freedom from employment would perhaps be fine if this freed us for creativity. But the distribution of resources, and the fact that only some are 'free' to make a living in the cultural industries while others are free to work in less pleasurable ways, ensures that remuneration in music, tourism or food is rather less than that afforded Madonna, The Spice Girls, or Kula Shaker.

30 It should be work like Kalra's that Featherstone has in mind when he writes: 'One could envisage a ... book on cotton which would focus upon the relations between Manchester capitalism and imperialist presence in the Indian and other colonies'. He interestingly continues: 'we should add that this and similar topics (chocolate, tea, etc.) are being addressed as student projects in cultural studies and communications courses' (Featherstone 1995: 156). Indeed, as it is non-tenured and sessional Asian researchers who have been teaching such courses, the absence of full-time employment and adequate teaching release for Black academics ensures the citation remains anonymous.

31 This is not to forget that there are other (internal?) hierarchies and appropriations at play here in sectors complex as well as profound – the discussion of these, however, is engaged elsewhere. See Kalra and Hutnyk 1998.

32 See Saurabh Dube, in Chapter 3 of this volume.

33 Of course subsumption arguments cannot simply be stated and left as self-explanatory guardians of what goes down. Complicated processes of cooption, recruitment of comprador classes, hegemonic cultural and political struggle and the myriad local variations that anthropologists love to point out would need to be accounted for in any comprehensive study. It is sufficient here to note that good, worthy, zealous, dim Crispian has been sequestered by the ideological division of such processes, aware of it or not (indeed, if he were 'taking the piss' it would be less offensive, but unfortunately the 'seriousness' with which Kula Shaker take themselves is never ever shaken).

34 Especially over Crispian's comments about the swastika being a great image, as reported by Stephen Dalto in the *New Musical Express* from a March 1997 interview (but see *NME* 4 April 1998 for analysis of Crispian's recantation, and his unconvincing excuse, as implied by the *NME*, that he himself is Jewish – he has a Jewish grandmother). Photographs and stories alleging his involvement with the National Front have not been mitigated by his claims that the band Objects of Desire, which included the alleged former NF member, Marcus McLaine (Crispian's mother's ex-lover), was 'a teenage thing' and that now Crispian 'loathes' the far right (*Vox*, May 1988). In an amazing response to one journalist's reporting of the original controversy, Crispian offered a long letter, subsequently posted on the Sony www page, which in part reads: 'I have travelled to India many times and have been influenced greatly by its people and philosophy, especially that of Bhakti or devotional love. It is my love of Indian culture, and its artistry, music, rich iconography and symbols that prompted my comments in the *NME* [about the legitimacy of the swastika and its ancient Indian origins]. My comments were not in any way a support of the crimes that are symbolized by the Nazis' use of the swastika.... I apologize to those who have been offended by my comment and humbly ask that they accept that I am completely against the Nazis.... Lately I have considered how confusing some of the things I have said appear, especially when they are taken as sound bites, and on occasion, out of context. Communication seems challenging at the best of times, and I now appreciate that my bundling of themes like the Grail, Knights Templars and Hinduism has not done much in the way of helping deep understanding. You are correct when you comment on my 'complicated and intriguing mystical worldview' saying that you 'find it hard to understand in simple terms' the co-mingling of all these ideas. I think the only way one can reconcile their relationship (if indeed one accepts that there is one), is if one looks at them from a mystical or spiritual point of view. There are of course lines of thought that suggest how Eastern ideas made their way to the West, especially via the Crusades, but it is true that for the most part they do not have a currency in modern thought. Thus in essence, the co-mingling is largely a personal expression of a desire to know and understand the deeper secrets of a spiritual or inner life. From the little that I know or understand, I see that somehow similar themes appear in different cultures and settings.... I appreciate that my own special mix of themes is at best eccentric' (Crispian Mills, letter to Mr Kalman, *The Independent*, 17 April 1997. Full text http://www.music.sony.com/Music/ArtistInfo/KulaShaker/reviews/inde_fax.html).

35 The oft quoted phrase 'The East is a career' appears in Disraeli 1871: 141. I take the citation from Chow 1993: 185, for whom it was located by Prabhakara Jha. There is however something disturbing in Chow's use of this phrase to make a point about students 'of the East': She writes: 'The difficulty facing us, it seems to me, is no longer simply the 'first world' Orientalist who mourns the rusting away of his treasures, but also students from privileged backgrounds Western *and* non-Western who conform behaviorally in every respect with the elitism of their social origin ... but who nonetheless *proclaim* dedication to 'vindicating the subalterns' ... they choose to see in other's powerlessness an idealized image of themselves and refuse to hear in the dissonance between the content and manner

of their speech their own complicity with violence ... even though ... [they] may be quick to point out the exploitativeness of Benjamin Disraeli's 'The East is a career', they remain blind to their own exploitativeness as they make 'the East' *their* career' (Chow 1993: 14–15). Chow then asks how we might intervene in the productivity of this overdetermined circuit. I hope some part of the answer is suggested in this book.

36 My reference here is to Gayatri Spivak's famous essay, 'Can the Subaltern Speak?' (Spivak 1988). I would point out that Crispian Mills is not the only one who is not subaltern at all. Those that do 'speak' (though they are not heard here, because of Crispian's verbosity), take the place of the subaltern who 'can' dance – and so they, keeping in mind the previous footnote, are hardly subaltern either. While I want to register the ways exotic versions of 'India' muffle the political articulations of bands like ADF and Fun^Da^Mental, they are themselves able to access media avenues with extraordinary reach (for example, the incongruity of ADF's single *Naxalite* – which references the history of peasant struggle in West Bengal – being beamed by satellite to receivers simultaneously in London and Calcutta). Nevertheless, here I play with the mode of address, and wonder not what matter who is speaking, but that it matters what is said, and with what purpose. Theodor Adorno might also be evoked – there is a big difference between the anger of writing poetry *about* Auschwitz, and aesthetics of reading poetry *after* Auschwitz – no matter whose poetry it is (see Hutnyk 1997).

37 It is no longer just a joke that the national dish is curry: the immigration departments, and the medical, dental and pharmaceutical industries are staffed by South Asians, the legal profession too, and the sound in the clubs is heavily Asian (and African diasporic) Jungle, Soul, Hiphop and Bhangra – though this inflected change is only rarely noticed in academia, parliament or the upper echelon corporate boardrooms of industry.

38 'What Brick Lane needs is more investment in housing, jobs and new local businesses – not just the curry houses' (*Eastern Eye,* 19 September 1997). Debate over changing the name Spitalfields to Banglatown still rages in in the local press (*East London Community News*, August 1998).

39 Against the saccharine multiculturalism of the Global Jukebox, Nation Records inaugurated their Global Sweatbox club night in London, March 1998.

# 9

## WISH YOU WERE(N'T) HERE?
### Discrepant Representations of Mirpur
### in Narratives of Migration, Diaspora and Tourism[1]

SEÁN MCLOUGHLIN AND VIRINDER S. KALRA

### Outward Bound

> They bear upon them the traces of the particular cultures, traditions, languages and histories by which they were shaped. The difference is that they are not and will never be *unified* in the old sense, because they are irrevocably the product of several interlocking histories and cultures, belonging at one and at the same time to several 'homes'. (Hall 1988: 310)

In the northern winter of 1994–5 we travelled to the disputed territory of Pakistani-administered (Azad or Free) Kashmir.[2] Our destination was Mirpur, a district which has seen large-scale migration to Britain since the late 1950s and early 1960s. Two young-ish males in their twenties, one visibly Sikh, the other of Irish heritage, our journey from Britain was for the purposes of doctoral research. Our trip to Mirpur saw us following in the footsteps of a variety of visitors from Britain who have all travelled to South Asia in search of a greater understanding of migrants' backgrounds. As we argue here, however, this surge of activity amongst anthropologists, local government officials and community workers has consistently and stubbornly reproduced one rather curious notion: that an analysis of culture brought from 'over there' (South Asia) is the best way to comprehend the experiences of people living 'here' (Britain).

Such an assumption was interrupted before we even arrived in (Azad) Kashmir. We were on the bus that would take us from the Panjabi city of Lahore to Mirpur – a five-hour journey – when we had the following encounter:

There were about ten men already seated on the bus, ourselves included, all waiting for the driver to arrive. There were also three young women just in front of us in the seats beside the driver. All were wearing *hijab* (the Islamic scarf). The bus was about to leave when another young woman boarded the vehicle and took her seat in the middle of the group of young women, one to her right and two to her left. She proceeded to greet those on her right with the formal Muslim salutation, '*as-salaam alay-kum*' (peace be with you). To the young woman on the left she simply said, 'Hi!'.

For the next hour or so we were witnesses to a conversation between Shazia (the young woman who had come late) and Arfana (the young woman to whom Shazia had said, 'Hi!'). They undertook their conversation in Shazia's Brummie drawl and Arfana's posh Lahori-Londoni accent. Interspersed with the conversation in English, were occasional bouts of Urdu, usually when the other two companions, Irfana and Nazia, were being included.

After an hour of listening in we gathered the courage to don our sociological hats in a more public manner and ask the group where they were from and where they were going to. Shazia answered that she and Arfana had been settled back in Pakistan for a few years now and that they were both studying medicine in Lahore. Like us, they were going to Mirpur. They had family there.

We also asked them which they preferred, life in England or in Pakistan. They, however, declined the opportunity to dichotomize the two places and reinforce the boundaries we had outlined for them. Shazia really liked Lahore because 'it's a happening place like Brum'. She was into music and had gone to see artists such as Ali Haider in both cities. Shazia could also indulge her other major leisure interest – eating out – without any trouble in Lahore: 'there's lots of places to eat here just like Pizza Hut in England and it's cheap as well by Birmingham standards'. Indeed, she even gave us an unsolicited quote on the local price of a bottle of vodka in what is a 'dry' Muslim country.

Arfana was less enthusiastic about Pakistan. She didn't like the hustle and bustle of Lahore even though she had once lived in London. In fact, she didn't feel that she had 'a home' at all and did not know where – or if – she would finally settle. Arfana's brother was in Spain and some of her family were in America. So while Shazia made few distinctions between here and there, Birmingham and Lahore, Arfana did not feel settled in any one place. What did move Arfana, however, was the question of religion. Indeed, our journey was undertaken during *ramazan*, the Muslim month of fasting (*roza*), and Arfana made a point of objecting to the bus driver playing his Hindi film music much to Shazia's disappointment. Islam was the identity that Arfana wanted to prioritize over all others and it fitted with her transnational consciousness: 'I can be a Muslim anywhere', she maintained.

This chance meeting with Shazia and Arfana prompted us to reflect on the accounts of young diasporized Asians that routinely emerge in a British context. Their reasons for being in Pakistan contradicted the widely held view that young people of Asian heritage – women in particular – are necessarily 'sent home' to be married off or disciplined in some way or other. Academic, state and media discourses in Britain regularly produce such young people as social 'problems', caught between the 'freedom' of British and the 'restrictions' of Asian 'cultures', and so alienated from both. However, Shazia and Arfana were two young women training to be doctors and they were travelling unchaperoned. Moreover, their conversation illuminated the constant sense of movement in their lives. Linguistically, they shifted effortlessly from English to Urdu, blurring the boundaries between the two languages with hybrid constructions of their own. Culturally, they bore the traces of both Pakistan and Britain in a way which reflected their multiple and translated histories. So when Pakistan appeared in their narratives it was only as one place amongst many, their experiences having been 'routed' through Britain, Spain and America as well. In short, their presence on that bus journey from Lahore to Mirpur was in no way symbolic of some inevitable return to their essential 'roots'.

This important distinction between notions of 'roots' and 'routes', which is now well established in the literature on migration and diaspora (Gilroy 1993), dominates the discrepant representations of Mirpur we examine here. Based on work in both Britain and (Azad) Kashmir during 1994–5, we focus on the travel narratives of migration, diaspora and tourism that were produced by quite differently positioned constituencies: the British-Mirpuri diaspora and its 'expert' observers; British-Mirpuri youth – mainly young men – visiting the district on holiday; and local Mirpuris themselves.

## Diasporizing Mirpur, Mirpurizing Britain

In the second half of the eighteenth century, Britain expanded its imperial project and colonised the Indian subcontinent through a process which had begun with the exploratory travel and 'trade' of the East India Company (CCCS 1982). It is against this background that the first evidence of a Mirpuri diaspora in Britain must be understood. Mirpur was never formally under British rule. Rather, Kashmir was one of the many princely states that peppered the imperial map of the Raj. Even within Kashmir itself, however, Mirpur has always been a peripheral area subject to agricultural and economic underdevelopment as well as political marginalization (Ballard 1983). Therefore, from the end of the nineteenth century onwards, labour migration from the district's small landholdings became a routine response to the problem of income generation in the area.

From as early as the 1880s Mirpuris sought work in adjacent Panjab and other parts of British-ruled India. Some found work on Bombay's docks with the Merchant Navy and created a niche for themselves as stokers aboard coal-fired ships. Others joined the British Army. Indeed, it was these sailors and soldiers in the colonial service who eventually pioneered migration to Britain during, and immediately after, the Second World War (Dahya 1974). In the late 1950s and early 1960s, largely unskilled workers followed these pioneers to Britain, hearing of the opportunities for work through extensive transnational village and kinship networks. They took jobs in low-paid sectors of the booming post-war economy such as manufacturing but had little intention of becoming settlers (Saifullah Khan 1977).

One of the reasons for the high volume of chain migration from Mirpur to Britain at this time was the forced displacement of around 100,000 people caused by the building of the Mangla Dam. Funded by the World Bank and completed in 1967, this project resulted in the immersion of about two hundred villages and old Mirpur town itself. New Mirpur town was built on the south of the resulting reservoir, while displaced Mirpuris were given inadequate compensation in the form of land in the Panjab and priority in the allocation of vouchers which would facilitate their entry to Britain (Kalra 1997).

Despite punitive immigration legislation and recession from the 1970s and 1980s onwards, a sizeable number of Mirpuris have now settled in Britain.[3] Therefore Mirpur has in many ways been comprehensively 'diasporized'. The corollary of this process has of course been the 'Mirpurization' of pockets of Britain evidenced by a cultural transformation of the landscapes and soundscapes of ordinary urban centres. In Bradford Kharri Sharif General Food Store has appropriated the name of the most famous *mazar* (sufi shrine) in Mirpur, and Mike's 'multiflavours' ice-cream van bears the inscription of the Pakistani flag and the *shahada* (the Muslim statement of faith) across its front (McLoughlin, 1997).[4] Old churches in Birmingham's inner city become new mosques and there is an Urduization of billboards in Oldham while the flag of (Azad) Kashmir dangles in the car windows of Luton.

It should be no surprise then that the so-called 'myth of return' (Anwar 1979) has fallen into abeyance. As a recent oral history project has put it, 'Mirpuris are Here to Stay' (Bradford Heritage Recording Unit, BHRU 1994). Nevertheless, while migration has taken Mirpuris along routes which have transformed their notion of 'home' for ever, local-global connections between the district and its diaspora remain. Indeed, the ability to maintain such connections has been substantially enhanced in recent years by advances in communications technology as well as the availability of relatively cheap air travel (Ballard 1990). Links continue materially through remittances and emotionally through marriages and other ties of family and kinship. The reproduction of cultural or political organizations and the circulation of religious or nationalist ideas should not be underestimated, either. For example, during the Rushdie affair Muslims in Britain were first informed of *The Satanic Verses* controversy with photocopies, faxes and telexes sent by a network of Islamic activists based in India (Bhatt 1997). So, as Gardner suggests in her study of migration from a Bangladeshi village, both *desh* (home) and *bidesh* (away), can be seen as 'different locations of the same society' (Gardner 1995: 8).

## 'No Entry': Bounded Britain Ahead

The periodization of the South Asian diaspora in Britain regards the emergence of British-born second and third generations as the culmination of the migration process. Into the 1990s, British-Mirpuris have been transformed from a migrant labour force into institutionally complete communities that are increasingly British-born (Anwar 1993). The hybridities and hyphenations of Mirpuri-Britain described above – which of course began with the travels of British colonizers – are an everyday reality for minorities. Nevertheless, places such as Mirpur are still routinely privileged as the originary reference points in accounts of the Asian presence in Britain, whether in academic or media, state or community discourse. Indeed, the location of British-Asian 'roots' almost exclusively in the Indian subcontinent has had the effect of racializing and ethnicizing minorities to such an extent that they are placed outside powerful constructions of Britain as an essentially white, English and (post-)Christian nation.

Of course, multicultural policies, which came into their own in Britain during the 1980s, have opened up new spaces for the representation and recognition of minorities. For example, multiculturalism has established the conditions of possibility for initiatives such as *Home from Home*, a recent oral history project which documents and validates the folklore of British-Pakistanis' travels from Mirpur to Bradford and back again (BHRU, 1997). Nevertheless, some have expressed concern about the terms on which this sort of representation and recognition has taken place. Crucially, it has been argued that the concepts underpinning multi-culturalism institutionalize popular assumptions about the 'essential difference' of racialized and ethnicized minorities from homogenizing constructions of the wider society. Multiculturalism has been associated almost exclusively with the 'culture' of migrant 'others' and the notion that 'their difference' is very much immutable and 'in the blood'. As Donald and Rattansi argue, multi-culturalism has

> conflated the question of culture with a particular understanding of ethnicity ... [where a] celebration of diversity tended to reproduce the saris, samosas and steel bands syndrome ... it defined alternative centres of cultural authority primarily in terms of their difference from the *norm of English culture*. (Donald and Rattansi 1992: 2, our emphasis).

The currency of such ideas has often found ready-made legitimation in the 'expertise' of the academy. *Between Two Cultures*, for example, is the definitive early collection of anthropological writing about dias-porized minorities in a British context (Watson 1977). Ultimately, it is remembered most for its unfortunate title which would seem to begin with the assumption that migrants are always contained by 'roots' and cannot improvise 'routes' in new directions. The name, *Between Two Cultures*, is therefore spuriously suggestive of a diasporic experience, especially for the children of first-generation migrants, with an implica-tion that people are condemned to be caught in the confusing position of being neither one thing nor another.

Some two decades on from the publication of *Between Two Cultures*, the essential 'cultural difference' of minorities – and the 'problems' 'they' cause both for society and themselves – remains the stereotype of British-Asians in the print media. Stories about 'arranged marriages' and 'inward-looking' traditional values draw upon the rhetoric of 'between two cultures' as a matter of routine. The more dramatic uprisings in Bradford during June 1995 received similar treatment. Young men in the predominantly Mirpuri and Pakistani district of Manningham took to the streets in protest at police harassment of a small group of their neighbours seemingly engaged in a harmless game of football. The con-frontation between British-Asian youth and the police that ensued was recorded at some length in the local, regional and national press. It was reported that Keith Hellawell, the Chief Constable of West Yorkshire understood events in light of the fact that:

> young Asians had lost touch with their cultural roots and religious traditions without being assimilated into British society. Cultural and religious leaders have been worried for 10 years or so that the younger generation don't

follow their teachings and feel they have great difficulty in controlling them (*The Daily Telegraph*, 12 June 1995).

Society has a problem. We have got a large number now of Asian youths who feel disenfranchised. They do not wish to follow their father's teachings and religion and yet perhaps feel alienated from the Western society into which they are trying to integrate. (*Bradford Telegraph and Argus*, 12 June 1995)

The fact that Hellawell identified British-Asian youth as being 'alienated' from their Asian heritage as well as their British environment has not prevented delegations of local government officials, social workers, teachers and other 'community workers' following anthropologists to subcontinental locations such as Mirpur. They come in search of cultural explanations of the riddle of pluralism which so perplexes the British polity. For example, Birmingham City Council has established a Friendship Treaty with Mirpur 'on the basis of equal partnership and mutual benefit' and a modest park has been built in the centre of town as a testament to this.[5] Other visitors, however, are less 'friendly'. Immigration officials, whose visits determine that elderly and sometimes sick parents may not join their children and grandchildren in Britain, have recently been joined by police officers investigating the relationship between the disappearance of Pajero jeeps in Britain and their growing popularity as a status symbol amongst returnees in Mirpur.

We must also include here one of the cheap but entertaining apocryphal stories which have grown up around the visits of the *goriyan* (whites) to Mirpur. When anthropologists of the future trace the 'myth of origin' of all touristic practice in the city, this tale will no doubt have its place. At Hotel Jabeer, an establishment owned by a Middlesborough-Mirpuri family and built in 1987 with migrants' remittances, we were told about two female teachers from Britain who stayed at the hotel during their fact-finding mission to the area. Having checked in at the hotel the two decided to take full advantage of the marvellous heat of a Mirpur summer before they experienced the local culture later in the day. It appears they promptly stripped off to their bikinis and sat out on the hotel veranda to soak up the sun. As Hotel Jabeer is located on the main Allama Iqbal Road, however, very soon a small but attentive crowd gathered; and like pupils sitting at a teacher's feet, they gazed in amazement at this lesson in 'sensitivity' to multicultural contexts. Is it possible that excursions or exchanges between Britain and South Asia do not routinely challenge white professionals who work with minorities to identify their own practices – rather than those of their clients – as the 'problem'?

Against this background, it is ironic that 'extended visits home' by British-Asian youngsters have been much maligned by right-wing educationalists such as Ray Honeyford. For Honeyford (1984) there is a necessary 'clash' between the desire of parents to 'maintain their culture' and the educational needs of children bound to grow up in Britain. The same double standards are applied to those for whom a visit home might actually be therapeutic, given – amongst other things – the trauma of the migration process itself and the experience of living in a racist society. For example, a mental health practitioner in the Greater Manchester area related to us the fact that social services had refused to pay for 'a visit to Pakistan' by her client, while continuing to fund 'proper holidays' elsewhere for white clients.[6] What this reflects, of course, is that the majority of people who travel to Mirpur each year are commonly assumed to 'be going home'. Indeed, one colleague at the University of Manchester reported to us a revealing enquiry by a student of popular culture. The student naïvely asked, 'Why don't Asians go on package holidays?'[7] This issue of tourism is one we shall return to presently.

## Alternative Arrangements and Imaginary Homelands

> Blocked out of any access to an English or British identity people had to try to discover who they were.... This is an enormous act of what I want to call imaginary political re-identification. (Hall 1991: 52).

British-Asian youth share with their parents the experience of racism in Britain and, as Hall has shown, minorities' resistance to racism has often been grounded in a 'return to roots'. So, for very different reasons to those considered above, an emphasis on 'roots' is also discernible in the perspectives of many parents and some young people of migrant heritage. As Shaw (1994) demonstrates in her study of Pakistanis in Oxford, first-generation parents are often afraid – however unrealistically – of the 'corrupting' influences of 'permissive' Western society on their children. At the same time, they are also fearful of the very real consequences of racial discrimination for those growing up in Britain. So it is, then, that many parents who appreciate the material benefits of living in Britain send their British-born children on holiday to Mirpur for a 'top-up' of *desi* (home) 'culture'.

Amongst the young people we spoke to on extended stays in Mirpur, only occasionally were their long stays a 'punishment' for 'bad behaviour' in Britain. There were some extreme cases, however which involved drug (ab)use or being in trouble with the police. More commonplace was the experience of those young men who had come to Mirpur to get married locally but were forced to stay, perhaps for as long as six months, while their spouses' immigration papers were put in order before they returned to Britain. Also more typical of the longer-term British-born visitor were those youngsters in elite private schools which are very much on the increase in Mirpur. Teaching in English as well as Urdu, one was even called the Sheffield Grammar School. Some pupils were living with ageing grandparents. Others lived in Mirpur with their mothers while their fathers remained working overseas. Visiting one such school we were told by pupils from Derby and Stoke that the main reason they had come (note, not 'come back'!) to Mirpur was the lack of discipline in British schools. They had come to get 'a stricter education than at home'. Kaiser, a young man of eight born in Derby was insistent: 'My mum says there was too much playing in the sand, painting and things. It's too free.'

Of course, some young people are actively concerned with the search for 'roots' themselves. For example, there are those – mainly students and young professionals – who are attracted to the idea of living in a Muslim country when confronted with the limits of developing an 'Islamic way of life' in a secular, (post-)Christian society. Usman, a young chemist from Luton in his twenties, had come to Mirpur in a bid to 'make a go of life in an Islamic country'. He considered himself to be more 'knowledgeable about religion' than most of his contemporaries whom he characterised as 'ignorant of true Islam'. Significantly, he wanted nothing to do with the *mazar* (shrine) of nearby Kharri Sharif, to which devoted pilgrims from all over Pakistan – and to a lesser extent Britain – travel in their thousands every year for the *urs mela* (death anniversary) of *pir* (sufi master) Muhammad Baksh. Instead, Usman had a background in the political Islam of Hizb ut-Tahrir (the Party of Liberation) back at university in London and his father-in-law was the *amir* (leader) of Jama'at-i Islami in Mirpur. He admitted, however, that his own quest for some sort of Islamic authenticity had come to an abrupt halt. Indeed, Usman was considering returning to England with his wife and child. 'The Muslims in Britain are more committed than the ones here', he complained, 'the mosques are empty most of the time in Mirpur.'

Usman's sentiments echoed the comments of some British-Pakistani youth who in recent years have signed up for a one-month Study Tour of Pakistan organized by the Overseas Pakistanis Foundation (OPF).[8] The tour is intended to give 'Overseas Pakistanis' with degree-level education a more positive image of Pakistan as a 'modern nation' and so attract them to take up short internships in the country's private and public sectors. Interesting reflections on the Study Tour are recorded in the OPF's magazine, *Yaran-e Watan*. For example, some invested heavily in the idea of 'roots', idealizing Pakistan as an imaginary, originary homeland, although others did at least show an awareness of hegemonic representations of the Third World in the West:

We are now proud to think that there is a place that we can call our true home where we can find out who we really are.... Being born in the West one often becomes confused as to where our loyalties ought to lie. (April 1993)

These tours must continue for they are a benefit to those young Pakistanis who are living abroad and are ignorant of their own roots. (April 1993)

I have truly gained an insight into the real Pakistan as opposed to a superficial view which I previously held. (April 1994)

The problem in the western part of the world is media coverage of developing countries. Third world countries are portrayed in such a bad way, hence creating a dim impression to the public. Fortunately, due to OPF we were able to dispel all misconceptions of Pakistan for ourselves. (September 1994)

I felt that I had left my family in London but had now come to my 'home' in Pakistan. (October 1994)

It is essential that we learn about our home country and strengthen our roots as each individual needs to know about their identity. While living in a western country many youngsters do find it difficult to identify themselves with their country of origin and so tours of this kind are essential in reinforcing our cultural and religious backgrounds. (October 1994)

Many found it difficult, however, to square their high (and fairly revivalist) expectations of what an Islamic country *should* be like – most especially as an empowering alternative to the materialism and racism of the West – with the realities of life in Pakistan amongst the secularized elite:

Being good Muslims we should have taken some time out to attend the Friday Jumma Prayers. (April 1994)

I am very reluctant to comment on the practice of Islam in Pakistan: I will just go so far as to say that the tour has left me with a feeling that disenchantment with, indifference towards and apathy towards Islam is on the increase in Pakistan. (May 1994)

Pakistan is 99.9% Muslim. It was formed on the basis of Islam. Yet, I thought the Islamic nature of Pakistan was almost forgotten during the Tour. Although we visited Mosques, no time was given to pray 'Salat' so that we could pay our respect to Allah and the Mosque. All of us come from Western countries and do not know how it is to pray in a mosque in a Muslim country. (July 1994)

Pakistan (land of the pure) was made for Muslims, even though alcohol is banned it is so readily available, the police should do something about this. (September 1994)

What these reflections demonstrate quite clearly is that for the young British-Pakistani-Muslims quoted here, their attachment to a notion of Islamic 'roots' has been 'routed' through their experiences as a diaspora living on the margins of British society and not through their exposure to the 'essentials' of 'Pakistani culture'. The quest for 'authenticity', however, was by no means characteristic of most British-Mirpuri youth we encountered in Mirpur. Their accounts had less to do with a search for 'roots' and more to do with 'having a laugh'. So while an emphasis on 'roots' emerges in the travel narratives of some constituencies visiting Mirpur, the practices of others are more characteristic of a 'routes' perspective which underlines the global nature of flows of people, goods, ideas and capital across national and cultural boundaries. We focus next, then, on the young British-Asians who, when accompanying their Mirpuri parents on visits 'home', were almost always going 'away'.

## Home from Home

When we first arrived in Mirpur, we – like others before us – were directed to Hotel Jabeer, which, as noted above, is run by a Middlesborough-Mirpuri family, having been built in 1987. The manager, a thirty-something called Mushtaq, long resettled in the city, told us that before Hotel Jabeer opened there were only Rs 40–50 (£1) per night places available in Mirpur. Many friends had advised his father, the owner, that it was a risk opening somewhere in the three-star, Rs 250 (£5) bracket. However, like the other two large hotels which now grace Allama Iqbal Road, the Jabeer does a good trade. Mainly, this involves hosting local and transnational weddings, business conferences and political meetings, as well as providing a fairly sophisticated refuge for those British-Mirpuris who want to stay in Mirpur city itself or take a break from the surrounding villages where most people's relatives tend to live.

The hotel was especially popular with small groups of young British-Mirpuri men, as it afforded them one of only a few opportunities to consume 'home-from-home' pleasures away from their families in a relaxed atmosphere. Two such young men from Manchester hailed us one morning as we were leaving for a day trip to the countryside. With the simple greeting, 'All right lads', bellowed from their balcony at the front of the hotel, their desire to make a 'British connection' had immediate effect. We arranged to meet them in their room later on in the day.

On entering Jaf and Zaf's room the same evening, we found that they had hired one of only two suites at Hotel Jabeer for the bargain price of £10 per night. Fed up with eating *dal-roti* all the time, they ordered fish and chips – a Hotel Jabeer speciality! They had also rented a video and video-recorder from a shop just over the road from the hotel, so all four of us settled down to watch an Arnold Schwarzenegger movie. It became clear that Jaf and Zaf were in Mirpur for the latter's wedding to his cousin, but they were not very impressed with what the place had to offer even if they were doing their best to make the most of it. As Jaf put it:

> Its not England is it? I'm so bored already. The only thing I like is looking at the birds but you can only see those in your own family. Otherwise, you've got to go to Jhelum for pussy. Still, we've found someone to get us some booze and the hash grows in the back garden. My uncle's even thinking of getting a satellite put in.

The talk, then, was often of 'back home' – not surprising, given their company – their cars, their girlfriends, their favourite clubs and even their Eid celebrations. Both Jaf and Zaf complained that they would rather be in England for the holiday (which marks the end of *ramazan*). Ideally, they would begin by driving flash cars, hired for the day, all the way to Blackpool before returning to Manchester and cruising along Wilmslow Road.

Our encounter with the likes of Jaf and Zaf was repeated many times during our stay in Hotel Jabeer as our own room gradually became known as a place for other 'young British geezers' to hang out and catch up on the latest news from Britain. Indeed, the conspicuous behaviour and consumption of these young men was perhaps most typical of those British tourists who holiday 'home from home' in the resorts of Greece and Spain. Mirpur town itself has changed so as to cater for these 'tourists', evoking images of bars on the Costa del Sol selling English Breakfasts the morning after the night before. So in Mirpur it is now common to find grocers selling 'luxury' items such as Kellogg's cornflakes, HP Sauce and Heinz Baked Beans which the 'locals' either find too expensive or have no desire to purchase anyway. At the same time, the names of other shops such as *London Tailors* and *British Jewellers* – written, of course, in Urdu script – reinforce the impression of a constant process of global circulation connecting the district to its diaspora. There is also a Duty Free Shop selling electrical goods run by the OPF – an overseas passport is required for entry – while plans for an international airport linking Mirpur with the rest of the world have been reported in the press (*The Pakistan Times*, 17 March 1994).[9]

The fact that young British-Asians on holiday in Mirpur, with rupees in their pockets and plenty of time on their hands, visit with the attitude that here they have a chance to do things they do not normally do, points to a certain kind of touristic experience. This is not to say that the notion of tourism can contain or explain all the complex activities and narratives of British-Mirpuris abroad. Nevertheless, it does suggest just one (seemingly) innovative way of disrupting dominant representations of a constituency which, as we have seen above, has so often been characterized as necessarily 'between two cultures'. As we have seen, for young travellers like Jaf and Zaf there was no quest for 'authenticity' or 'roots' behind their journey to Mirpur. Nevertheless, for all their complaints about the district, they, like other young British-Mirpuris we met, moved relatively easily in a variety of transnational and multicultural contexts, switching between English, Urdu and Panjabi as they readily made connections both with relatives living locally and with us. Indeed, the skill with which they navigate situations of cultural difference would suggest that the young Britons most evidently 'between two cultures' are in fact those monocultural 'backpackers' who suffer emotional and psychological traumas when all too quickly confronted with the discrepancies in *Lonely Planet*'s all 'exotic', all romantic imaging of India (Hutnyk 1996).

Even amongst young men like Jaf and Zaf, however, who had never really harboured a desire to visit their parents' villages or inhabit an idealized Islamic homeland, there were some we met who were being forced to reconsider their connections beyond Britain. For example, Adil, a young Oldhamite, admitted that in the wake of attacks on Bosnian-Muslims in the heart of Europe he had felt a dread of repatriation to Pakistan. Adil's experience perhaps begins to explain just one of the reasons why so many people settled in Britain still maintain emotional and financial investments in places like Mirpur (McLoughlin, 1996). Indeed, one young boy in Mirpur with relatives in Bradford, someone who had never seen 'Burn Muslims, not Books: Pakis Go Home' graffiti, enquired as to why the English hated 'Pakis'. Bad news travels fast, too.

## The Scars of Tourism

British-Mirpuri holidaymakers, like 'expert' observers of this diaspora, begin their journeys in the West and travel to a Third World country. So, if accounts which emphasize 'routes' as well as 'roots' interrogate the culturalist-racist notion that while settled 'in' Britain, Mirpuris can never be 'of' Britain, it is important to recognize that such accounts do not include the voices of local Mirpuris themselves. The fact is that migrants' remittances have skewed the local economy of the district. So while the British-Mirpuri diaspora supports Mirpur itself, at the same time it also contributes to forces which undermine the economic development of the area.

On our visit to Mirpur, it gradually became apparent that agriculture is in decline, industrial development is virtually non-existent and land prices are determined in virtual pounds sterling. The problem is a lack of infrastructure. Indeed, the Pakistani administration has failed to intervene while revelling in the significant – though admittedly falling – foreign exchange that remittances bring. The money on deposit in Mirpur's many banks is soon whisked away to fund projects in either Islamabad or Karachi. Mirpuris overseas buy land but rarely choose to build on the piece of 'home' they have secured. This is not to say that Mirpur gives the immediate impression of underdevelopment. Rather, the *bazaar* developments and service industries that have emerged supply only the demands of capital-rich transnational families, *nouveaux riche* tourists who spend only part of their year in Mirpur. The large ostentatious houses – many of which remain empty – Pajero jeeps and satellite dishes are signs of little more than conspicuous consumption.

In a diasporic context we have seen that the young British-Mirpuris referred to above often experience racism, Islamophobia and social exclusion. On holiday in Mirpur, however, these same youngsters often attract the cynicism and derision of locals. Many of the young men that we met in Mirpur had had their 'difference' objectified for them by relatives or passers-by in the street. Shamas, a young man studying in Bradford, recalled how on his first visit to Mirpur one relative had called him a *'valayti* chicken', an English weakling unable to endure the strenuous daily tasks that rural-dwellers routinely do. Some referred to 'corruption' and reported being 'skanked' by locals who always charged *valayti* visitors over the odds. As Shamas related, 'They see you coming; the way you walk, dress, have your hair [he had a pony-tail] and talk and they're supposed to be your own people.'

To Iftikhar, a young insurance salesman in Mirpur with no desire to migrate to Britain, the likes of Shamas sometimes appear to be 'extravagant boorish louts' and 'people who have forgotten their language and culture'. He maintained that: 'They come here and act like they are DCs [District Commissioners – senior civil servants] whereas we know that in England a DC is a dish cleaner, in a take-away restaurant.' Local Mirpuris' relationships with such tourists, then, are characterized by both dependency and disdain. On one hand, there is a recognition that even today the economy remains dependent on remittances from overseas. On the other hand, there is a realization that visitors – including the likes of ourselves – come with their own agendas: to take what they want and then leave. As Barrister Qurban, a local political activist, argued:

> We get very tired of people like yourself coming here demanding information about these people who have left. When are you ever concerned about the problems that we have here?... There is economic underdevelopment because of the political status of Kashmir and the only input we get from the government is to support schemes for these immigrants. What use is a duty-free shop when the local people cannot go in there and, even if they do, they cannot afford to buy anything?

It is important, therefore, to recognize that our account of British-Asian youth does not come at the cost of recognizing Mirpuris' concerns about local issues such as economic development. Mirpur's economy, after 30 years of mass migration, bears little resemblance to anywhere else in (Azad) Kashmir. Ballard (1985) has characterized it as a 'third-world paradox'; an area with infrastructural underdevelopment but a huge capital base. With the growth of global tourism and the deterritorialization of capital (Lash and Urry 1994), however, Mirpur is only a particular example of a widespread phenomenon. Like so many areas of the world scarred by tourism, it has become dependent on the ongoing traffic of international travellers.

## Return Journeys

In the various travel narratives of migration, diaspora and tourism that we have discussed here it is perhaps the theme of discrepancy that emerges most strongly. Our account has attempted to go beyond the question of 'roots' and 'routes' by highlighting discrepant representations of Mirpur without privileging any one narrative over another. Indeed, one of the main points that we try to make is that all representations are situational. Therefore each representation of Mirpur in turn deconstructs another, revealing that the operation of power amongst differently positioned local, national and global constituencies is always open to contestation.

We began with an attempt to disrupt the common perception that the British-Asian diaspora is necessarily confined by a primordial attachment to subcontinental 'roots', insisting that such notions routinely have the effect of locating minorities outside hegemonic constructions of the British nation. Of course, it is not only the British establishment which makes this appeal to 'roots'. Rather, the narratives of some British-Mirpuri parents and youth also make claims about the authenticity of a 'homeland' located outside Britain. Such accounts, however, are routinely prompted by the experience of social exclusion and racism in Britain. They represent an alternative, a search for something better. When the reality of such alternatives is confronted during extended stays in Mirpur, moreover, it is often a case of the grass being greener on the other side.

From the entangled experiences of young British-Asians who visit places like Mirpur, a range of narratives which emphasize a 'routes' perspective, tends to emerge. Very far from being caught 'between two cultures', as some have suggested in the past, the young people we spoke to produced situational and improvised accounts of identity and belonging which straddled 'here' and 'there', 'home' and 'away'. Of course while they were in Britain, Mirpur had certain attractions – a more lavish lifestyle for example – but whilst in Mirpur, the reverse was often true. Either way, as translated and hyphenated persons, British-Mirpuri youth exhibited the ability to operate in a number of cultural contexts, shrugging off the labels that others – officials, parents and 'locals' – have periodically attempted to attach to them.

It does of course bear repeating, finally, that the all-important shift in context from Britain to Mirpur that travel involves has had at least one other consequence. It has transformed a constituency living on the margins of British society into a relatively powerful 'touristic' elite whom many of the locals in Mirpur have come to scorn and ridicule, while all the time acknowledging that they are bound to such visitors in a relationship of dependence. So it is, then, that Mirpur, (Azad) Kashmir can not be reduced to the all-consuming nature of its British diaspora or indeed the associated trope of 'authenticity' that the conventional focus on diaspora often seems to reproduce.

# Notes

1  This chapter draws on material that we collected for our respective PhD degrees, both awarded by the University of Manchester in 1997. For details see bibliography. Virinder would like to thank the British Cotton Growers Workers Welfare Fund, and Seán would like to thank the University of Manchester and the Economic and Social Research Council (award: R00429424215), for their support in 1992–6. Thanks are also due to all those who helped, fed and entertained us whilst we were in Mirpur and beyond, especially Saeed Kashmiri, Masood Bilal Lodhi, Ishtiaq Ahmed, Masood Alam Raja, the staff of Jabeer Hotel and the staff of the Overseas Pakistanis Foundation (OPF).

2  At the independence and partition of the Indian sub-continent in 1947 the status of Kashmir was left in dispute, so the state was divided between Pakistan – hence (Azad or Free) Kashmir – and India. (Azad) Kashmir is effectively controlled by, and administered from, the Ministry of Kashmir Affairs in Islamabad. It has been used as a political tool in the relations between Pakistan and India since partition in 1947 (Akbar 1991, Akbar 1996, Lamb 1992). Indeed, Pakistan and India have fought two wars over Kashmir, in 1948 and 1965. The conflict has only come onto the political agenda in Britain due to the large 'Azad' Kashmiri/Mirpuri settler population.

3  In the last two decades however, some Mirpuris have been more attracted to transient sojourns in the Middle East.

4  The *shahada* is: *la ilaha illallahu muhammad urrasul ullah*: 'There is no god but Allah, Muhammad is the messenger of Allah'.

5  The source here is a letter from Birmingham City Council to Mirpur Development Authority, dated 6 April 1993.

6  Thanks to Tahirah Parveen for this insight.

7  Thanks to Roger Ballard for this insight.

8  OPF was established in 1979 to promote the welfare of overseas Pakistanis and their dependants. Significantly, one amongst only five regional offices is located in Mirpur.

9  It seems unlikely, however, that such a project could ever go ahead. A significant amount of the international air traffic regularly coming through Pakistan's capital, Islamabad, relies on holidaying migrants and their families bound for (Azad) Kashmir. Therefore, Islamabad seems unlikely to devolve such a lucrative business opportunity to Mirpur, especially given Pakistan's marginalization of (Azad) Kashmir's economic interests generally in recent times. What seems more likely is an air-borne commuter service between Islamabad and Mirpur.

# 10

## JOURNEY THROUGH LIFE
### The Self in Travel

SHIRIN HOUSEE

Travel for those of us living in diasporic conditions unravels numerous possibilities. These possibilities encompass a travelling self which is always questioning, or subject to question by, its own positionality. A travelling migrant self has to learn to accommodate a sense of not belonging with a search for belonging. This quest is not only about looking for the physical sense of the 'home', but also about feeling accepted, feeling at 'home'.[1] As so poignantly described by Trinh T. Minh-ha:

> Every voyage can be said to involve a re-siting of boundaries. The travelling self is here both the self that moves physically from one place to another ... and the self that embarks on an undetermined journeying practice, having constantly to negotiate ... between a here, a there, and an elsewhere (Trinh 1994: 9).

In contradistinction to Trinh's focus on the notion of the 'exile' I concentrate on the experience and modalities of travel for the black migrant which, often marginalized, proposes a broader consideration than holiday touring on the pleasure periphery of mass tourism.[2] Travel accounts deploy narratives which are predominantly written by, and for, the universalized white or Western male traveller. This is reflected in the resources of the tourism industry, guide books, travel tours, the expected hotel guests and so forth. The complexities of black travel experience are very rarely accommodated within dominant travel discursive formations. Even the established counter-discourse recognized in travel writing – that of women's travel experience – still remains largely within the hegemonic influence of white male travel. In this chapter I explore neglected horizons of travel to counter the Eurocentric and gender bias in the literature. At the same time, I examine how travel experiences are the very stuff of identity construction. As I journey through life, I pick and choose my travelling memoirs. For those of us who are twice diasporized migrants to Britain, we know only too well that our place of 'origin' is frequently the subject of interrogation. We are often asked, 'Where are you from, originally?' 'Originally, as in London, or Mauritius or India?' I would reply. It soon becomes clear that these questions about our origins are intimately tied to our identities. Through these questions, I began my search. Like the piecing together of a jigsaw I have assembled the stories, the photos, the memories of parents and of childhood. As these stories gradually unfold, I realize that I also simultaneously (re)construct them. These experiences and processes of life history are co-constitutive.

This chapter charts the historical and contemporary moments that have configured my present. It is divided into three sections mapping key crossroads on this journey. The first is an arrival story which focuses on travel to Britain – my early experience of living in a white host society. Here, the issues for me are very much about the making of the black migrant, the 'outsider', and how these identities are constructed and reconstructed by the interplay between ourselves and the various forces of socialization, our parents, our family, and our schooling. The conventions of tourism are considered in the second section as I begin to unravel some of the complexities of my travelling encounters. As a black female traveller my experience is certainly more than that of leisurely holidays. It is about the way in which gender, racialization, perceived ethnicity, and certain privileges determine my reception in areas of the world that I visit. In this context I also confront the complexities of my political desire – the motivation to negotiate the contradictions of transnational placement through formation of solidarities and shared experience with others. The final section is a point of departure which looks to one 'home': the 'over there' in Mauritius. I explore some of the ways in which Mauritius is represented, and how the migrant is perceived when returning 'home'. The return home not only raises issues about the physical sense of home, but also the modalities of experience of the returnee.

## From Mauritius I Came...

I begin with my first transnational journey – from Mauritius to England. As a Mauritian kid arriving in a new country at the age of five, I had little choice in this matter. As economic exiles, our dreams, or more precisely my parent's dreams, were about an economically better life with improved life chances, especially educational opportunities. For children, in particular, this movement came to mean more than shifting home and school; it was about the gradual awareness of complexities and contradictions which come from being part of, and in so many cases being outside of, the majority host community.

My most vivid experience of being in England begins with school. Not understanding a word of English, I was expected to 'join in' and to 'mingle' with the children. Tangled feelings of wanting to belong, and yet not; of wanting to be the same, but yet different; of wanting to 'fit in', yet being 'left out'. Language was an important signifier of how one 'fitted in', but other barriers too became obvious: like skin colour, cultural dress differences and so on. 'Fitting in' and not being 'left out' constituted a strong theme of my early childhood. It was a process of learning about what was private and public, and what was Eastern, 'your own', and Western, 'their own'. Children soon become adept at shifting in and out of varied cultural milieus, quickly learning the limits of situational acceptability. The process of negotiating very distinct life worlds was more complicated, however, than the 1970s sociology literature on 'culture clash' would like us to believe.[3] It was certainly about the articulation of many cultures, but in ways the self-appointed experts could not see. As children, we were already expert in the negotiation of difference, culture and meaning. Sometimes this entailed the 'symbolic' and literal 'redressing' of our differences. In other words, some of us would untie our hair plaits and take off our trousers (worn underneath our skirts) in order to fit in with the rest – processes not simply about letting go of 'owned' culture and assimilating, but about 'role playing'.

Sometimes we would proudly display our differences, whilst at other times, we would act out the similarities, knowing that this was about neutralizing our differences in the hope of easier access and acceptance. Trinh notes:

> To be named and classified is to gain better acceptance, even when it is a question of fitting in a no-fit category.... Foreignness is acceptable once I no longer draw the line between myself and the others. First assimilate, then be different within permitted boundaries (Trinh 1994: 13).

One permitted boundary for me was the way Mauritius and Mauritians could be granted a distinct authenticity. This was useful when the racists called me 'Paki' or 'Nigger', because I would, however inconsequentially, correct them by informing them of my country of birth. I heard myself say, 'Actually I'm not from Pakistan or Africa or the Caribbean, but Mauritius.' As a child I did not realize that slanderous words such as 'Paki' and 'Nigger' were simply references to all dark-skinned peoples; and that therefore my corrections were misplaced.

To other, less overt racists, my perceived differences were almost acceptable, and sometimes even celebrated. It seemed I was all right because I was not like all the others. I became an exotic other, the island girl from the land of sea, sand and palm trees. Curiously, this categorization felt safe. For some time, I could hide inside their paradise dreams. I was not associated with those other black children, who came from those lands crassly portrayed as blighted by 'natural' disasters, floods, droughts, political wars (East v West Pakistan), famine and poverty. I was often asked, 'But why did you leave?' (Fools, as if at five you have a choice.) 'It's a place where we would love to go on holiday.' The interesting point here was that I was told to go home by the ultra-racists, while those that liked me wanted to go home with me!

Institutional formations consolidated this process of differentiation: a process which ensured that on one level we were 'all the same', as part of the 'black others', but yet, on another level, we were different to each other. This was made ever so clear by the teachers sometimes treating us the same as the black 'mob' and yet at other times clearly distinguishing our national and/or cultural differences. This actually meant that, some of the time, some of us were more acceptable than others, and in my case this could mean acceptance that was based on Mauritian particularity. Constant reference to our difference shaped the contours of subjectivity, sometimes more acceptable, other times less so. Back and forth the valuations swirled: my place of birth had become an issue of 'interesting' difference to many; my 'blackness' an issue of contempt and dislike to almost all; and my 'authentic otherness' an issue of intrigue, mockery and also, in some contexts, a cause for acceptance, sociological scrutiny, and multicultural policy.

Identities are only momentarily static. Other times they are fluid, enabling movement from one subject positioning to another. These shifts correspond closely to experiences of acceptance and rejection. The personal is intricately entwined with the social milieu. Thus, each moment of identity formation is negotiated within a given political space, and its construction is always relational. If we identify ourselves as black, it is because we are in a white world. We are gender conscious because, in a man's world, the female gender is positioned differently and unequally. We identify situationally, according to different people, in different places, at different times. It is in this sense that identities are always in the making. They borrow from the past, whilst also taking from the present. Identity formations therefore belong, in the words of Kaur and Kalra, to two trends of

> correspondence, where ideas of a shared past, similar backgrounds or comparable present-day circumstances are stressed ... [and] difference where,

either through antagonism, resistance or cultural superiority complexes, particularities are stressed. These need not be rigid oppositions ... [but also] an oscillation of the one and the many, the fixed and the unfixed, the essentialised and the de-essentialised, and the particular and the hybrid, in constant processes of suturing and fracturing (Kaur and Kalra 1996: 220).

Kaur and Kalra describe this process as 'latticed identities'. I now go on to explore the implications and shifting strands of such identifications on my travels abroad as a black woman with a British passport. Black is not always a rigid form of identification; it is invoked in a relational way in contradistinction to white male travels – the latter often assumed and narrated without the adjectival prefixes as part of hegemonic control. Furthermore, a stress on black female travel is not to assume an essentialist realm of experience based on distinct differences *in* women, but to note the emphases which characterize black female travel as centring on specific concerns, based on gender, ethnicity, nationality and shared experiences.

## Black Tourism: the Unexamined Horizon

Experiences of travel place us within public spaces of negotiation. As we walk, talk, and meet with strangers in public, we tread carefully – both with curiosity, and with caution. Below, I unravel these complexities by looking at the way in which black tourists negotiate these spaces on their travels.

Given a certain level of economic privilege concomitant with increased access to the global apparatus of the leisure industry – planes, hotels and package deals – travel opens up wider horizons for playing out the scenes of complex cultural and identity negotiation. My first tourist exchange between host and black traveller focuses on my visit to a then erstwhile communist regime in 1983 during a college trip to the Soviet Union. As a starry-eyed socialist, I was excited by the prospect of comradeship. Being of the persuasion that oppression had to do with capitalist class regimes, I was hoping that international comradeship could cut across colour bars and gendered differences and offer a truly egalitarian vision. I was wrong, however: as a traveller with fellow students, black and white, I learnt more than the usual insight into Soviet life. I learnt that socialism, too, had its racialized boundaries. On the streets of Moscow and Leningrad, black students were stared at in ways that reminded us that even in this world hierarchical differences prevailed. Like all tourists we were there to appreciate this different regime, yet we learnt, simultaneously, that the black traveller was received with curiosity and a latent aggression. As we gave the 'tourist gaze' (Urry 1990) to the Kremlin, we found that the 'gaze' was upon us. Significantly, these 'stares' were not altogether different from those we recognized at 'home'. They were much like the 'stares' encountered on the streets of London, Birmingham and Manchester. Why should they be different? As black tourists, we still remained the foreigners – more foreign than white British tourists. Sadly, Soviet socialism had not lifted the boundaries of racial difference and inequality.

On the other hand, on our train journey to Leningrad we encountered a situation where a Soviet woman from the Eastern states came to greet us. We realized that what prompted her to come to us was my friend's Muslim emblem. Despite the fact that our communication was limited to handshakes and smiles, this bonding worried the Russian guards on the train and things became tense. Whilst the guards questioned this friendship we acknowledged a sense of solidarity that surpassed national political boundaries. Indeed, as she defiantly stared back at the guards, we felt that her allegiances were closer to ours than to the Soviet bloc. Sharing with the 'Other'[4] was also about being familiar with hierarchies of power.

## The Package Holiday Scenario

Racialized exchanges are also apparent in the signification we deploy in the package holiday scenario. The boundaries of exclusion are conspicuous for holidaying migrants. In our places of residence, we know where it is safe to live, to walk and to eat. In the holiday enclaves, however, we are not always sure where the lines of demarcation are. We have to find them out, sometimes the hard way. Those unsaid rules of where it is safe to sit and to walk are left to the vagaries of experience and negotiation, some of these spaces remaining strictly out of bounds for the foreigner.

In my early twenties, holidaying in places like Crete, Portugal, Tunisia and Turkey through the facility of the package deal immediately set me and my companions apart from the local communities. The holiday places the holidaymakers in the safe havens of tourist service. Yet I am never sure whether it is the holidaymakers that are protected from the local communities or vice versa. It is probably an arrangement of mutual consent. The package tourists stick to their own packages, while local entrepreneurs mostly just want to make a deal.

During our walks across the tourist sites, we meet white British holidaymakers. These encounters are characterized sometimes by indifference, sometimes by hostility. In passing, we look at each other, and we think, 'Are these the home-grown racists that we left in England?' And we wonder what they are thinking – could it be, 'What are these Pakis doing on our holiday?' Holidaying with other British folk places us in many ambivalent and contradictory situations. Sometimes we feel the need for British solidarity. We gather together as white and black tourists displaying our British passports to enter or return from the enclave. Through fear of being singled out as 'illegal' immigrants we show our passports. The convenience of paper endows us with a British identity. Ironically it is at this moment that Britishness becomes a signifier for protection and privilege. At other times, we want to disassociate ourselves completely from travellers who exhibit themselves as the all-powerful imperial ones, whose language is supposedly universal, and whose chauvinist attitude is often shown through their abusive behaviour.

This bulldog-headedness is sometimes shown in their mistreatment of local people. Despite the passports we carry as our 'security', we never feel less British than when cringing with embarrassment during such moments. In Tunisia a white British holidaymaker went on stage during a Karaoke evening and immediately engaged in racist abuse: first by calling the compère 'Ali', then saying to the audience that the stage had a strange smell coming from Ali's direction. The predominantly white and British audience found this amusing and laughed.

It is no surprise that racism travels, but this racism has clear economic parameters which are probably not only a residue of colonial times, but also correlate with the international class and race privileges of today. These racial supremacists are travellers from the West, who, like myself, have the financial capacity to make journeys across the world. For some, however, this access is concomitant with a social attitude that suggests that those from the West are best. The 'lager lout' scenario of 'Brits abroad' appears to have emerged from a patriotic nostalgia and arrogance which seems to cut across class positions. In Britain we would try to shelter ourselves from such blatant racism by only frequenting clubs, cafés and restaurants which we knew well or had made our own. Yet, here we were in the South still embraced by the imperial racism of the North.

## Exchanges between Hosts and Black Female Tourists

In an attempt to avoid such consequences of the all-inclusive package holidays, we would often embark on independent excursions to escape other tourists. Many interesting incidents have occurred on these (never empty) meeting grounds.[5] Some of these incidents are race-specific, some are gender-specific and some are based upon religious or national differences. Our identity, or more precisely the way in which our identity is perceived, informs the way people receive us. In some places the local residents of 'remote' villages would stare at us with curiosity, interest or trepidation – we suspect, but are not sure, that this reception is due to the colour of our skin. Whilst, in other places, people approach us readily and even begin to speak in their mother tongues – assuming we are locals. It seemed to me that often these encounters and exchanges across difference, at other times across (supposed) similarities, offered a previously unavailable opportunity for transnational connection and the formation of unlikely solidarities. More often than not, these connections were made with those workers in the tourism sector who were in a position of providing services to us and yet found us different to the other (white) tourists they served. Within the international flows of an (albeit unequal) tourist industry and across the divisions of tourist and local, visitor and host, we sought to find, and found others seeking, a commonality beyond the brochures. In other words, repeated invitations to local cafes and restaurants, and long, friendly chats with workers in hotels and cafes, could be understood as examples of local people asking: 'Who are you? Where are you from? How can we get to know you better?'

In Britain, Britishness (or rather, Englishness) is seen as the given norm and, more importantly, a norm that we all should be familiar with. Its cultural capital is considered superior to others whose cultures remain on the undifferentiated margins. Under these hierarchical circumstances the exchange of 'cultural difference' seems much more voyeuristic and suggests consumption of the (exotic) 'Other' rather than an equitable two-way exchange. Of course, our interest for host communities could be due to our being temporary visitors as well as relatively few in number, hence any fear of 'swamping' of those communities was not really an issue. Yet there were other dimensions to which we were often alert: that sometimes interest in us suggested the potential of affinity with the peoples of the South as something we desired and worked towards. Warm and friendly invitations based on connections between non-Western people was the recurrent theme of experiences shared with us by many tourism workers. Solidarity was not just forged on a romanticized basis, for it drew on two main considerations: first, there was an issue of shared experience of hostility and racism *vis à vis* Western people; second this bonding was often based on assumed cultural or religious commonalities. Such liaisons introduce means by which a wider solidarity in travel could arise, and constitute practices which appeal to the migrant resident in the North.[6]

## Gendering our Differences

Perceived commonalities in travel encounters, however, were not without their drawbacks. I remember many occasions in Turkey, Malaysia, and Tunisia when men and women would look at me with judging eyes, expecting or suggesting modes of acceptable behaviour. The assumption was that I was like 'their women', and should behave accordingly. Judgements would be made of me that would not necessarily be made of white Westerners – for example, an Asian woman wearing a bikini causes much more fuss than a white woman. Of course, this could be due to the novelty of blacks/Asians on holiday beaches, but I have the sense that it was less acceptable because I am Asian and, perhaps, also because they assumed I was Muslim, and more like their own. In this sense Asianness and Islam played a role in how we were perceived but, more importantly, our perceived 'cultural identity' led to certain expectations of behaviour. In Malaysia, for example, I felt that a headscarf was an essential part of my dress. Had I not dressed accordingly, reception from the local residents (particularly the men), would certainly not be one I welcomed. The message clearly was, 'You're one of us and so behave as such.' Having contended with similar patriarchal expectations in the country of my upbringing, I understood the rules premised on gender segregation.[7] The challenging aspect of being the traveller in a foreign place, however, is that one can choose not to contend with these rules. Putting on the scarf, I negotiated culture and identity, sometimes grudgingly, sometimes for the sake of convenience or out of respect, not always with ease.

In this sense, therefore, forging alliances with the local community had to be based on recognized, and somewhat renegotiated, rules of acceptable and unacceptable behaviour. For example, I found it sometimes acceptable to wear a headscarf if it meant I could enjoy being one with the people. This, however, does not mean that I would also tolerate particular sexist harassment. Therefore, 'being one with the people' is not necessarily an uncompromising relationship. As black/Asian women travellers, we may choose to shift in and out of cultural roles. It could also be argued here that a black woman travelling in a country outside 'home' has a greater choice in crossing those cultural boundaries. She does not have to contend with community condemnation in the same way – she is, after all, a traveller who can afford to travel, and due to the mass aspect of travel, anonymity guarantees a degree of escape from communal codes of conduct.

Yet some barriers in social communication are retained. I speak here of the way women are often almost invisible in the presence of other male travellers. Many of the holiday places I visited were gender segregated. My contact with the local community often meant contact with men, who worked in hotels or restaurants, attended beaches, and provided other services. In such encounters, conversation was often directed to men, or via men. This form of women's 'invisibility' was often difficult to challenge. Dealing with it required an acknowledgement of the fact that, in such segregated communities, men were not confident when talking to women of the general public (as opposed to women in their family). In such circumstances it is important to recognize that this is not exactly the same brute sexism as found in the West.

It is also the case that the issue for women travellers is not always about being made invisible, but, perhaps in circumstances not of their own choosing, it is about not wanting to be visible. This has to do with feeling (un-)safe. In this sense, we sometimes choose to be invisible because visibility may lead to harassment. As happens anywhere else in the world – in England on our way home at night, or walking on the beaches in Turkey – we are forced to make judgements as women, on when and where it is safe to travel. Clearly, safe spaces for women travellers are not a feature of these pleasure peripheries.

Harassment of all women cuts across class and race lines. Our move-ments are organized by the overlapping effect of all these signifiers. Travel without men, however, adds a further dimension: lone women travellers and/or women-only travel groups, black or white, are often seen as sexually available. Framed within polarized positions in the dominant local patriarchal code, women travellers (usually white) are seen as loose and promiscuous. At the same time, Asian women are often seen as pure, innocent and to be protected in a perverse manner which suggests the control fantasy of desire and possession. The general message, however, seems to be that any woman who is not with a man is an available one. The way in which my women friends and I deal with this is by simply avoiding certain spaces. In other words, women, mindful of their own safety, limit their movements, particularly if they are on their own. The irony here is that we travel across the world, yet in the holiday resorts, we still curtail our movements, and as black women we find that the options become even more limited unless we actively respond through the assertion of our rights, tempered with common sense, respect and negotiation.

Images constructed by the social norms and moral codes found within the various cultures are strongly supported, if not promoted, by the tourist media messages. The tourist industry sells its holiday by suggesting that holidaying, at least for single young white adults, is about sexual freedom. These images are oppressive and rely upon rigid sexist assumptions which have damaging effects (Crick 1988). Despite the specificity of the experience of sexism, sexual harassment is universal and to be combated whatever its forms. This is the ground on which solidarity is built. In those places where women feel vulnerable, even intimidated, it is our commonality that draws us together. The gaze is not a threat in every case: those women-to-women stares are often a way of saying 'it's good to see other women here'.

## Privileges and Expectations

Like other holiday makers, black female tourists are seen as wealthy – or able to buy a foreign holiday at least. But unlike white tourists, our cultural commonality seems also to bring with it false expectations. Once it was established that we were British citizens, many local residents in Turkey or Tunisia would ask us how they too could migrate to Britain or Europe. Legal privileges became associated with economic and travel privileges. We were the travelling black tourists, who could afford to travel the world, and economically we were seen as equal to the white tourists. In this sense, they had seen in us the possibility of non-Western peoples achieving global manoeuvrability and economic success.

For people in the South, (lack of) finance, along with the enforcement of Fortress Europe, mean exclusion: many continue to be prevented from crossing the border. Tourism or international travel may well have made the world 'smaller', but only for those so privileged, who are mainly from the West. For the rest of the world, global access remains the privilege of a minority. For the majority, escape to the West is a fantasy built largely through media channels and, specifically, the dominant images emanating from the tourism industry. Arjun Appadurai, through his notion of 'mediascapes' to describe global flows of magazines, television and film productions, newspapers, the Internet and so forth, helps to clarify this 'imagined world':

> Mediascapes ... provide large and complex repertoires of images, narratives and ethnoscapes to viewers throughout the world, in which the world of commodities and the world of news and politics are profoundly mixed.... The lines between the realistic and the fictional landscapes they see are blurred, so that, the further away these audiences are from the direct experiences of metropolitan life, the more likely they are to construct imagined worlds (Appadurai 1993: 330–1).

Travelling as a tourist raises many issues about identity and positionality – one's racial, gender, religious, cultural and class positions all come into question. The holiday experiences that I have discussed above have explored how these identifications have been expressed during our exchanges. There is an inherent contradiction built into my travels as a black/Asian woman. On one level, our freedom of movement is curtailed by our gender, due to considerations of safety and harassment, and by cultural assumptions based on commonalities of race and religion. But on another level, the liminality of holiday experiences can also bring with it a sense of 'freedom' and welcome connections of potential solidarity. In our home towns we may often feel restricted by the moral and religious codes set by our local communities, and these restrictions influence our dress, our behaviour and even the places to which we travel. On holiday, however, we need not demonstrate such commitments so readily and we look for new connections, new experiences across conventional divides. In this sense cultural boundaries become more fluid by way of temporal residence and freedoms of anonymity. Repercussions of community gossip are of little relevance in the travel experience, and one can look forward to leaving the particular strictures of racism in Britain behind.

## Mauritius, Mauritians, Mauritianness, Mauritianality...

In the following section I discuss some of these pertinent issues in connection with notions of 'home', identity and sense of belonging. Here my travel takes me back to the place where I was born – Mauritius. For the returning migrant, travel 'back home' often leads to questioning our assumed identity. Much of this is based on how we see ourselves and how relatives and friends view us. In places like Turkey and Tunisia I was able to negotiate my presence. Yet in Mauritius I assumed a given identity, received from my parents – a positionality that required in my experience comparatively little negotiation. In this final part of the chapter I explore the ways in which my migrant identity is dialectically mediated, being from the two worlds of the 'over there' of Mauritius and the 'over here' of Britain. This process, I argue, allows for transmutations of ideas about identity but also the transportation of these categories.

As I narrate my journey to Mauritius, this story is both about the physical travel to Mauritius and the emotional travel 'home'. I travelled 'back' to Mauritius to go 'home' and to visit relatives. Many of the people I stayed with, or with whom I met during that visit, were workers in the travel sector, servicing the wants of wealthy Western visitors. For most people, Mauritius is known through literature which represents the island as part of the pleasure periphery, a holiday place for fun and play, where all that is available is to be appropriated and appreciated as entertainment. My experience of travel is not catered for in the same ways, as consumerist images survive by asserting a separation of traffic and so defying cultural transmutation. For me, the visit disrupted some cherished images and some unexamined notions of my identity, further refracting many of the issues raised in the earlier parts of this chapter.

Mauritius is an island state in the Indian Ocean. It was uninhabited before European sailors and merchants arrived in the late 1400s. Mauritius knows no other history than that created by colonial processes. It had no indigenous population to exploit, and no native industry to offer trade. Its settlers were unwillingly deployed there and the past history of these people is not one to be envied: most came forcibly as slaves or indentured labourers. As a country made by others, it has experienced four changes of 'ownership' since its initial occupation in 1498. Mauritius was first known to Arab sailors, but was later invaded by the Portuguese, Dutch, French and British, a colonial legacy which means that Mauritius today is populated by people from Africa, India, Europe and China, as well as groups that are of 'mixed origins'. Contemporary Mauritian society is made up of a number of cultural practices, languages and religious beliefs (Eriksen 1992, Addison and Hasareesingh 1993).

Saccharine multiculturalism, multi-ethnicity and hybridity form the dominant discourse on Mauritius. Glossy holiday brochures offer a good example of how this 'mixed' society is generally represented to the world. Mauritius and Mauritians are seen as one – the island and its islanders. Rarely seen as ordinary people going about business, working, schooling, arguing, chatting and laughing, islanders have become objects marketed as part of a 'paradise dream'. This imagery of paradise is supported by a set of particular visual representations that place the black subject secondary to sand, sea, sun and palm trees in ways completely dislocated from other possible representations. Mauritius, for many, is only ever the holiday island. This kind of representation, argues Hall,

> has positioned the black subject within its dominant regimes of representation, the colonial discourse, the literature of adventure and exploration, the romance of the exotic, the ethnographic and travelling eye, the tropical language of the tourism, travel brochure and Hollywood (Hall 1990: 223).

By highlighting such discourses, we can begin to counter their extensive prevalence, yet narrow demarcations. The processes Hall identifies can be observed in specific detail operating in the following seemingly innocuous Mauritius holiday brochure:

With so many nationalities, cultures and religions happily co-existing, it is difficult to find a day without some festival or celebration.... Collectively, they make Mauritius the unique place it is – not just another exotic island in the sun, but an island nation, shaped by the richness of Asia, Europe and Africa, yet fully independent (Government of Mauritius 1993).

In such brochure-speak, Mauritian cultures are only celebrated in an abstract way for their 'differences' and their diversity and commended for their supposed harmony and unity, as suggested by another similar document:

The people are unique for their sheer diversity: Indians, Creoles, Muslims, French, Chinese and an intoxicating range of mixture. Beautiful people with soft features, infectious smiles and disarming personalities.... [P]reserving their original cultures ... [they] achieve a unity in diversity which offers the rest of us an inspiring vision of tomorrow's cosmopolitan world (Government of Mauritius 1993).

The images and the language of the brochures are a powerful influence in the creation and perpetuation of the myths of identity. Even at the point of recognizing the people of Mauritius they confirm the stereotypes of the present, of the unchanging, fixed image of happy-friendly natives, and of the authentic and exotic. Laced within the language of an idealized multiculturalism, the brochures exploit fantasy notions of festive island richness to sell holidays. The promise of spectacle, the 'everyday a celebration' routine, shows that the 'indolent native' ideology lingers on in the brochure as the flip side of the island girl dream. Travel agencies, like other marketing agencies, exploit the fact that 'difference and diversity' sells. Such objectification of a place and its people is the means of creation of the 'Other' and the 'exotic', embedded within movements of 'discovery' and 'appropriation'. Hence, this island romance is fundamentally about the unequal relationships between 'the West and the rest'. Kabbani (1986) and Said (1978) have suggested that the colonial past is responsible not only for economic and political domination but also, through its ideological configurations, for the myths, stereotypes and fantasies that have shaped the West's view of the 'Orient'. The holiday brochures of Mauritius are a contemporary example of these ideological configurations of the 'Other' which have had a direct founding impact on the ways my own identity was formed and is received in the North. These structures and processes of 'othering' influence our subjectivities and fit us up in particular ways – as a multicultural ideal, with 'celebrations' of 'unity in diversity'. The brochures depict us in fixed frames, produced as objects for touristic consumption within the preferred ideological fashions of a contemporary 'cosmopolitan' West. And like other consumer goods, Mauritius and Mauritians fall prey to the sharks of the holiday marketing industry.

Of course I did not arrive in Mauritius independently of these kinds of images, however much I also had an additional – 'cultural' – connection to relatives and 'origins'. The dichotomous relationship between the 'over there' in Mauritius and the 'over here' in England raises pertinent issues of belonging. Through narratives of the 'over there' an image is constructed for those who live 'over here', as memories blinkered by nostalgia are presented as unchanging accounts of life before migration. Through stories of how life *was* in Mauritius, an (imagined) image of how life *is* in Mauritius is created; as explained by Hall:

> Cultural identities, in terms of one, shared culture, 'one true self', hiding inside the many other selves ... reflect the common historical experiences and shared cultural codes which provide us as 'one people', with stable unchanging and continuous frames of reference and meaning, beneath the shifting divisions and vicissitudes of our actual history (Hall 1990: 223).

The process involved here might be called the 'bridging' of cultures. The metaphor of the 'bridge' suggests the way in which the 'over there' is brought across 'here' and the 'over here' 'there'. But this bridging is also something that is transformed in the process of travel. The fixities and nostalgic images of the 'one true self' are challenged through the experience of crossing this bridge. It is not only about movement from one place to another (and return), but also about who we meet, who we become, and about the fusions and transmutations that take place in between and during those journeys on the (transnationally connected) bridge. This allows a complex two-way traffic of ideas, thoughts, people and capital, but also the transformations of these categories through both the weight of received images – including the brochures – and the interactive social relations of actual people.

During my visits home I saw myself as part of the majority – the 'self', not as part of the 'Other', the minority. Yet, despite my quest to assert my Mauritian identity, I was seen by local inhabitants as a 'black British', *Anglaise noire*, not a Mauritian. As with our friends from Turkey and Tunisia, we were envied for having travelled widely, sometimes for having escaped the iniquity of Third World economics. The irony here, is, that whilst I saw myself as a Mauritian, they saw me as someone who did not have the required cultural background, experience, or fluency in the languages. In their eyes, I was not a 'real Mauritian', but maybe at best an English Mauritian. 'Unity in diversity' rhetoric had its limits.

In Britain my Mauritianness was less queried, but, rather became a resource with which to assert my difference and integrity as part of

Britain's multiracial community. Such affirmation of cultural difference became a way of defining identity, and also a means of overcoming the demeaning assumptions and colonial legacies of a racist society. Cultural identification – usually a fluid social response – under volatile situations becomes a means of politicized mobilization founded upon relatively fixed and unitary premises.

Thinking about cultural identity as being fluid is to accept the many junctures and disjunctures between the 'over there' and 'over here'. It is about accepting a cultural world in the making, but also about recognizing that these cultural worlds, separated by distance, may yet perhaps meet on the 'bridge'. On our journey 'home' we carry with us not only the luggage made up of clothes and gifts, but also the baggage weighted by renegotiation of the cultural teachings of our parents, and the reconsideration of received images. It is important to recognize that behind the brochure identity of Mauritius as island paradise there are people with other politics, identities, differences and experiences. Those who work to provide the sun, sand and sea services for package tourists are the ones we should strive to connect with, and not receive as part and parcel of the package. Similarly, our identities are not only pre-packaged; instead of the convenience of ready-made identifications, straying from the planned path into cafés and conversations with local workers is the point of departure from which a transnational political orientation can be extended. A politics of travelling identity would include a reimagination of Mauritius, and indeed of travel worlds, as a place, in MacCannell's words, 'vibrant with people and potential and tense with [a history of] repression' (MacCannell 1992: 2) or, in Trinh's words quoted earlier, a negotiated 'here, there and elsewhere' (Trinh 1994: 9).

Travelling back and forth between my various destinations highlights debts to various homes. I am the product of the 'over here' and now, and the 'over there' and then, maybe also of the everywhere of a possible future. As this travel story tells us, moving across the world is also a movement within ourselves. In travel my identity was negotiated – sometimes Mauritian, sometimes British, sometimes of the South, sometimes of the West. I found my desire for 'home', as much as my explicit search for political and cultural commonalities across trans-national connections, something constantly in creation. My travel in the world is a (re)questioning of the boundaries and borders which cut across culture, gender, religion, ethnicity, nationality and black position-alities, and imaginaries which allow or limit these movements.

# Notes

I would like to thank John Hutnyk and Raminder Kaur for their reconstructive work on this chapter, originally given as a talk in the South Asian Seminar Series, International Centre for Contemporary Cultural Research, University of Manchester. In addition I thank Paul Grant for his very meticulous scrutiny of the chapter, and Mukhtar Dar, Uma Kothari and Sanjay Sharma for comments on earlier drafts. I dedicate this chapter to my boys, Jammal and Qamraan: they are my inspiration for writing about our 'place of belonging'.

1 The references to 'home' are for me very much about an imaginary concept based on notions of belongingness, of being wanted, of being as it were 'at home'. It does not refer to any specific geographical or physical presence, although it may include an emotional attachment to certain places. In this sense we can occupy many homes, here, there, and in a just world everywhere and anywhere!

2 The term 'black' here is a political category used to mobilize against racism. I have sometimes prioritized black over other identities. Here I am trying to relay a shared experience that brought us together not only in terms of mobilizing against racism, but, also by the recognition of our commonalities. I do not think (contra the arguments of people like Tariq Modood of the Policy Studies Institute) that black has silenced my Asian experience. Instead I understand black to be a unitary platform where the debate about our 'differences' is played out in discussion. Whilst I do not subscribe to an essentialist 'Other', I do not want to lose sight of the commonality of experiences which has been for me part of a wider black experience. Specific references to categories such as Pakistani, Indian, Asian or Caribbean refer to supposedly specific cultural /national differences. Such references were for me about an affirmation of difference *vis-à-vis* white/ English homogeneous cultures.

3 See Virinder Kalra and Seán McLoughlin in Chapter 9 of this volume.

4 The term 'Other' refers here to people of/from the 'Third World' who have a certain commonality of experience *vis-à-vis* a colonial history. This is not to assume that 'Third World' is submerged within a singular identity of 'experience', but, that the 'Other' is often constructed as different, inferior, less civilized, exotic – to the European/Self. It is the case that people from the Muslim states of the Soviet Union often found their relations with the dominant Russian cultural groupings unequal. There is not sufficient space to go into this in grater detail, but it is not a 'clash of civilizations' (European vs Muslim) or simply an ideological dispute.

5 The reference here is to MacCannell: 'the double movement of tourists to the periphery and formerly marginal peoples to the centres ... the 'Empty Meeting Ground' ... is not really empty. It is vibrant with people and potential and tense with repression' (MacCannell 1992: 2).

6 There are other reasons for validating such solidarities – and these should not need to be spelled out for anyone with an internationalist bent. They involve everything from mutual support across boundaries and borders, to the development of shared analyses and critical perspectives, through to campaign activism and support for revolutionary struggle. Such internationalism is as relevant today

as it ever was. Of course, organizationally, much more is required for internationalism than coffee chats in 'foreign' cafés. The point is that such connections support internationalist sensibilities – what follows from this goes beyond the domain of academic description offered here.

7 Significantly, though, I was never really 'made' to feel Muslim at school, I was Asian/black. There were never enough of us from different religious backgrounds, so we united as black. Interestingly, in those days – in the late 1960/1970s – schooling processes were too busy trying to assimilate us, so to be recognized as different was quite a luxury in some ways when it came later with 'multicultural education'.

# 11

## PARKING THE SNOUT IN GOA

### RAMINDER KAUR

She sat there scanning the sea of plump, puckered, pink flesh. Familiar faces on foreign lands lay horizontal like supermarket salmon. But to Yasmin's jaded sunglasses, they appeared as slivers of cod with Saxon chips on their shoulders. The writing paper in her hands having burnt her retina and patience up waiting for Linda, Yasmin finally announced that she was popping down to Anjuna. Linda didn't say anything, but carried on absorbing UV. Yasmin cast her a cursing glance. Linda was hard now, resilient, like unbeaten leather that needed to be tacked into shape. She could even take the midday sun. But she needed a bit of moral support under pressure from the packs of Indian wolves in sheep's clothing on the parched beaches – they never did get the dress code quite right. She said that she couldn't stand their insistent bleating, rotating her skull on its metal ball bearing to mime them, 'Picture please. Excuse me, photo please.... And those were the polite ones!' and she reverted back to the sturdiness of her corpulent neck stump.

She should feel flattered – not many other Peeping Toms were going to give her a look in, Yasmin mused. Linda had been in Asia two months now, trekking northwards in aeroplane aisles, on her way to Earls Court like all the other Aussies in exile. Filling up their hunchbackpacks with more hilariously paranoid stories about unruly natives, suspicious food and public inconveniences; their uncontrollable belching fuelled them further through numerous passport controls with ease and customary stamps of approval.

And now Linda had a Leni Riefenstahl-amongst-the-Nuba-look about her, despite all her precautionary tubs of Vaseline – Vaseline petroleum jelly, Vaseline hand cream, Vaseline ass lubricant – which Yasmin would, without fail, tread on as she made her nocturnal visits to the bog in the room they shared.

They met in one of those make-do shacks out East where the food was cheap and the plates were plastic. Yasmin had been in Goa two

weeks, and after a bit of splashing out in her first week, she was trying
to go steady with her fluctuating rupees. Well, after all, they had to last
her a year out East – at least until she'd gathered up all the material she
needed to please the corporations back home. And Goa wasn't as cheap
as some of the other sites she could have chosen in South Asia.

Linda was sitting drinking *feni* for breakfast, and effervescing at the
mouth whilst she tried to cut through a chapati with her knife and fork.
They were the only customers at the caff, so it was almost inevitable
that Linda would fire her recent Balinese jungle adventures in Yasmin's
direction – near-death episodes of the hairy spider crawling up her belly
when she was fast asleep ... trapped in a train toilet with a dozen
lascivious men banging away at the door ... the jungle trip where she fell
into a leafy trap laid out for boars....

Now Linda's pendulum personality needed a dose of Westernism
again, to nurse her wounds before parading her graffiti-inscribed
bandages amongst like company, the emblem of her heroism. Goa
seemed to be the nearest spot of civilization on the northward route,
renowned for its *sossegados*, mind-expanding pills and full-moon parties.
A place where Linda could meet some fellow sceptic aisle trekkers with
whom she wouldn't have to use epileptic sign language.

Why did she ever let Linda move into her little box-room? Linda's
charm had worn off like as fast as the paint on those golden Kashmiri
bracelets. Now she was just an irritation. It was time to find another
room mate; failing that, another room, preferably with a Goan family;
autochthonous, with plenty of garrulous informants – that'd be the best.

Yasmin flung her cloth bag over her left shoulder, and shovelled her
feet across the sand to catch the boat to Anjuna – 'famous for palm
sands and natural splendour for runaway hearts of the cities', declared
the tourist guide. (Local and ethnic hippie residents knew that 'runaway
hearts' was actually a euphemism for pilfered goods from elsewhere
which unfailingly turned up on the local market. But as yet Yasmin was
outside this world of local knowledge.)

The fisherman's boat was phutt-phutting (*phatta phatta*) towards the
shore. It was Wednesday – amnesty day for saline fish. A day on which
enterprising fishermen cast their hooks to pluck the northern ones
gasping out of their waters; and leave them at Anjuna flea market to get
fleeced again.

'See if I can get in with any locals there,' Yasmin thought to herself,
blanking the weekend 'bachelors' in their Sunday-best tricolour three
pieces who were veering up with instamatic intent towards the empty
space that she'd just vacated. They were looking for somewhere to park
their starched trousers and open their lunchboxes, no doubt, but

photography was less messy. Their compound eyes preyed in on Linda, lying there in her exclusive spot, as they made their click-clicking descent to a swelling chorus of 'Beauty-phool', 'Wonder-phool', 'Bloody-fool!'

'I said, fuck off out of my sight. You're blocking the sun. Eh! Yasmin! Yasmin! Tell these darkies to fuck off, will ya? In your Indian. Oiii! You're not taking a fucking photo! Oh for God's sake!'

Yasmin carried on walking, squeezing her cloth bag to see that *her* camera was still in there, and ventured up towards the lapping sea. Deep blue-green-grey sea, where over-water shouting sounded like a *distant dream*. . . .

On the boat, the two healthy yet wizened fishermen steered with the outboard motor as their unbuttoned nylon shirts flapped in the breeze. Yasmin was the only passenger. It was nearly midday, and presumably their other customers had either not yet woken up, or fallen asleep on the beach – the unlucky ones would wake up hours later with nasty rashes and peeling skinbags, still in pursuit of the glowing, enviable tan.

Yasmin looked over the side at the frothing waters, and longed for a proper cappuccino. She was disgusted at her homesickness for cafés in Soho. This is pathetic, she thought. Home over there? Missing it? This was her chance to prove after a *rite de passage* in the field that she could reach those higher echelons of approved and tested professionals. She was one of the chosen few, snip-snipped carefully to be a professional informant, cut out for the job of understanding criss-cross-cultural humanity. Yet the one cloud in the sky chose only her, casting its foreboding shadow.

'Where are you from?' she was repeatedly asked, without the cautious reservations of the PC Brigade! So she always needed to be ready with responses which didn't entail customized verses from those gurus of the diaspora, Duppy Conqueror Hall and Swami Bhabha. 'I'm from the shipwrecks down at the bottom of the sea', she liked to think as she stuck her head over even more to see what might lay in its buried treasure chests.

She didn't see her reflection, just the sediment of looted years, evangelical visitations, and colonial conquistadores disrupting the peace and tranquillity of Goa's *beautiful* people. All of them Saint Francis Xavier's feet-kissers, no doubt. After making their confessionals, they'd hang, draw and quarter a few more natives that wouldn't convert, and chase them into the hinterlands. They'd keep the beach areas for themselves and build 'Golden Goa, Queen of the East, Rome of India'. Their power-crazed dreams of building the West in the East was later overridden by a somewhat inconvenient plague. The glorious city of the East became a cadaverous shadow of its former self. Then this Rome was plundered, its lighter inhabitants kicked out for good by the Indian armies. That was in 1961, when the East–West traffic got even more congested. Migrants from the East were treated like dogs in the West, and hippies, repulsed by the West, came over to seek the mystic pleasures of the East. A marriage of unequals. A marriage of convenience. Public Convenience.

Saint Francis Xavier's mortal body had lain putrefying over the last four hundred years in a silver casket in the Basilica of Bom Jesus in Old Goa. A miracle! Truly a miracle! A body without preservation! But that didn't explain why godly powers didn't protect him from the devotee who bit his toe off with relish as she bowed her head at his feet in obeisance. Nor the fact that his feet also seemed to be on their last hinges. Yasmin checked herself for being too cynical: 'Can't scoff. Got to at least try and believe. Otherwise nobody will ever talk to me here. Nor take me seriously back home' – in the 'over there' fortress, ethnography 'over here' its buttress.

A giant splash of the wave gave her a motherly slap for her errant thoughts. She dried her face with her cloth bag, and dug out her Factor 30 Photostable Filtration, water-resistant, anti-cell ageing Ambre Solaire. My conscientious relatives would go bananas if they saw me looking like a *banderi*, she thought. Appreciative of white skin, but not white blood, she never quite worked out their niggling complexes.

But it was too late. Yasmin was already degrees browner. Not healthy brown like those slices of Danish after the rashes had gone, but tea brown, too brown. With recuperative zeal, Yasmin placed strategic blobs on her facial promontories. With one eye open and her right hand making creamy clock-wise motions, she absorbed the pretty Portuguese-style churches which proudly peppered the landscape. Hindu temples lay prostrate on four pillar posts in the crowded undergrowth. And land-grabbers from skyscraper-city Mumbai stuck their concrete digits up at everyone.

In front, row after row of beach shacks were visible through the spitting spray. An investment in a fridge freezer for the beach trade seemed a safer option for the shack owners than biking foreigners around, groins to backside. But business bigwigs had started complaining about all those shacks – 'environmental hazardness', 'aesthetic eyesoreness', 'loud nuisanceness' – and now their future lay in Parsi balances, mass produced by the extended monopoly of Tata and Birla families.

It was going to take another fifteen minutes to get to Anjuna. For a moment, Yasmin felt inspired and thought she might do a bit more writing. She took out her pad of paper, and wrote:

Boats are long and wooden, about seven foot by four foot. Coconut wood.

But the spark had obviously died. She tried to capture the moment and her fleeting thoughts. Despite all her strained efforts, captivating writing wasn't coming easy. It was the last thing she wanted to do, but sub-admonition guns fired off 47 bullets at the back of her mind. She perspired, and persevered.

'Did you make this boat?'

'No we just fish. A man makes them – the only man left in Goa who does it any more.'

'Oh really! Where does he live?'

'Over there.' The fisherman waved his arm in the random direction of the entire village they had just left.

'Where?'

And again a nonchalant 'There!'

The two men were quite amused and bantered in Konkani, with bursts of peeling laughter.

Yasmin, still looking for some kind of boatyard, snapped her head round, like one of those lizards moving in electronic bursts on the wall of her room. And she stared at this other wall – their wall of impenetrability. Fretful thoughts raced through her five hundred metre mind – distrusting their mirth, mistrusting their steering. But a gust of unexpected wind burst in before they got to the end, and her papers went flapping into the sea. It seemed to be the will of Lord Srinivas.

'Aargh!' She tried to fish them out again.

'Leave it! You want to drown?' The men tried to stand firmly as Yasmin attempted a panicked doggy paddle with manic intent from the side of the boat.

Yasmin looked up at the two men – they were both grinning at each other with their *feni*-rotten teeth – from her compliant position. Two miles out from land, and about to career around an isolated rock face, Yasmin suddenly felt a swell of sticky panic rising from her gut. She tried to get up on hind legs. God, they could do anything they wanted to me here! She felt sick on her rising bile of paranoia. She was disgusted at her lack of spine. They're indigenous, for God's sake. Why can't you just get on with them?

She tried to smile it away, but then thought that she'd compose a frown with a stern look. Which she did. And with her arms crossed regally and her back erect as a mast, she sat stone-faced as the boat sailed past the rock face and up towards the next beach....

Was she glad to get off the boat? Refresh and start again, she thought. The paper wasn't too much of a loss – just a few observations. But not

enough participation, she mused mournfully. She ventured up towards
the flea market. Further up the beach, she saw a crowd of people. It
looked like an *incident* – an incident that Yasmin just had to be at, according to her Manual of Good Practice. 'You have to accumulate to
speculate' was her resounding overture to the regulated chaos which
quick flip-flop paces sped her towards.

It was a film crew making a show of themselves. Yasmin sat down
and thought she'd treat herself to a free open-air film. Men in label-jeans
and baseball hats rubbed torsos with women with Tibetan snow cream
on. But this one was an old-style troupe, old-style women lapping up
the waves with frozen, buxom smiles. Not the waifs from VTV satellite
land, or the clones of Miss Universe Sushmita Sen and Miss World
Ashwarya Rai. Phew! What women they were. International visas for a
year, entitled to buy citizenship in the West, with passport photos to
boot that enabled trips to heaven and back.

Only in India do beauty shows have the clout of a UNESCO summit,
Yasmin mused. But now the queens had blown it. Now they were back
with the Indian bratpack. Now their only free flights were with Air India.
And it was only in Bollywood that film producers danced up to them
like clapping seals, especially for that Ashwarya Rai. It was common
knowledge that every guy in urban India loved ol' Ash. After all, she'd
done so much for the Indian nation. An Ambassador of India, except
that she went further than those four-wheeled relics of imperialism.
She'd attracted more businesses to India than any government tax break.
Look at that new knickers line from New York! India's getting ready to
be a world player in the twenty-first century. Roarrrr!

Yasmin slapped her running thoughts down.

She asked one of the boom holders what the film was – Shaktiman!
India's first home-grown superhero was making his maiden appearance
on film. Shaktiman, otherwise known as Bumbling Press Photographer
Ganghadhar, stood with his brown velour trousers and knee-length suede
boots astride, his isosceles arms and hands at the hip which was spilling
out of a large steel studded belt, and a giant metallic flower on his chest.

'*Avtaar nahin. Insaan hai!*' he boomed.

Cut!

Shoot! Female reporter, Geeta Vishwas, feigned shock horror at
villainous fiend, Electric Man, who ascended in a stupendous helicopter
from the sea which she had thought had sunk.

Cut!

Shoot! The crusading, indestructible Shaktiman, hanging precariously
from ropes attached to a crane, scooted into the sea to grab the
helicopter's base, and throw it off balance. Bent on revenge, another

make-do crane was bending with the weight of Electric Man's helicopter chassis.

Cut!

Shoot! Geeta implores Shaktiman to stay. Hawaiian-type nymphs come out of the sea, and start echoing Geeta's high-pitched melodious words: '*Aap kaun hai, Shaktiman*'.

('*It's a bird. It's a plane. It's a bird. It's a plane*', the chorus of nymphs echoed along to nymphomaniac movements on the wet sand.)

'*Jis ne mera badan ko jaan diya.*'

(*Chorus: Shaktiman, Shaktiman forever, forever!*)

'He is a modern-day Hanuman,' said a frail octogenarian who'd come down from his beach veranda to get a closer squint at the watery scene.

'Oh really?' Yasmin was delighted that such an old man could speak English to her.

'Seven *rishis* adopted him when he orphaned in plane crash in mountains.'

Yasmin shuddered at the recent memory of her own Indian Airline flight to Goa.

'So does he fly as well?'

'No,' he quavered with the glee and enthusiasm of a child. 'He is not like your Superman.'

'Mine!'

'Yes, yours. Shaktiman is a moral man, well-reading in the scriptures. Because they trained him in seven secret disciplines and made him *siddhi purush*.'

'A *siddhi prosh*?'

'*Siddhi purush*. It means man with super yogic strength.' He was getting carried away on his own super-humanism. '*Siddhi purush* is real. Not just an idea. Shastra say that people like him can exist for he can raise his *kundalini*.'

The wise man was doing his good deed of the day – putting one more errant member of the younger generation back on the path towards enlightenment before he had his afternoon siesta. Yasmin wallowed contentedly in the arcane knowledge he imparted, and gave him encouraging grunts at measured moments.

'*Kundalini* is *shakti*. It can be raised by practising yoga. Patanjal Yoga. Now Shaktiman has power to be anything he wants. Once in my life, I too had *kundalini*. But now I must go to have my nap.'

Yasmin felt deflated at the old man's decision to depart. In her two weeks of being in Goa, she hadn't come across anyone as old and knowledgeable as he was. To her he was the authentic article – seemed 'untouched' by touristic stupidities. What's more, he spoke English when

Konkani without *kundalini* was an uphill grapple. She thought about going after him with her desirous imagination, to find out where he lived for future participant observation. The old man toddled up the beach, his bright yellow t-shirt catching the sun's rays: 'God Bless Shaktiman' it said, 'Sponsored by Parle Biscuits'. Yasmin had second thoughts.

'Now I want some real action.' The director's megaphone blasted through her thoughts. 'Shaktiman, you must take the Hydraulic Hose Pipe and....'

'First I need some more waterproofing for my boots,' replied the Crusader.

'OK! OK! OK! Shankar! You ass! Hurry up and spray him. Quickly!'

'Yes sir! Spraying sir!'

Yasmin moved away from the scene in the making, and took a just-in-case photograph. It was a distraction after all, not what she was really into.

Quite drained by the series of near non-events, Yasmin sat down at a nearby shack for a papaya *lassi*. Hallucinogenic blends of hard electronic rhythms and Eastern sitar and tabla were blasting out in the recent appropriation called 'Goa Trance'. Looking round, it seemed as if she had walked into the den ... of the underbelly ... of the dregs ... of the scum of society – the pits. Your average Jungle Barries, Lord Charlies, Wild-haired Shamans and other fugitives from the materialist West were skinning up for visceral thrills, and getting more ethnic by the minute in tune to their blurred visions of the East. A tall German with boils and Teutonic Plague, in tattered bright rags and trinkets, sat opposite her and smiled a diagonal smile. He was talking to his friend – an Englishman – but kept his dilated retina fixed on her.

'This is all I need! Look at the state of them. I bet he's looking for a bit of available Asian flesh!' Yasmin was infuriated.

The ethnic tourists had taken off their PC yoke, and revelled in the fact that here they didn't have to say Sex Worker. Here they were kings, benign dictators. Here they could order the easy life off a waiter. But they still wondered where they all were – the available women of the East? Except for those that demanded 'One Mark for One Woman only at Baina beach. Foreign currency is quite alright.'

Yuk! imagined Yasmin. She'd heard about the beach in Vasco – lined up with small shacks, five foot four long, just enough to accommodate the women's pre-nubile bodies on the rack – where even sows wouldn't go through their filth without a plastic mask. Still desperate *firanghis* made special bike trips to pick up a woman for each day of the week. Maybe the one staring at Yasmin was looking for someone who was a little older. Maybe even an adult.

These were the very same white men whose colour spoke of mountains of greens. Complicitous native men sold birds at 'cheap, cheap'
rates. Duplicitous *firanghis* bought them even cheaper by the dozen,
giving the lie to their free loving image. And if permanent residency was
the intention, then an array of 'very good marriage options' were
paraded. Those 'options' that were 'lucky' enough, were pulled out of
the squalor, dressed up in roses, and asked to massage blistered feet
lined up against walls – the walls of the *firanghi*'s 'typical' Goan bungalows, recently acquired with their new-found permanent residencies and
ration cards. Bungalows were transformed into palatial stop-off, drop-
in centres for their friends overseas, or for those half-baked 'ethnic
*firanghis*' who were returning from Nepal with another-six-months-
renewal-of-daisy-chain visas. And adjoining gardens boasted of giant
pools, available girls, and endless supplies of very soft drinks.

Yasmin could overhear them saying things that fuelled her wrath at
being trapped in their Orient-seeking gaze, confirming all her other
assumptions about privileged scum out of its territory. They were talking
about right-on novels, organizing the next full-moon club-hopping
pilgrimage, and about the scarcity of Enfield motor bikes in Europe.
They mused about enterprising ideas with the purpose of increasing their
average age of mortality out in Asia. Still attempting Eastern careers with
their inherited import–export schemes, they were renegade yuppies, not
hippies; white man's burden, 1990s style.

Yasmin gave her order – a Papaya Juice Special and a Pastry – and
started reading the four-page newspaper lying on the next seat, scouring
it avidly for facts and figures. Five minutes later, she got out her other
pad and tried her hand at writing again whilst a pack of Mumbai meatpackers – trousers packed with stuffed meat – strode into the caff with
a recently acquired smarminess.

> It used to be Bombay, but now they've taken out the Bomb – it was too
> close for comfort. And put a Mum in its place – Mumbai – short for
> Mummyboys.

Yasmin carried on swimming in her verbal diarrhoea. Maybe if I start
off writing absolute shit, points will begin to surface, she comforted
herself.

The Men with Wads were here, regular visitors of state-of-the-art
gymnasiums to widen their pencil necks, scouting around for *chalu*
'chicks' in their packs of ten. They were still stuck in a warped Seventies
American vernacular. Stuck because since 1990, each recent Western
decade's bag of commodities – music, music videos, films, styles,
fashions – had suddenly swamped the cities' muddle-class masses. Now

all was middled and messy. But Seventies vernacular sounded 'cool'. Mixed with Eighties music and Nineties dress, it was even more 'cool'. College kids with baseball caps, dark Ray-bans and loud Reeboks listened to Michael Jackson on their imported Sony Walkmans. Liberalization without complete liberation from parents was making its mark.

What was to happen next was inevitable. Spotting a lone woman on the horizon, one of them was pushed forward, whilst the others tried to be subtle with their leers. Yasmin rolled her eyes to the ceiling, and tried to slip under the table.

'Whatt are you drinking?....Where you from?'

Yasmin made her disgust visible in the gathering wrinkles around her nostrils.

'Nott ttarking?'

'England. Now will you please leave me alone. I'm trying to write.'

'That's cool. To your boyfried, is ittt?'

'What's it to you?'

'How long have you been in England?'

'Since at least Maharaja Dilip Singh's days.'

'Cooool! What does your dad do now?'

'Well, my grandad used to be a sailor. Then he got off, and sold knick-knacks door-to door with my dad.' Convincing herself that perhaps he could be of methodological interest after all, Yasmin's acquired stiff upper lips began to thaw.

'And now he has his own business, I should think.'

'No, now he's a fork-lift lorry driver.'

'So he's not a business man.'

'No.'

The 'Oh' that emanated from him went on a downhill slide to arrogant oblivion.

'Looking for visa strategies, are you?' Yasmin teased.

'No one's interested in your England, babe. It's a colonial underdog now. America's where it's all at.'

She thought, 'Why don't they go back to their wives?' then checked herself for her presumptuousness: their mummies?

'Excuse me. I'm very busy.' When he didn't take the hint, Yasmin moved to another table.

The degeneration of the Great in Britain was a global fact, even in the South. Superiority complexes of Brits in Goa, however, didn't stand up to their meticulous counting of change, careful divisions of bills, and mingy one-rupee tips. They were nearly as bad as the *Bhingtakar* (peanut-sellers/domestic tourists) or Mumbai meatpackers.

The lads irritated Yasmin with their hollow shell of mimicry. Nonetheless, it gave her something to write about – totally irrelevant to her task in hand, but you never know, it might come in handy in the writing-up.

Rich man, Poor man, Tailor, Tinker and Modern Day Mimic man.

On to something, but not quite hitting it, Yasmin thought strenuously. America ruling the global roost – or so they'd like to convince everyone, as beamed out on their satellite police stations. But once upon a time, it was Britain, up to the Second World War at least, but they never got their clammy hands on this piece of land. That's why there are not many Goans over in England. Understandably quite a few in Lisbon, up until Portugal, too, decided to revoke their Portuguese passports to Goans this decade....

Yasmin did not have time to read up about Portugal, until she got here. England, of course, she knew a lot about. But the information seemed too familiar, mundane and, well, not gripping enough, even though she thought she knew it all. Maharaja Dilip Singh exiled and indoctrinated in Victorian Britain. Dilip and Ranjit – Victorian cricket team champions of the highest order. Sailors, peddlers, soldiers – travellers seeking adventure and fortune, all pre-Second World War, contrary to post-1960s 'rivers of blood' ideologues. And this is aside from elite students travelling to Cambridge and Oxford because of the prestige attached to British institutions – havens of erudition that quickly turned into revolutionary hotbeds, keeping square-toed Scotland Yard constables on their feet tracking down those *wily* Asians. Politicos such as Gandhi, Nehru and Tilak stirred the brew in Britain. Uddam Singh's transnational vendetta to assassinate Governor General O'Dwyer at point-blank range in the heart of the empire resounded throughout colonial corridors of power. Then there were artists such as Amrit Sher-Gil and her coterie who went to Paris to paint it red. And now the elites want to go to America to crunchcode for Microsoft, for Disney experiences and shopping trips!

Admittedly, the American Consulate queues were the longest human chains in India, especially if you had an Indian passport: a sure passport to suspicions, delays, and rejection, unless you owned a bank, of course. Despite their West-imported goods, South Asian travellers carried their indelible markers on their skin everywhere.

On the point of transferring more thoughts on to paper, the waiter arrived with the papaya juice and pastry. Yasmin, on her usual quest to strike small talk with the local Goans, asked, 'Do you have any rooms here?'

'No sorry. We only have one room and someone has booked it for three months to commit suicide.'

'Oh. I'll try later.'

Only in Goa – where life's casualties came to die.

Yasmin ate her tasty pastry, developing a distaste for tourists comparable to her distaste for dog shit. For she wasn't anything like them, of course. She was a traveller with a packaged conscience. Her manic Manicheanism reached its polar extremes as she pictured herself nurturing a self-censured bonhomie with the local inhabitants. Self-regulated because she had already been subjected to their curiously polite surveillance and gossip, despite her vainglorious efforts at striking friendships. All was captured on brightly exposed Hi-8 for slow-motion chats during those hot patio afternoons. Foolishly, under the friendly sun, she bares all – everything about her experiences, which ricochets around from patio to patio. She is even seen inviting men back to her room for an *alloo chat* and *chai*. Then, without warning, poisoned tongues lash at her frost-glass panes – window screen vipers relishing the storm: 'She always has visitors. What is she doing here? She's much too happy for a woman. She must be doing drugs from that hippie bag of hers.' Shobha De bitchery was just the tip of their unrepentant butchery.

Well that's India for you. Or maybe it's just Goa: Goans playing Indian whispers where 'I saw her getting a lift on his Honda' easily converts to 'I saw her licking his honker'. I suppose that's the cross I have to bear for being out here on my own, she pacified herself, and thought about paying someone to go round with her. She gulped back her drink, paid, and left to scoffing wolf-whistles in US-Mumbai accents.

The flea market looked tempting with its colourful and kitsch ware. Large kaleidoscopic sheets hung from washing lines, and threadbare scarves and sarongs dressed up the beach, indicating patches of small-time enterprise. Tibetan refugees who'd trekked the mountains fleeing the sunrise of another imperial sun, set up camp to begin a mercantile Buddhist life. Kashmiri tradesmen, with memories of a former paradise setting for tourism's lucre, left their war-torn beauty spot when only hard-up backpackers with death wishes were visiting. Lambadi gypsies wandered about from state to state selling their hand-made ethnic chic wares with brisk awareness. And moth-eaten hippies with one-way tickets to nirvana were selling anything that fell off the back of an auto-rickshaw to replenish their paths to material enlightenment. They nursed hallucinations of going dirty with the 'natives' when the 'natives' prized clean living.

Yasmin knelt down to look with keen interpretation at some of the Lambadi quilted blouses – round glass – to ward off the evil eye; backless and tied up with string – to allow for ease of breast-feeding? Maybe not....

'How much?'

'Too much. You must buy from here,' another man intervened and almost half-nelsoned her to his scarf-patch on the beach.

'We have the latest only. All tourists buy from us.'

'Thank you, but I'm *not* a tourist.'

Seething with anger, but not enough convincing arguments, Yasmin left and strode purposefully towards the sea. The boat with the *feni*-rotten teeth was making its way to the shoreline. Yasmin fished around in her bag to see how much money she had left. The purse wasn't there. Panic-struck, she shook her bag out – her note pad, pens, camera, hair clip, keys and condoms came tumbling out. But no purse. What was worse, the wizened fishermen must have seen her in her plight, and started shaking the boat with all too familiar laughter. Yasmin fumed a steam-ship siren, and stormed round towards the long and windy road.

The journey back was about five miles. Maybe she could thumb a lift off one of the locals, she thought. She passed a large white Tata with Mumbai number plates. One of the locals was screwing the headlamps off for his stall on the beach. Yasmin quite stunned, stared at him, as he carried on singing and unscrewing.

'What you looking at?' he replied after some minutes of surveillance. Yasmin shrugged, and walked off, smiling. It was a Tata big enough to seat an extended family – or a group of Mumbai meatpackers.

The walk was exhausting, but pretty. It was nearly evening time. The sun got up fast, and went down even faster. There was only about three hundred rupees in her purse – three days' rent. She didn't feel too upset. In fact, she felt almost ... happy. She wouldn't have made this walk back, through the maze of tiled bungalows, had she not got stranded, saying charitable hellos to all the women in their zingly, frilly frocks on the veranda, taking photographs of their pretty white crosses or multi-coloured tulsi-plant holders in their front gardens, and the pretty Goan faces that seemed destined to be on Benetton ads.

Around the bend, they'd be a few motor-taxis whirring past, shouting, 'You want lift'. And sure enough, an old Enfield cruised past.

On the ride home, she kept her mouth shut, despite her urge to find out about *this* Goan's life history. Otherwise, 47 fireflies would go bulleting in with their exhaust pipes flaming. When she got back to her room, she rifled through her suitcase, and managed to stitch up the fare – less ten rupees. The cabbie waited patiently, and dismissed her short-changing with a 'You must be from England. Even though you could even be Indian.'

Yasmin scurried under the spotlight glare the man thrust upon her, and showed him the door. She wasn't quite ready for self-reflexive presentations. It was too early for that sleight of hand. Tomorrow, she'd have to go to the bank to exchange her traveller's cheque, and possibly open up a bank account for long-term budgeting, if she was going to stay there a long time and initially, at least, become a fly on the wall with any degree of success.

Yasmin flung herself on the bed and stared up at the anxious, lopsided fan, creaking as it whirred. Fortunately, it hung more over Linda's bed than her own. Her mind reeled off images of helicopters landing from outer space, as she remembered Shaktiman. Well, they'd soon progress, just as she had. Her body cringed at the memory of the time that she used to pronounce Said as if he was a participle in the past perfective. She looked at the pile of books lying at her side in their sprawled filing system. Books by Clifford and Marcus, Geertz, Srinivas, and Malinowski were close at hand. Uninspired, Yasmin reached over to read her pre-fieldwork brief again – to remind herself once more of what had brought her to Goa.

### Parking the Snout in Goa

'Tourism is like the camel which looks for a place to park its snout and ends up taking over the whole tent...'

In recent years, Goa has seen an explosion of the tourist industry from its post-60s drifter-hippie travel, to the mass packaging of its green and lush territories for national and global consumption. Global, political and economic onslaughts have affected Goa particularly by means of increased promotion drives for foreign tourism since a 1971 resolution taken on the advice of a United Nations Development project commission. From 1975 package tours began to include days in Goa within their itineraries, and direct charter flights to Goa's Dabolim airport began to take off in 1986. These processes are both instigated and propelled by national reconfigurations, particularly since the early 1990s in the form of liberalization programmes, rampant *laissez faire* capitalism in official and 'black' markets, and the increase in size of the Indian middle classes – all of which have direct bearing on the tourism industry. Goa has become a dumping ground for the effects of concrete restructurations at the global and national level – a site prized for its idyllic and bountiful setting as an escapist release from these structurations and yet, ironically, a site marked for their concrete installations.

Engaging with Goan residents, this research will account for indigenous perspectives and opinions on the neck-breaking rise of tourism. In the process, it will attempt to counter nation-state and global agendas by noting the precedents and consequences of such agendas, and working towards a more solidarity-based nomadic coalition against their violences.

Yasmin was puzzled as to why she could write in libraries in England, but not here. It all looked so easy and seamless on paper, but it was a totally different world to the one she was trying to inhabit. Her sutured brain had obviously been mashed up by the tropical temperatures.

So where were all these 'solidarity-based nomadic coalitions'? Where were the autonomous zones? Where was the siblinghood? The Goans seemed to be wanting the tourism, even if they'd complain and mock the tourists' buffoonery and bullishness. She wondered if her colleagues out in fields scattered around the South of the globe were also undergoing similar blues, and thought about writing to them. But even that didn't come easy. She took out her baleful blue biro and wrote:

> Travel – travail – sounds like hard work. Writing about travels – even harder work.

'Utter shit!'

Why did she have to pick something totally impossible? Her ideals didn't match the reality. Her theories didn't match the observations. Her pro-active report didn't match her reactionary temperament. Goa, where all souls seemed marketable – everyone in it for themselves. She wondered what it was exactly that made her any different from the psychedelic spectacles around her? Well, I came here because I care. Not to plunder about and make a spectacle of myself. At least I have a sense of ethics and care about the local community, she thought. Her corporation-funded conscience perched on her left shoulder screamed out in laughter at her, until she realized it was Linda outside trying to open the door in a pissed stupor. Eventually, and gracefully, Linda stumbled in through the door.

'Oh, Yas, you couldn't do me a big, big favour?'

'What?' Yasmin pretended to be asleep.

'Just let me have the room for half an hour. Please. I've got someone with me.'

'Why can't you go back to his place?'

'He's Goan. He's really sweet, and you know the score, lives with his folks in one of those cute Catholic cottages.'

'What's wrong with the beach?'

'There's some beach jerks wandering about out there. Purleeze, Yas.'

'OK! OK!… Just don't pull that long face on me. Half an hour and I'm counting.'

Yasmin with bottled-up wrath, slipped on her flip-flops, grabbed her cloth bag, and went outside. A perfect set of snazzy teeth thanked her profusely with a glint in his eye, and Linda shut the door in a frenzied giggle.

Yasmin sat on the hanging wicker basket in the veranda, swinging to herself. Linda, in predictable fashion, was sampling a piece of the sweet Orient, and, by now, probably licking his *gulab jamuns*. The play and reruns of clashing, acquiring continents made her physically and epistemologically sick....

Yasmin became even more conscious of the fact that she still hadn't found a decent Goan family to live with. The Rohit Resort 'Best Thing in Goa after Fish Curry Rice' was great for a friendly kick-off. But it was too near tourists, and not near those that counted. Or did they?

She took out her diary, and wrote,

> Tourism is really taking off. Overnight, it seems more and more women are becoming beauticians, and men taxi drivers.
>
> There are about 10,000 people in the village – ever-expanding at the seams, about 80 per cent of the residents are directly or indirectly involved with touristic activities.
>
> That includes drugs, but foreigners are just as complicit in this international trade, if not more.
>
> The governments, central and state, are hell-bent on selling whatever they can to capture more foreign exchange. Tax incentives, shaking hands with old colonial masters, inviting businesses with the promise that, 'Any one who will invest in Goa will be a successful businessman' are plastered on advertising hoardings, newspapers, and circulars.
>
> What's going to happen to indigenous lifestyles, organic growths and strategies of self-sufficiency? Is there anyone out there who wants to talk to me about these things?

Her oversized question pierced through the paper. At least, this time she wrote something marginally coherent. But the squeals from her room were getting increasingly off-putting, so Yasmin decided to take a walk on the beach.

She walked past the Babreshvar mandir, with its canopy of tree branches and fish-eyed ogreish grin on the gate. Her present landlady had informed her that Babreshvar came out at night: 'He stalks the beach after midnight, and sits on the coconut branches. If he lands on you, people go mad and see people with their feet facing backwards'. Yasmin's upbringing in a culture of critique predisposed her to scepticism. Nonetheless, she thought it'd be quite splendid if this would happen to her so that she could write her 'thick' descriptions about it later on.

Further on, there was the Hindu crematorium with its corrugated iron roof and white-washed walls. Yasmin made a note to get up next time there was an early morning bell ringing, so she could check out the rituals. A dog was sniffing around the passage way. The dog jolted when he saw Yasmin, composed himself, then sneered a salivating snarl.

Yasmin swiftly changed her course, and walked towards the dark bushes near the dunes. She could hear someone panting from within, then some shouts: 'Oii! Can't a man have a shit in peace?' Yasmin was about to fall on to the farting *firanghi*, then darted away, embarrassed that she was denying the man the one luxury in his life – to have a crap in paradise.

Her swift and rapid changes of course had her on the beach in no time. In the ink of the night, the sea looked godly. She sat down to take in its magnificence with long inhalations. A dog was barking in the distance, and a familiar cry repeated itself, ending with a wolf-like howl. Human or dog-like, Yasmin wasn't sure. But the guttural hushes and splushes of the sea drowned it all out into insignificance. The breeze stirred. Branches flew. Yasmin sat, absorbed in lungfuls of sea-air.

In the distance, a family of lean torchlights were approaching. They spotted a squatting shadow on the beach, and began to tread with accelerated intent.

'*Eh! Tu kiddhe korte?*'

Yasmin snapped out of her reveries of her plans for the next day, and stood up ringing with alarms. There were four torchlights advancing towards her. She thought it better to run rather than demonstrate her bravery. The torchlights darted after her in a manic roller-coaster-with-headlamps way. It wasn't long before they had reached Yasmin's frantic moonlit shadow. One tumbled on top of her. The ogreish torch-men picked Yasmin up roughly by her neck, and started blubbering things in Konkani. Whatever it was, it sounded threatening.

'Leave me alone! Fuck off!' she yelled.

Then she flung her fist at one of their noses, and ran off again, only to be descended upon by a volley of thumping fists. Then twittering birds in halo rings above her head lifted her up into an inky void.

The next thing she knew, she was in a little shack with racks and an overdose of khakiness, caught and incarcerated in a beach *chowki* by the Local Beach Patrol. Just like their counterparts back 'there', corpulent officers joined forces with weedy officers, wickedly gleeful that they could play out scenes from Kangaroo courts. Only here they'd never seen a kangaroo before, so they couldn't even be good at being bad.

'What is your name?'

'Yasmin Grewall…. Look I was doing nothing wrong. Just sitting.'

'You assaulted one of our officers….'

'That was a mistake. I didn't know who you were.'

'Where is your father?'

'He's in England.'

'On business?'

'He works there.'

'Ah! Living there?'

'Yes. He'll be coming later,' she lied.

'What does he do?'

'He's a fork-lift lorry driver.'

'So he's left you to travel on your own?'

Their feigned moral indignation was mixed up with the salacious prospect of man-handling *azadi* goods.

'No, well I'm not a tou-….'

Yasmin's panicking sense of regret – she hadn't bothered to get a research visa – suddenly throttled her. Harvesting the fruit of foreign knowledge at a price had seemed inconsequential. The thought of having no spare cash on her at the moment when she might need it most, flogged her into quiet submission.

'I'm here with my friends … as a tourist.'

The skinny officer looked at her, bemused. But the corpulent constable breathed out authority. Judging by the seniority of the size of his girth, this guy was serious by about forty inches. His slit eyes sawed into her, and his feet could almost have been facing backwards. Each vessel in his eye ball told a story: 'Can't get a pasty, so try a bit of nasty on her. More rare, aren't they. Are they like our women? Or their women. Let's poke her and find out.'

But momentarily, professional reputation took over. They opened up her cloth bag, and the Malinowskiesque truth came tumbling out. The plump police officer picked up the dog-eared journal:

'October 20th, Friday night…. There are about 10,000 people in the village…. Drugs…. State and central government…? What is this – spying?…You're not from Pakistan, are you?'

Their compound eyes saw hexagonal. Their intention to dig up buried guilt complexes reached the verge of lip-licking satisfaction.

'Explain yourself, woman!'

Naked to the skin. Stripped to the bone. She chased her rabid tail round and round.

*Yasmin Grewall went on to become an expert in 'thick' descriptions and analysis for prisoners of rationality; and her ethnographic field notes became the stuff of authoritative legends in very restricted circles.*

## Note

Thanks to Koushik Banerjea and John Hutnyk for comments on this chapter.

# CONTRIBUTORS

**Koushik Banerjea** lectures on Ethnicity, Culture and Identity, and Popular Music, Diaspora and Identity at Birkbeck College, University of London. He has recently completed a novel, *Malice in Wonderland*, and is a contributor to *Dis-Orienting Rhythms: the Politics of the New Asian Dance Music* (Zed Books 1996), along with Shirin, John, Raminder, and Virinder.

**Saurabh Dube** teaches History and Anthropology at El Colegio de Mexico. His books include *Untouchable Pasts: Religion, Identity and Power among a Central Indian Community* (SUNY Press 1998) and, as editor, *Pasados Postcoloniales* (El Colegio de Mexico, forthcoming).

**Joyoti Grech** is a poet, short story writer, playwright and workshop leader. Her work appears in *Black Women, Writing and Identity* (Routledge 1994), *Inside Ant's Belly* (Nate 1994), and *Flaming Spirit* (Virago 1994) amongst others. She attained her MA at SOAS, University of London, and has been involved in solidarity work with the Jumma Peoples Network.

**Shirin Housee** teaches in the Sociology Department at Wolverhampton University. She is doing research on tourism and cultural representation in Mauritius and is currently writing on gender, 'race' and cultural identity configurations.

**John Hutnyk** teaches in the Anthropology department of Goldsmiths College, University of London. He is the author of *The Rumour of Calcutta: Tourism, Charity and the Poverty of Representation*, and a co-editor, with Sanjay and Ashwani Sharma, of *Dis-Orienting Rhythms: the Politics of the New Asian Dance Music*, both published by Zed Books in 1996.

**Virinder S. Kalra** is a lecturer in Sociology at Leicester University and his book *From Textile Mills to Taxi Ranks: the Local Impact of Global Economic Change* will be published soon by Ashgate.

**Raminder Kaur** is a (script-)writer and artistic director of Chandica Arts. Her new productions include *Draupadi's Robes, Bullets through the Golden Stream, Pregnant Pauses*, and a collective script, *Futures*. She recently completed her PhD, 'Performative Politics', at SOAS, University of London.

**Seán McLoughlin** teaches about the interrelationships between religion, politics and society at Liverpool Hope University College. He has a PhD in Social Anthropology from the University of Manchester and is currently writing a book on discrepant representations of British Muslim identity.

**Peter Phipps** is completing a PhD on post-colonial theory as a global intellectual commodity in the Department of Social Theory at the University of Melbourne. He scrounges odd bits of academic teaching work where he can.

**Navtej K. Purewal** lectures on Development and South Asian Studies at the University of Manchester. An incessant border-crosser herself, she is also co-author of the course, *Teach Yourself Panjabi* (Hodder and Stoughton 1998).

# BIBLIOGRAPHY

Addison, John. and Hasareesingh, Kissoonsingh (1993) *A New History of Mauritius*, Editions of De L'Ocean Indien, Mauritius.

Adorno, Theodor W. (1991) *The Culture Industry: Selected Essays on Mass Culture*, ed. J. M. Bernstein, Routledge, London.

Ahmed, Akbar (1997) *Jinnah, Pakistan and Islamic Identity*, Routledge, London.

Akbar, Mohammad (1991) *Kashmir: Behind the Vale*, Viking, Delhi.

Akbar, Mohammad (1996) *India: The Siege Within*, UPSBD, Delhi.

Amado, Jorge (1979) *Tieta: A Melodramatic Novel in Five Sensational Episodes, with a Touching Epilogue*, trans. B. Merello, Avon Books, New York.

Amin, Shahid (1995) *Event Metaphor, Memory*. Chauri Chaura 1922–1992, University of California Press, Berkeley.

Ang, Ien (1996) *Living Room Wars: Rethinking Media Audiences for a Postmodern World*, Routledge, London.

Anwar, Mohammad (1979) *The Myth of Return: Pakistanis in Britain*, Heinemann, London.

Anwar, Mohammad (1993) 'Muslims in Britain: 1991 Census and Other Statistical Sources', *Centre for the Study of Islam and Christian-Muslim Relations (CSIC) Papers*, No. 9, Selly Oak Colleges, Birmingham.

Anzaldua, Gloria (1987) *Borderlands/ La Frontera: the New Mestiza San Fransisco*, Aunt Lute Books, San Francisco.

Appadurai, Arjun (1981) *Worship and Conflict under Colonial Rule: A South Indian Case*, Cambridge University Press, Cambridge.

Appadurai, Arjun (1990) 'Disjuncture and Difference in the Global Cultural Economy', in *Global Culture: Nationalism, Globalization and Modernity*, ed. M. Featherstone, Sage, London.

Appadurai, Arjun (1993) 'Disjuncture and Difference in the Global Cultural Economy', in *Colonial Discourse and Post-Colonial Theory: A Reader*, ed. C. Williams, Harvester Wheatsheaf, Hemel Hempstead.

Apter, Andrew (1993) *Black Critics and Kings: The Hermeneutics of Power in Yoruba Society*, University of Chicago Press, Chicago.

Arshi, Sunpreet and Carmen Kirstein, Riaz Naqvi and Falk Pankow (1994) 'Why Travel? Tropics, En-tropics and Apo-tropaics', in *Travellers' Tales: Narratives of Home and Displacement*, eds M. Mash, L. Tickner, J. Bird, B. Curtis, and T. Putnam, Routledge, London.

Ayandale, Emmanuel (1966) *The Missionary Impact on Modern Nigeria 1842–1914*, Longman, London.

Ballard, Roger (1983) 'The Context and Consequences of Migration: Jullundur and Mirpur Compared', *New Community*, 11 (1/2): 117–36.

Ballard, Roger (1985) *The Context and Consequences of Emigration from Northern Pakistan*, unpublished ESRC report, University of Manchester.

Ballard, Roger (1990) 'Migration and Kinship: The Differential Effect of Marriage Rules on the Processes of Punjabi Migration to Britain', in *South Asians Overseas*, eds C. Clarke, C. Peach, and S. Vertovec, Cambridge University Press, Cambridge.

Banerjea, Koushik and Banerjea, Partha (1996) 'Psyche and Soul: A View from the "South"', in *Dis-Orienting Rhythms: The Politics of the New Asian Dance Music*, eds. S. Sharma, J. Hutnyk, and A. Sharma, Zed Books, London.

Baudrillard, Jean (1983) *Simulations,* Semiotext(e), New York.

Bayly, Susan (1989) *Saints, Goddesses and Kings. Muslims and Christians in South Indian Society 1700–1900,* Cambridge University Press, Cambridge.

Bell, David and Gill Valentine eds (1997) *Consuming Geographies: We Are What We Eat,* Routledge, London.

Bhabha, Homi (1994) *The Location of Culture,* Routledge, London.

Bhatt, Chetan (1997) *Liberation and Purity,* University College London Press, London.

*Block Reader in Visual Culture* (1996) Routledge, London.

Blundell Valda, John Shepherd and Ian Taylor eds (1993) *Relocating Cultural Studies: Developments in Theory and Research,* Routledge, London.

Bradford Heritage Recording Unit (BHRU) (1994) *Here to Stay: Bradford's South Asian Communities,* City of Bradford Metropolitan Council, Arts, Museums and Libraries.

Bradford Heritage Recording Unit (BHRU) (1997) *Home from Home: British Pakistanis in Mirpur,* City of Bradford Metropolitan District Council, Arts, Museums and Libraries.

Brodsky-Porges, E. (1981) 'The Grand Tour: Travel as an Educational Device, 1600–1800', *Annals of Tourism Research,* 8 (3): 318–29.

Bureau of Tourism Research (1995) *Backpackers in Australia: Occasional Paper Number 20,* BTR, Department of Sport, Recreation and Tourism, Commonwealth of Australia.

Butalia, Urvashi (1994) 'Community, State and Gender: Some Reflections on the Partition of India', *Oxford Literary Review on India: Writing History, Culture, Post-Coloniality,* eds A. Loomba and S. Kaul, Vol. 16, Oxford University Press, Oxford.

Camus, Albert (1962) 'Carnets 1935–37', NRF/Gallimard No. 26.

Catanach, Ian (1997) *Famine and Disease before and after 1947,* oral presentation at the South Asian Studies Association conference, Translatings: Ideas of India Since Independence, Museum of Sydney.

Caufield, Mina Davis (1974) 'Culture and Imperialism: Forging a New Dialectic' in *Reinventing Anthropology,* ed. D. Hymes, Vintage, New York.

Centre for Contemporary Cultural Studies (CCCS) (1982) *The Empire Strikes Back,* Hutchinson, London.

Certeau, Michel de (1984) *The Practice of Everyday Life,* trans. S. Rendall, University of California Press, Berkeley.

Chambers, Iain (1990) *Border Dialogues: Journeys in Postmodernity,* Routledge, London.

Chow, Rey (1993) *Writing Diaspora: Tactics of Intervention in Contemporary Cultural Studies,* Bloomington, Indiana.

Clastres, Pierre (1989) *Society Against the State: Essays in Political Anthropology,* trans. R. Hurley, Zone Books, New York.

Cleaver, Harry (1979) *Reading Capital Politically,* Harvester Press, Sussex.

Clifford, James (1989) 'Notes on Travel and Theory', *Inscriptions,* 5:177–88.

Clifford, James (1992) 'Travelling Cultures' in *Cultural Studies,* eds L. Grossberg, C. Nelson and P. Treichler, Routledge, London.

Clifford, James (1997) *Routes: Travel and Translation in the Late Twentieth Century,* Harvard University Press, Cambridge.

Cohen, Erik (1972) 'Towards a Sociology of International Tourism', *Social Research,* 39:164–82.

Cohen, Erik (1974) 'Who is a Tourist? A Conceptual Clarification', *Sociological Review,* 22(4), pp. 527–60.

Cohen, Erik (1979) 'A Phenomenology of Tourist Types', *Sociology,* 13: 179–200.

Cohen, Erik (1979) 'Rethinking the Sociology of Tourism', *Annals of Tourism Research,* 4 (4): 184–94.

Cohen, Erik (1982) 'Marginal Paradises: Bungalow Tourism On The Islands of Southern Thailand', *Annals of Tourism Research,* 9: 189–228.

Cohn, Bernard (1980) 'History and Anthropology: The State of Play', *Comparative Studies in Society and History,* 22: 198–221.

Cohn, Bernard (1986) *An Anthropologist among the Historians and Other Essays.* Oxford University Press, Delhi.

Cohn, Bernard (1996) *Colonialism and its Forms of Knowledge. The British in India,* Princeton University Press, Princeton.

Coll, Steve (1998) 'On the Grand Trunk Road':
http://www.mojones.com/mother_jones/JA94/coll.html.

Comaroff, Jean and John Comaroff. (1986) 'Christianity and Colonialism in South Africa', *American Ethnologist*, 13: 1–22.

Crick, Malcolm (1985) '"Tracing" the Anthropological Self: Quizzical Reflections on Fieldwork, Tourism and the Ludic', *Social Analysis*, 17: 71–92.

Crick, Malcolm (1988) 'Sun, Sex, Sights, Savings and Servility: Representations of International Tourism in the Social Sciences', *Criticism, Heresy and Interpretation*, 1 (1): 37–76.

Crick, Malcolm (1991) 'Tourists, Locals and Anthropologists', *Australian Cultural History*, 10: 6–18.

Crick, Malcolm (1994) *Resplendent Sites, Discordant Voices: Sri Lankans in International Tourism,* Harwood Academic, Chur.

Crick, Malcolm (1995) 'Anthropologist as Tourist: Identity in Question' in *International Tourism: Identity and Change*, eds M. Lafant, J. B. Allcock, and E. M. Bruner, Sage, London.

Dachs, Anthony (1972) 'Missionary Imperialism: the Case of Bechuanaland', *Journal of African History*, 13: 647–58.

Dahya, Badr (1974) 'The Nature of Pakistani Ethnicity in Industrial Cities in Britain', in *Urban Ethnicity*, ed. A. Cohen, Tavistock, London.

Davidson, Robyn (1980) *Tracks,* Jonathan Cape, London.

Davidson, Robyn (1981) *Tracks,* Granada, St Martin.

Dawson, Graham (1994) *Soldier Heroes*, Routledge, London.

Deleuze, Gilles and Guattari, Felix (1986) Nomadology: The War Machine, trans. B. Massumi, Semiotext(e), New York.

Diller and Scofidio eds (1994) *Visite aux Armees: Tourismes de Guerre/ Back to the Front: Tourisms of War*, FRAC, Basse-Normandie, France.

Dirks, Nicholas B. (1996) 'Foreword', in *Colonialism and its Forms of Knowledge: The British in India*, ed. B. Cohn, Princeton University Press, Princeton.

Dirks, Nicholas B. (1987) *The Hollow Crown: Ethnohistory of an Indian Kingdom*, Cambridge University Press, Cambridge.

Disraeli, Benjamin (1871) *Collected Edition of the Novels and Tales by the Right Honourable B. Disraeli, Volume IV: Tancred or the New Crusade*, Longmans, Green.

Donald, James and Ali Rattansi (1992) *'Race', Culture and Difference,* Sage Publications (in association with the Open University), London, 1–8.

Du Gay, Paul, Stuart Hall, Linda Janes, Hugh Mackay and Keith Negus (1997) *Doing Cultural Studies: The Story of Sony Walkman*, Sage, London.

Dube, Saurabh (1992a) 'Myths, Symbols and Community: Satnampanth of Chhattisgarh', in *Subaltern Studies VII. Writings on South Asian History and Society*, eds P. Chatterjee and G. Pandey, Oxford University Press, Delhi.

Dube, Saurabh (1992b) 'Issues of Christianity in Colonial Chhattisgarh', *Sociological Bulletin*, 41: 37–63.

Dube, Saurabh (1993a) *Caste and Sect in Village Life: Satnamis of Chhattisgarh, 1900–50, Occasional Paper 5, Socio-Religious Movements and Cultural Networks in Indian Civilisation,* Indian Institute of Advanced Study, Shimla.

Dube, Saurabh (1993b) 'Idioms of Authority and Engendered Agendas: The Satnami Mahasabha, Chhattisgarh, 1925–50', *Indian Economic and Social History Review*, 30: 383–411.

Dube, Saurabh (1995a) 'Paternalism and Freedom: The Evangelical Encounter in Colonial Chhattisgarh, Central India', *Modern Asian Studies*, 29: 171–201.

Dube, Saurabh (1995b) 'Propiedad, Enemistad y Conflicto: Litigos y ley en los ultimos años del Chhattisgarh Colonial, en India Central', *Estudios de Asia y Africa*, 30: 433–63.

Dube, Saurabh (1995c) 'Rite Place, Rite Time: On the Organisation of the Sacred in Central India', *Calcutta Historical Journal*, 17: 19–37.

Dube, Saurabh (1996a) 'Colonial Law and Village Disputes: Two Cases from Chhattisgarh', in Social Conflict: Oxford Readings in Sociology and Social Anthropology, eds N. Jayaram and

S. Saberwal, Oxford University Press, Delhi.

Dube, Saurabh (1996b) 'Telling Tales and Trying Truths: Transgressions, Entitlements and Legalities in Late Colonial Central India', *Studies in History*, 12: 171–201.

Dube, Saurabh (1997) 'India: Historias desde abajo', *Estudios de Asia y Africa*, 32.

Dube, Saurabh (1998) *Untouchable Pasts: Religion, Identity and Power among a Central Indian Community, 1780–1950*, State University of New York Press, Albany, New York.

Dube, Saurabh n.d. (a) *Everyday Encounters. A Diary of an Indigenous Christianity*, forthcoming.

Dube, Saurabh n.d. (b) *Historical Cultures, Ethnographic Pasts*, forthcoming.

Dunayevskaya, Raya (1973) *Philosophy and Revolution*, Columbia University Press, New York.

Dunayevskaya, Raya (1981/1991) *Rosa Luxemburg: Women's Liberation, and Marx's Philosophy of Revolution*, University of Illinois Press, Urbana.

Eaton, Richard (1984) 'Conversion to Christianity among the Nagas, 1876–1971', *Indian Economic and Social History Review*, 21: 1–44.

Eriksen, Thomas (1992) *Us and Them in Modern Societies: Ethnicity and Nationalism in Mauritius and Trinidad & Beyond*, Scandinavia University Press, London.

Falk, Pasi and Colin Campbell (1997) *The Shopping Experience*, Sage, London.

Fanon, Frantz (1963) *The Wretched of the Earth*, Penguin, Harmondsworth.

Featherstone, Mike (1995) *Undoing Culture: Globalisation, Postmodernism and Identity*, Sage, London.

Fekete, Liz (1998) 'Let Them Eat Cake', *Race and Class*, 39 (3): 77–82.

Forrester, Duncan B. (1980) *Caste and Christianity. Attitudes and Policies on Caste of Anglo-Saxon Protestant Missions in India*, Curzon Press, London.

Foucault, Michel (1966) *The Order of Things*, Vintage Books, New York.

Foucault, Michel (1981) *The History of Sexuality*, Vol. 1: An Introduction, Penguin, Harmondsworth.

Frow, John (1991) 'Tourism and the Semiotics of Nostalgia', *October*, 57: 123–51.

Fussel, Paul (1980) *Abroad: British Literary Travelling Between the Wars*, Oxford University Press, New York.

Gardner, Katy (1995) *Global Migrants, Local Lives*, Clarendon Press, Oxford.

Gennep, Arnold Van (1909) *The Rites of Passage*, University of Chicago Press, Chicago, 1960 reprint.

Gilroy, Paul (1993) *Small Acts, Thoughts on the Politics of Black Cultures*, Serpent's Tail, London.

Gilroy, Paul (1993) *The Black Atlantic: Modernity and Double Consciousness*, Routledge, London

Giroux, Henry A. (1992) *Border Crossings: Cultural Workers and the Politics of Education*, Routledge, London.

Graburn, Nelson H. (1977) 'Tourism: The Sacred Journey', in *Hosts and Guests: The Anthropology of Tourism*, ed. V. Smith, Basil Blackwell, Oxford.

Graburn, Nelson H. (1983) 'The Anthropology of Tourism', *Annals of Tourism Research*, 10: 9–33.

Graburn, Nelson H. (1989) 'Tourism: the Sacred Journey', in *Hosts and Guests: The Anthropology of Tourism*, ed. V. Smith, University of Pennsylvania Press, Philadelphia.

Greenwood, Darydd J. (1989) 'Culture by the Pound: An Anthropological Perspective on Tourism as Cultural Commoditization', in *Hosts and Guests: The Anthropology of Tourism*, ed. V. Smith, University of Pennsylvania Press, Philadelphia.

Guattari, Felix (1996) *The Guattari Reader*, ed. G. Genosko, Basil Blackwell, Oxford.

Hall, Stuart (1990) 'Cultural Identity and Diaspora', in *Identity, Community, Culture Difference*, ed. J. Rutherford, Lawrence and Wishart, London.

Hall, Stuart (1991) 'Old and New Identities, Old and New Ethnicities', in *Culture, Globalization and the World-System*, ed. A. D. King, Macmillan, Basingstoke.

Hall, Stuart (1992) 'The Question of Cultural Identity' in *Modernity and its Futures*, eds S. Hall, D. Held and A. McGrew, Polity, Oxford, pp. 273–327.

Harris, Cheryl I. (1993) 'Whiteness as Property', *Harvard Law Review*, Vol. 106: 1709–91.

Hasan, Mushiral (1997) 'Partition: The Human Cost', *History Today*, Special Issue 'India and the British: The Subcontinent Under and After the Raj', Vol. 49 (7), September.

Hayward, Philip (1997) *Music at the Borders: Not Drowning Waving and their Engagement with Papua*

*New Guinean Culture*, John Libbey and Co., Sydney.

Henderson, Mae ed. (1997) *Boundaries, Borders and Frames: Cultural Criticism and Cultural Studies*, Routledge, New York.

Honeyford, Ray (1984) 'Education and Race – an Alternative View', *The Salisbury Review*, Winter, 6: 30–32.

hooks, bell (1995) *Killing Rage, Ending Racism*, Penguin, Harmondsworth.

Horne, Donald (1984) *The Great Museum: The Re-Presentation of History*, Pluto Press, London.

http://www.2launch.com/kula.html

http://www.geocities.com/SunsetStrip/7772/

http://www.gws.or.jp/home/miyuki/kula.html (Japan):(includes picture of Sir John Mills handprints in the concrete pavement of a London street, and a tif file of a $60 ticket for a KS show in Japan – comment, 'pretty expensive huh?')

http://www.hello.no/html/what_up!kula_shaker.html (Norway)

http://www.kulashaker.co.uk/kulashaker/grape/newep.html

http://www.music.sony.com/Music/ArtistInfo/KulaShaker/

http://www.shef.ac.uk/~shep/music/interviews/kulaint/index.html

Hubel, Teresa (1996) *Whose India? The Independence Struggle in British and Indian Fiction and History*, Duke University Press, Durham.

Hutnyk, John (1996) *The Rumour of Calcutta: Tourism, Charity and the Poverty of Representation*, Zed Books, London.

Hutnyk, John (1997) 'Adorno at Womad: South Asian Crossovers and the Limits of Hybridity-talk' in *Debating Cultural Hybridity: Multi-cultural Identities and the Politics of Anti-Racism*, eds. P. Werbner and T. Modood, Zed Books, London.

Hutnyk, John (forthcoming) 'Capital Calcutta: Coins, Maps and Monuments', in *City Visions*, eds. C. Bell and A. Haddour, Longman, London.

Iyer, Pico (1988) *Video Night in Kathmandu and Other Reports from the Not-so-far-east*, Knopf, New York.

Juhnke, J. C. (1979) *A People of Mission. A History of General Conference Mennonite Overseas Mission*, Faith and Life Press, Newton.

Kabbani, Rana (1986) *Europe's Myths of the Orient*, Macmillan, London.

Kalra, Virinder (1997) *From Textiles Mills to Taxi Ranks: Experiences of Labour among Mirpuris/(Azad) Kashmiris in Oldham*, PhD thesis, Department of Religions and Theology, University of Manchester, forthcoming as a monograph with Ashgate, Aldershot (1999).

Kalra, Virinder and John Hutnyk (1998) 'Brimful of Agitation, Authenticity and Appropriation: Madonna's Asian kool', *Post-Colonial Studies*, 3 (special section).

Kaplan, Caren (1996) *Questions of Travel: Postmodern Discources of Displacement*, Duke University Press, Durham.

Kaur, Raminder and Virinder Kalra (1996) 'New Paths for South Asian Identity', in *Dis-Orienting Rhythms: The Politics of the New Asian Dance Music*, eds S. Sharma, J. Hutnyk, and A. Sharma, Zed Books, London.

Kincaid, Jamaica (1988) *A Small Place*, Farrar, Straus and Giroux, New York.

King, John (1996) *The Football Factory*, Jonathan Cape, London.

Kovel, Joel (1994) *Red Hunting in a Promised Land*, Basic Books, New York.

Kristeva, Julia. (1986) 'Women's Time' in *The Kristeva Reader*, ed. T. Moi, Basil Blackwell, Oxford.

Lafant, Marie-François and Nelson Graburn (1992), 'International Tourism Reconsidered: The Principles of the Alternative' in *Tourism Alternatives: Potentials and Problems in the Development of Tourism*, eds V. Smith and W. R. Eadington, University of Pennsylvania Press, Philadelphia.

Lafant, Marie-Francoise (1995) 'Introduction' in *International Tourism: Identity and Change*, eds M. Lafant, J. B. Allcock, E. Bruner, and M. Edward, Sage, London.

Lamb, A. (1992) *Kashmir: A Disputed Legacy 1846–1990*, Oxford University Press, Karachi.

Lapp, J. J. (1972) *The Mennonite Church in India*, Herald Press, Scottdale.

Larson, Pier M. (1997) '"Capacities and Modes of Thinking": Intellectual Engagements and Subaltern Hegemony in the Early History of Malgasy Christianity', *American Historical Review*,

102 (4) 968–1002.

Lash, Scott and John Urry (1994) *Economy of Signs and Space,* Sage, London.

Lett, James (1989) 'Epilogue', in *Hosts and Guests: The Anthropology of Tourism,* ed. V. Smith, University of Pennsylvania Press, Philadelphia.

Lewis, Martin and Karen Wigen (1997) *The Myth of the Continents. A Critique of Metageography,* University of California Press, Berkeley.

Lipsitz, George (1994) *Dangerous Crossroads: Popular Music, Postmodernism and the Poetics of Place,* Verso, London.

Lohr, J. J. (1899) *Bilder aus Chhattisgarh und den Central Provinzen Ostindiens,* place of publication not mentioned.

Long, Elizabeth (1977) *From Sociology to Cultural Studies,* Blackwell, Massachusetts.

Lowe, Lisa and David Lloyd (1997) *The Politics of Culture in the Shadow of Capital,* Duke University Press, Durham.

Ludtke, Alf ed. (1995) *The History of Everyday Life. Reconstructing Historical Experiences and Ways of Life,* trans. W. Templer, Princeton University Press, Princeton.

MacCannell, Dean (1976) *The Tourist: A New Theory of the Leisure Class,* Schoken Books, New York.

MacCannell, Dean (1992) *Empty Meeting Grounds: The Tourist Papers,* Routledge, London.

Malinowski, Bronislaw (1922) *Argonauts of the Western Pacific: An Account of Native Enterprise and Adventure in the Archipelagos of Melanesian New Guinea,* Routledge, London.

Manor, James (1971) 'Testing the Barrier Between Caste and Outcaste: The Andhra Evangelical Lutheran Church in Guntur District 1920–40', *Indian Church History Review,* 5: 27–41.

Manto, Sadat H. (1950/1990) *Nimrud ki Khudhai,* Saqi Book Depot, Delhi.

Marcuse, Herbert (1970) 'The End of Utopia', *Ramparts,* April: 28–34.

Marx, Karl (1844/1979) *The Economic and Philosophical Manuscripts of 1844,* Progress Press, Moscow.

Marx, Karl (1857/1974) *Gründrisse der Kritik der Politischen Ökonomie,* Dietz Verlag, Berlin.

Marx, Karl (1857/1986) 'Economic Manuscripts of 1857–8' in Marx and Engels *Collected Works,* Vol. 28, Lawrence and Wishart, London.

Marx, Karl (1857/1987) 'Economic Manuscripts of 1857–8' in Marx and Engels Collected Works, Vol. 29, Lawrence and Wishart, London.

Marx, Karl (1867/1967) *Capital: A Critique of Political Economy, Vol. 1: The Process of Capitalist Production,* ed. F. Engels, trans. S. Moore, and E. Aveling, International Publishers, New York.

Massumi, Brian (1992) *A User's Guide to Capitalism and Schizophrenia,* MIT Press, Cambridge.

Mattelart, Armand (1991/1994) *Mapping World Communication: War, Progress, Culture,* University of Minnesota Press, Minneapolis.

Mattelart, Armand (1996) *The Invention of Communication,* University of Minnesota Press, Minneapolis.

Mattelart, Armand and Michele Mattelart (1986/1992) *Rethinking Media Theory,* University of Minnesota Press, Minneapolis.

McClintock, Anne, Aamir Mufti, and Ella Shohat eds (1997) *Dangerous Liaisons: Gender, Nation and Postcolonial Perspective,* University of Minnesota Press, Minneapolis.

McGuckin, Eric (1996) *Anthropologists and Other Tourists: Fieldwork and Tourism in Dharamsala,* India, oral presentation, American Anthropology Association Annual Meeting.

McLoughlin, Seán (1996) 'In the Name of the Umma: Globalisation, 'Race' Relations and Muslim Identity Politics in Bradford', in *Political Participation and Identities of Muslims in non-Muslim States,* eds, W. A. R. Shadid, and P. S. van Koningsveld, Kok Pharos, Kampen, The Netherlands.

McLoughlin, Seán (1997) *Breaking in to Bounded Britain: Discrepant Representations of Belonging and Muslims in Bradford,* unpublished doctoral thesis, Department of Social Anthropology, University of Manchester.

Mehta, Gita (1979) *Karma Cola: Marketing The Mystic East,* Jonathan Cape, London.

Menon, Ritu and Bhasin Kamla (1996) 'Abducted Women, the State and Questions of Honour' in *Embodied Violence: Communalising Women's Sexuality in South Asia*, eds. J. Kumari and M. De Alwis, Zed Books, London.

Mitchell, Timothy (1991) *Colonising Egypt*, University of California Press, Berkeley.

Morris, Meaghan (1988) 'At Henry Parkes Motel', Cultural Studies, 2: 1–47.

Mulvaney, D. J and J. Calaby (1985) *'So Much that is New': Baldwin Spencer 1860–1929, A Biography*, Melbourne University Press, Melbourne.

Munn, Jessica and Rajan Gita (1995) *A Cultural Studies Reader: History, Theory, Practice*, Longman, Harlow.

Nash, Dennison (1977) 'Tourism as Form of Imperialism', in *Hosts and Guests: The Anthropology of Tourism*, ed. V. Smith, Blackwell, Oxford.

Niranjana, Tejaswini (1994) 'Integrating Whose Nation? Tourists and Terrorists in "Roja" ' *Economic and Political Weekly*, 29 (3): 79–82.

Obeyesekere, Gananath (1992) *The Apotheosis of Captain Cook*, Princeton University Press, Princeton.

Oddie, G. A. (1975) 'Christian Conversion in the Telugu Country, 1869–1900: a Case Study of one Protestant Movement in the Godavery-Christian Delta', *Indian Economic and Social History Review*, 12: 61–79.

Pakistan-India Peoples' Forum for Peace and Democracy (PIPFPD) (1998) Home Page: http://brain.brain.net.pk/~pakindo/

Pandey, Gyanendra. (1989) 'The Colonial Construction of Communalism: British Writings on Banaras' in *Subaltern Studies VI. Writings on South Asian History and Society*, ed. R. Guha, Oxford University Press, Delhi.

Phipps, Peter (1991) 'Travelling Subjects: A Deconstructive Ethnography of Budget Travellers in India', Honours thesis, Departments of Political Science and Anthropology, University of Melbourne.

Pi-Sunyer, Oriol (1981) 'Tourism and Anthropology', *Annals of Tourism Research*, 8: 271–84.

Prashad, Vijay (1997) 'The Tarnished Rays of 1947', *Himal*, 10 (4): 56–7.

Pratt, Mary Louise (1992) *Imperial Eyes: Travel Writing and Transculturation*, Routledge, London.

Prins, Gwyn (1980) *The Hidden Hippopotamus: Reappraisals in African History*, Cambridge University Press, Cambridge.

Riley, Pamela J. (1988) 'Road Culture of International Long-Term Budget Travellers', *Annals of Tourism Research*, 15: 313–28.

Robbins, Bruce (1986) 'Feeling Global: John Berger and Experience', in *Postmodernism and Politics*, ed. J. Arac, University of Manchester Press, Manchester.

Robertson George, Melinda Mash, Lisa Tickner, Jon Bird, Barry Curtis, and Tim Putman, eds (1994) *Travellers' Tales, Narratives of Home and Displacement*, Routledge, London.

Rodney, Walter (1981) *How Europe Underdeveloped Africa*, Harvard University Press, Washington DC.

Rosaldo, Renato (1989) *Culture and Truth: The Remaking of Social Analysis*, Beacon Press, Boston.

Rushdie, Salman (1981) *Midnight's Children*, Picador, London.

Sabean, David Warren (1990) *Property, Production, and Family in Neckerhausen, 1700–1870*, Cambridge University Press, Cambridge.

Sahlins, Marshall (1995) *How "Natives" Think. About Captain Cook, for Example*, University of Chicago Press, Chicago.

Sahlins, Marshall (1985) *Islands of History*, University of Chicago Press, Chicago.

Said, Edward (1978) *Orientalism*, Penguin, London.

Said, Edward (1993) *Culture and Imperialism*, Vintage, London.

Saifullah Khan, V. (1977) 'The Pakistanis', in *Between Two Cultures*, ed. J. L. Watson, Basil Blackwell, Oxford.

Savage, Peter (1993) *The Safe Travel Book*, Lexington Books, New York.

Scott, David (1992) 'Conversion and Demonism: Colonial Christian Discourse on Religion in Sri Lanka', *Comparative Studies in Society and History*, 34: 331–65.

Seybold, Theodore C. (1971) *God's Guiding Hand. A History of the Central Indian Mission 1868–*

*1967*, Herald Press, Scottdale.

Shanin, Teodor ed. (1983) *Late Marx and the Russian Road*, Monthly Review Press. New York.

Sharma, Sanjay, John Hutnyk and Ashwani Sharma eds (1996) *Dis-Orienting Rhythms: The Politics of the New Asian Dance Music*, Zed books, London.

Shaw, A. (1994) *The Pakistani Community in Oxford*, in R. Ballard (ed.) and Desh Pardesh, Hurst, London.

Singh, Kirpal (1989) *The Partition of the Punjab*, Punjabi University Publication Bureau, Patiala.

Smith, Valene ed. (1989) *Hosts and Guests: The Anthropology of Tourism*, University of Pennsylvania Press, Philadelphia.

Spivak, Gayatri Chakravorty (1988) 'Can the Subaltern Speak?' in *Marxism and the Interpretation of Culture*, eds C. Nelson and L. Grossberg, University of Illinois Press, Urbana.

Spivak, Gayatri Chakravorty (1990) *The Post-colonial Critic: Interviews, Strategies, Dialogues*, Routledge, London.

Stoler, Ann (1989) 'Rethinking Colonial Categories: European Communities and the Boundaries of Rule', *Comparative Studies in Society and History*, 31: 134-61.

Storey, John ed. (1994) *Cultural Theory and Popular Culture*, Prentice-Hall, Hertfordshire.

Taussig, Michael (1991) *Shamanism, Colonialism and the Wild Man*, University of Chicago Press, Chicago.

Teas, Jane (1988/1974) '"I'm Studying Monkeys; What Do You Do?": Youth and Travellers in Nepal, Anthropology', *Kroeber Anthropological Society Papers* 67–8, University of California Press, Berkeley.

Tharu, Susie (1994) 'Rendering Account of the Nation: Partition Narratives and Other Genres of the Passive Revolution', *Oxford Literary Review Special On India: Writing History, Culture and Post-Coloniality*, Vol. 16, eds A. Loomba and S. Kaul, pp. 69–91.

Theroux, Paul (1975) *The Great Railway Bazaar: By Train Through Asia*, London, Hamilton.

Theweleit, Klaw (1987) *Male Fantasies, Vol. 1: Women, Floods, Bodies, History*, University of Minnesota Press, Minneapolis.

Trinh T. Minh-ha (1994) 'Other than Myself /My Other Self', in *Travellers' Tales, Narratives of Home and Displacement*, eds. G. Robertson, M. Mash, L. Tickner, J. Bird, B. Curtis, and T. Putnam, Routledge, London.

Urry, John (1995) *Consuming Places*, Routledge, London.

Urry, John (1990) *The Tourist Gaze*, Sage, London.

Van den Abeele, George (1980) 'Sightseers: The Tourist as Theorist', *Diacritics*, 10: 1–14.

Van der Veer, Peter (1988) *Gods on Earth. The Management of Religious Experience in a North Indian Pilgrimage Centre,* Oxford University Press, Delhi.

Von Tanner, Th. (1894) *Im Lande der Hindus oder Kulturschilderungen aus Indien,* German Evangelical Synod of North America, St Louis.

Visvanathan, Shiv (1988) 'On the Annals of the Laboratory State' in *Science Hegemony and Violence: A Requiem for Modernity,* ed. A. Nandy, Oxford University Press, Delhi.

Watson, John L. ed. (1977) *Between Two Cultures,* Basil Blackwell, Oxford.

Weightman, Barbara A. (1987) 'Third World Tour Landscapes', *Annals of Tourism Research*, 14: 227–40.

Wexco Publications (1980) *The Complete Travellers Guide*, Wexco, London.

Whitehead, Henry (1913) 'The Mass Movements towards Christianity in the Punjab', *International Review of Missions,* 2: 442–53.

Williams, Raymond (1981) *Culture,* Fontana, London.

Wilson, Monica (1969) 'Co-operation and Conflict: The Eastern Cape Frontier' in *The Oxford History of South Africa,* Vol. I, eds. M. Wilson and L. M. Thompson, Oxford University Press, Oxford.

Wolpert, Stanley (1989) *A New History of India*, Oxford University Press, Oxford.

# INDEX